Side profile. (Scale: 1/600)

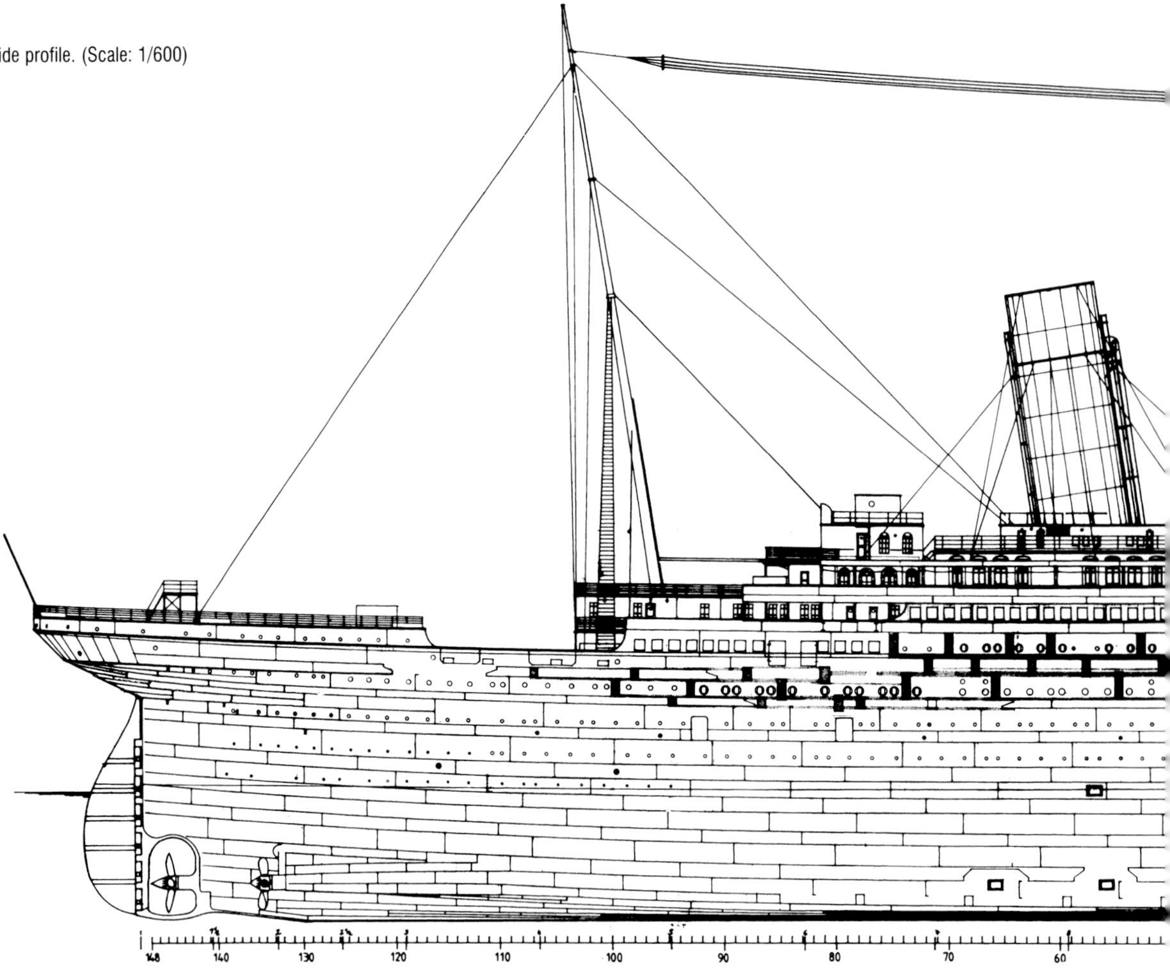

The lines plan shows the hull cut into a bow and stern section at the centre frame and the two sections drawn on top of each other. (Scale: 1/300)

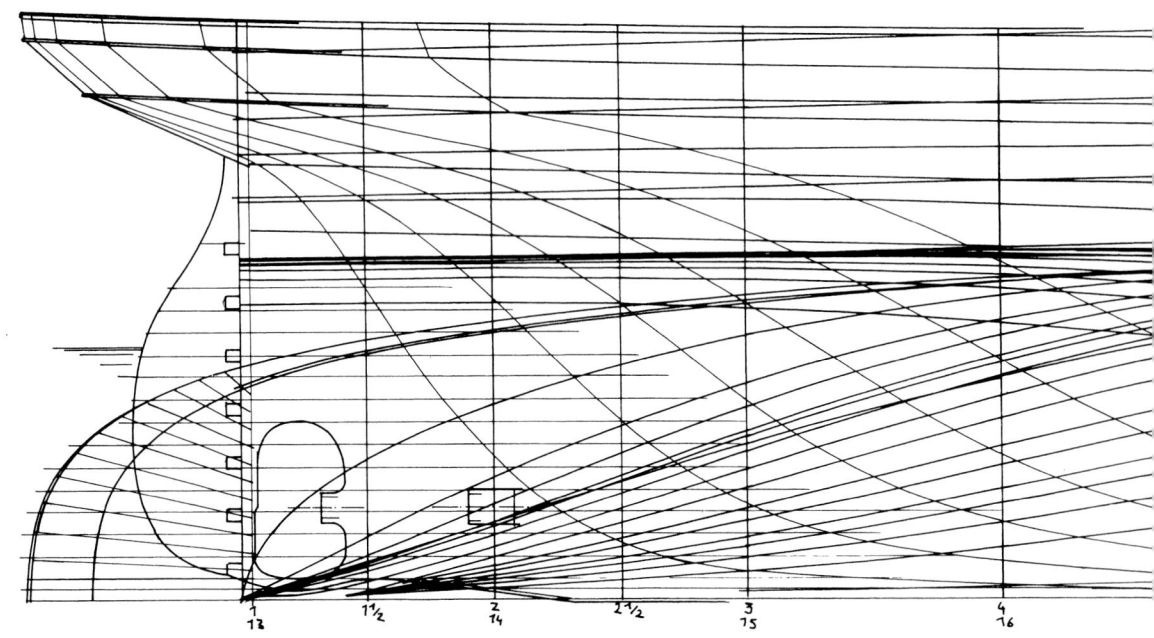

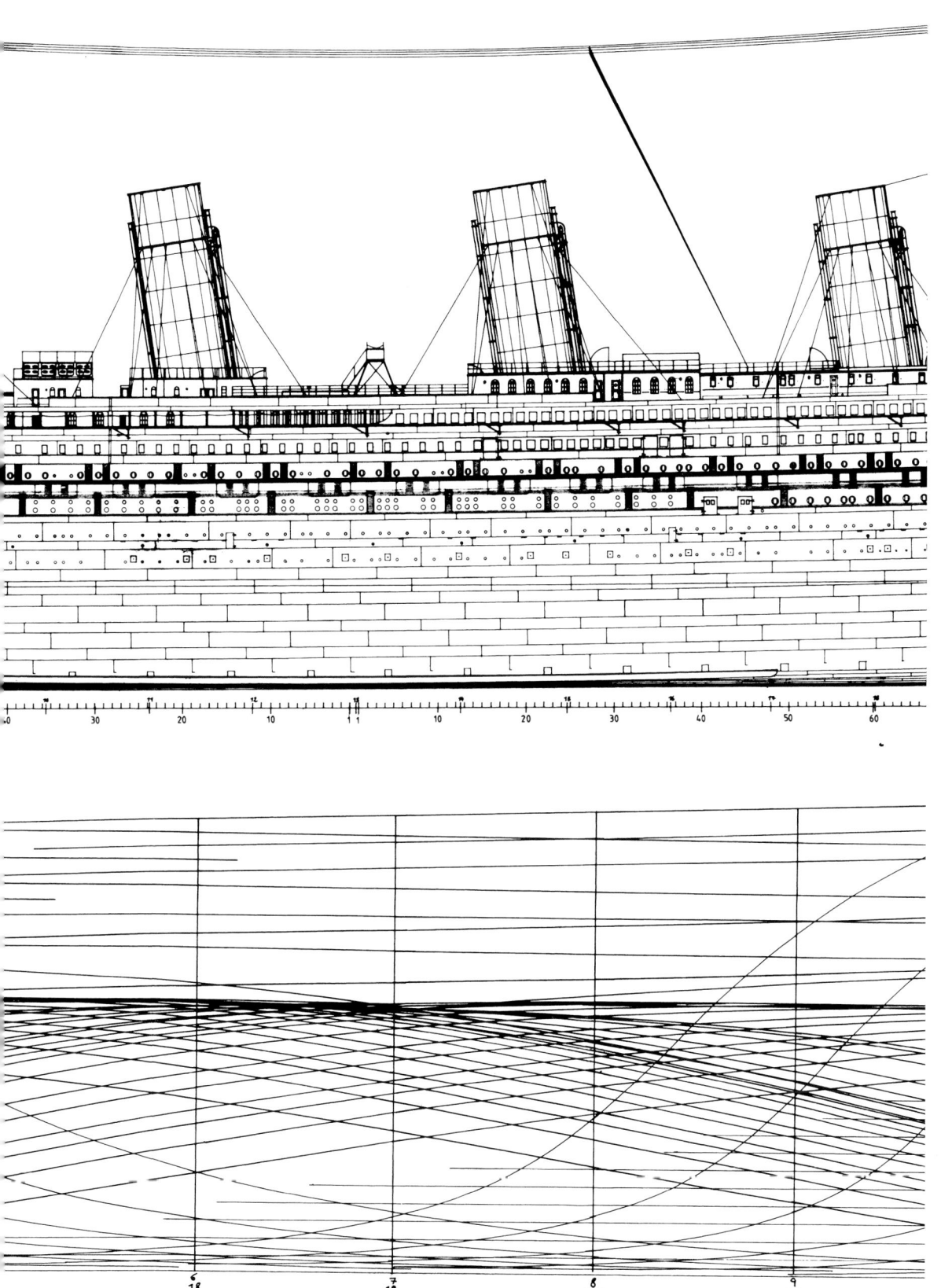

Peter Davies-Garner is a full-time modelmaker who trained as an architect, and much of his modelling has been for architectural practices. His particular fascination with *Titanic* led to his most remarkable work, the 18ft museum-quality model that is now on display at the Titanic Experience in Branson, Missouri, and is the subject of this book. He lives in Germany where he works for a company that designs and produces fall-arrest systems.

RMS TITANIC
A MODELMAKER'S MANUAL

PETER DAVIES-GARNER
FOREWORD BY KEN MARSCHALL

Seaforth
PUBLISHING

DEDICATION

For all at Harland & Wolff who built and designed a ship forty-eight times the size of the model I built, and which in her day was the finest ship in the world, RMS *Titanic*.

First published in 2005 by Chatham Publishing

This paperback edition first published in 2018 and reprinted in 2022 by
SEAFORTH PUBLISHING
Pen & Sword Books Ltd,
47 Church Street,
Barnsley S70 2AS

www.seaforthpublishing.com

Copyright © Peter Davies-Garner 2005

ISBN 978 1 5267 3733 5 (PAPERBACK)
ISBN 978 1 4738 0803 4 (KINDLE)
ISBN 978 1 4738 1769 2 (EBOOK)

A CIP catalogue record for this book is available from the British Library

The right of Peter Davies-Garner to be identified as Author of this work has been asserted by him in accordance with the Copyright, Designs and Patents Act 1988

Printed and bound in the UK by Short Run Press Ltd, EX2 7LW

All rights reserved. No part of this book may be reproduced or transmitted in any form or by any means, electronic or mechanical including photocopying, recording or by any information storage and retrieval system, without permission from the Publisher in writing

---

FRONTISPIECE

Olympic (left) and *Titanic* (right) together for the last time, March 1912. *Titanic* is undergoing yet another alteration to her design: the forward half of her promenade deck is about to be enclosed. This would be the most immediate difference between the two sisters. *Olympic* is being nudged into the drydock to undergo repairs to one of her propellers.
(Photograph: Terrell Wright)

Contents

Foreword		*VI*
Introduction		*VIII*
1	The Loss of *Titanic*	1
2	Builders' Models	11
3	The Hull, Propellers and Display Base	16
	Propellers	21
	Display Base	22
4	Shell Plating and Rudder	25
	Rudder	40
5	Well Decks	42
6	Poop Deck	55
7	Forecastle Deck	66
8	B Deck	75
9	Promenade Deck	82
10	Boat Deck	92
11	Deckhouses	100
	Officers' Quarters	101
	Lounge Roof	110
	No 3 Funnel Deckhouse	114
	Tank Room	115
	No 4 Funnel Deckhouse & First Class Smoking Room Roof	118
	Second Class Entrance Boat Deck	121
12	Funnels	124
13	The Lifeboats and Davits	131
	30ft Lifeboats	132
	25ft Cutters	135
	27.5ft Engelhardt Collapsibles	138
	Davits	138
14	Masts, Rigging and Flags	142
	Masts	142
	Rigging	144
	Flags	146
Appendices		*148*
	I Model Kits	*148*
	II Colour Chart	*149*
	III Recommended Reading	*150*

Foreword

Building an 'accurate' model of *Titanic* is an enormous, if not impossible, task. The legendary liner is the most recognised ship in history, yet many of the general public would be surprised to learn that most of *Titanic*'s deck spaces were not photographed. Aside from deck plans which do exist, artists and modelmakers have had to rely on photographs of her nearly identical sister-ship *Olympic*, and sometimes her less similar sister *Britannic*, to fill in the many gaps. *Britannic* was not around very long and never carried a paying, camera-toting passenger, and onboard photographs of her are extremely rare. *Olympic* ferried passengers across the Atlantic for over two decades, but despite this long and successful career, rivet counters like myself continue to be stymied by the lack of photographic documentation for numerous nooks and crannies on deck.

The discovery of *Titanic*'s wreckage was a welcome boon for modelmakers, yielding much new data on the ship's structure. The information gap has further narrowed in recent years thanks in large part to several websites devoted to ferreting out these details (see www.Titanicmodel.com). But despite such dedicated research, some areas and 'mystery fittings' remain a frustrating enigma. And there is no one left to ask – the people who designed and built these ships are long gone. Nearly a century later, some details of *Titanic*'s structure may never be known.

That is why taking on a project like this – recreating this famous ocean liner at such a titanic scale – is such a daunting task. It has been attempted before, but to *accurately* replicate something involves intense research, dedication, focus, patience, not to mention the most basic of all requirements – paying attention to the photographic record. There are many who simply do *not* pay attention. As a hopeless perfectionist, I do not have much patience with such modelmakers. Peter Davies-Garner is most emphatically not one of them.

I first learned of Peter's *Titanic* model in April of 2003 while having lunch with Günter Bäbler, president of the Swiss *Titanic* Society, who was on a two-day layover in Los Angeles. He had brought his good friend Brigitte Saar with him from Germany, specifically to see the large-format 3-D film *Ghosts of the Abyss* which had just been released here in the US but would not be shown in Europe for nearly eight months. Günter had seen it already, Brigitte had not. She had actually dived on *Titanic* a few years earlier and wanted to write a review of the movie for their society journal, *Titanic Post*. I had participated in the *Ghosts* project and dived on *Titanic* myself, so we were eager to experience the film together.

After watching the movie, the three of us walked to a nearby restaurant and enjoyed a meal. We discussed *Ghosts*, and Brigitte and I shared diving stories. At one point Günter slid a white envelope over to me, containing several snapshots. He told me there was a guy in Germany who was building a very large model of *Titanic* and who would be interested in any comments or criticisms I might have....

Oh no, I thought. In my nearly four decades of *Titanic* study I've seen many, many models of the ship. None could even remotely be considered 'perfect', and some, despite flag-waving pronouncements of unsurpassed accuracy, were riddled with errors so obvious that any first-year *Titanic* student would blush. So when Günter handed me that envelope, I wondered, what can I say that's nice about *this* one? Then I pulled out the photographs.

It was instantly apparent that I was looking at something quite different. Unprecedented, in fact. Instead of the dozens of blatant mistakes I routinely saw in other models, I noticed only a few subtle things, things even the most experienced of *Titanic* researchers might have missed. I tried to act cool, but my jaw must have dropped more than once.

Seeing these photographs was almost like looking at dramatic fresh views of the real

FOREWORD

ship. Someone, it appeared, had finally, *finally* done it right. I knew the challenges. I have tried modeling the ship myself and advised on many *Titanic* model projects for individuals, kit companies, exhibitions and motion pictures. The frustrations were many. Budget or time restrictions invariably prevented a fully satisfying result, or worse, attention simply was not paid to the reference material I provided.

The time and care lavished by Peter on this museum-quality model is evident in every square inch of it. He drafted detailed drawings of most pieces before construction. Every hull plate appears in its accurate length and width, its unique rivet patterns faithful to that particular plate. Little is more important to a model's appearance than a smooth and correct sheer (that 'sag' in the hull between the bow and stern), and his is as smooth, graceful and accurate as could possibly be recreated. It is a pure joy to behold.

Peter has excelled in clearly observing what was really there. Instead of plowing through and mass-producing fittings such as ventilators and motors, he noticed the subtle differences between them and included those differences. And he has sensibly applied his research and modeled those mysterious, unknown areas of the ship as they most likely once appeared.

The model is not 100 per cent spot-on, nor could it ever be. No one knows this more than the builder himself. There will always be those small, obscure mystery areas. And new information – revelations, in fact – come to light all the time, proving some previous assumptions, no matter how educated, to be incorrect. Understanding *Titanic*'s structure is an ongoing process of discovery, interpretation, chance, epiphany. We will never know it all.

I have not met Peter Davies-Garner. I have no idea what he even looks like. But when he asked if I were interested in writing the foreword of this book, I did not hesitate. The images alone speak volumes about the meticulous care he has taken. This model, unprecedented in its accuracy, and the drawings that accompany the book, are such noteworthy achievements that I am honored to do so.

Ken Marschall
Redondo Beach, California
January 2005

Introduction

For a ship that was built nearly a century ago, it is surprising how poorly documented *Titanic* is today. This is perhaps the reason why no complete work has yet been produced, aimed at the large number of model shipbuilders who would like to model this famous doomed liner.

In 1996 I started to draw my own set of plans, and a year later I was fortunate enough to have access to the Harland & Wolff plan archives. While I was there I saw some 200 working drawings of *Olympic* and *Titanic*. There were many plans missing, mostly detailed drawings. Contemporary photographs and wreck footage fill some of the gaps, but are there are still a few areas which remain unclear.

In September 2001 I was commissioned to build a 1:48 scale model of *Titanic* for 'Titanic - The Exhibition' (www.Titanicshipofdreams.com) in Orlando, Florida, the contract requiring the highest possible degree of accuracy. The completed model is featured in this book. Some of the discoveries made while researching and building this model were quite fascinating, such as the two drinking fountains on the aft well deck and the huge hot air fan on the port side next to the foremost funnel, which had been a complete mystery until then. These discoveries were made in consultation with the TRMA (*Titanic* Research and Modelling Association – www.Titanic-Model.com), in particular Bruce Beveridge and Scott Andrews.

Living in the Internet age has been a great advantage. I recall the days when letters of questions were sent to museums or shipyards in the hope that they would end up on some knowledgeable soul's desk, who could then provide me with the correct answers – although this was rarely the case. Today questions can be posted on a message forum set up by enthusiasts for enthusiasts, and sometimes I have the reply after about ten minutes with a superb image attached to it.

But certain issues are still unclear. The correct shade of 'White Star buff' (some sources state 'White Star pink'), the colour of the funnels, still is cause for endless debate amongst *Titanic* enthusiasts. I used the artist Ken Marschall's amazing paintings as a guide to get as close as possible. I do not know if this is the correct colour – and this is due solely to the limitations of colour printing. Only when someone can produce a chip of paint from a funnel of a White Star liner will we know what colour they really were (providing the chip of paint is unweathered).

The bridge roof is another issue which enthusiasts have been debating for years with the answer still unresolved (yes, I know, some will now cry out 'It IS clear!'). The fact is that in most cases the bridge roof was covered with canvas and enamelled to seal it. However, there is a photograph of *Titanic* in which part of the roof is visible and in this photograph one can clearly see what appear to be deck plank seams.

A 100 per cent accurate model of *Titanic* will probably never be built. However, I believe I can safely say that my model is one of the closest yet.

This book is aimed at everyone who has an interest in the *Titanic* and modelmakers who wish to build a scratch-built model in any scale, as well as those who use model kits as a basis. The plans will help model kit builders spot the inaccuracies in their kits. The techniques described in this book are generally applicable to all scales, though I have included further methods of building the hull and small deck fittings which were not used for building the model described in this book and which should be useful for smaller models. The biggest problem I encountered was getting as much information possible within the limited space I had without having to miss something out, resulting in a book that would be affordable for the younger generation of ship modellers. Historians who advised me whilst building this model soon named it the 'Orlando Model', and so in this book the model is referred to by this name.

Acknowledgements

I would like to thank the following, as without their help the model and this book would not have been possible. I apologise to anyone who has been missed out, but will ensure that they are included in future editions.

Scott Andrews, Günter Bäbler, Bruce Beveridge, Axel Breest, Paul Burns, my sister Mo Croasdale (for proof-reading my manuscript and converting it into a language which most people can understand), my brother Chris Davies-Garner (for giving me access to his photocopier at the most ridiculous times of day and night), John McFadyen (for the jacket illustration), Robert Gardiner of Chatham Publishing (for his faith in me after all), Robert Hahn, Brian Hawley, James Lane, Ray Lepien (for cheering me up), Paul Louden-Brown, Julian Mannering of Chatham Publishing (for his patience), Ken Marschall (whose e-mails are a delight to read), Tom Nicolai, Jeremy Nightingale, Loren Perry, Bob Read, Steve Rigby (for opening the doors), Brigitte Saar, Bill Sauder, Eric Sauder, Claes Jöran Wetterholm (who generously gave me permission to use some of his photographs), Stuart Williamson, and Terrell Wright (who has the most amazing collection of *Titanic* and *Olympic* real-photo-postcards, and who also generously supplied many previously unknown photos of *Titanic*).

My thanks go also to those who assisted in building this model. They were a very dedicated and talented group of people. I couldn't have wished for a better team.

Ebru Baykal (for cad-drawings for photoetched items), Elwyn Davies (who sadly did not win his battle against cancer to see the finished model), Martin Dicks, Michael Fehr, Jörg Graffe (for bench seats and lifeboats), Mathias Hegerath, Steve Rigby, Marie Luise Rogmanns, and Klaus Thyssen.

Last, but most certainly not least, my most sincere thanks go to my darling wife Annette for putting up with all this and, of course, to my mum.

Peter Davies-Garner
January 2005

Deck Layout.
Key:
1. Aft well deck.
2. Forward well deck.
3. Poop deck.
4. Second Class entrance B-deck.
5. Second Class smoking room.
6. Private promenades.
7. Forecastle deck.
8. Promenade deck aft.
9. Promenade deck centre.
10. Promenade deck fore.
11. Veranda cafes
12. First Class smoking room.
13. First Class lounge.
14. First Class entrance.
15. First Class state rooms.
16. Boat deck aft.
17. Boat deck centre.
18. Boat deck fore.
19. Second Class entrance boat deck.
20. First Class smoke room roof.
21. No. 4 funnel deckhouse
22. Aft staircase skylight.
23. Engine room skylight.
24. Tank room.
25. No. 3 funnel deckhouse.
26. Lounge roof.
27. Officers' quarters.

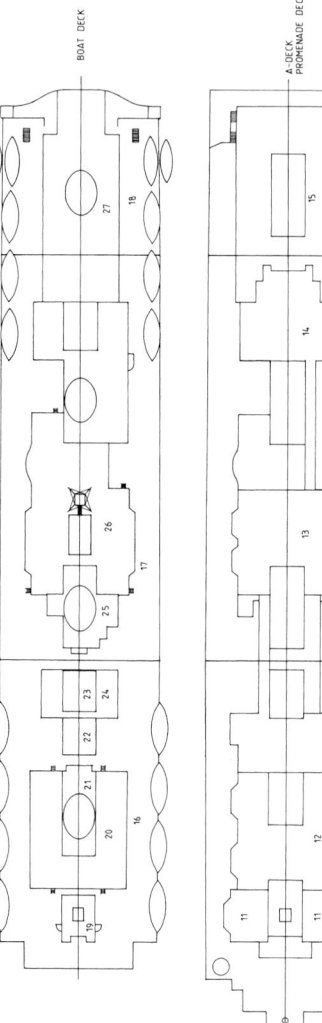
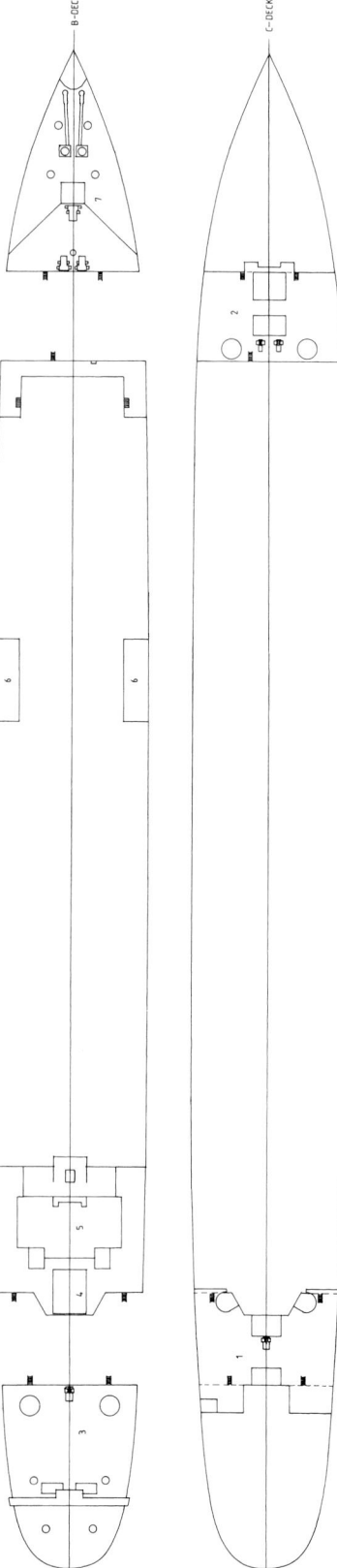

1 The Loss of *Titanic*

High above in the crow's nest, in the freezing cold night air, lookout Frederick Fleet noticed a dark mass against the black background of a moonless night straight in front of him. He rang the bell three times, the signal for danger ahead, and immediately picked up the phone connecting him with the bridge.

'What did you see?' asked a calm voice on the other end.

'ICEBERG, RIGHT AHEAD!' Fleet shouted into the phone.

'Thank you,' answered the calm voice and hung up. For the lookouts in the crow's nest, time suddenly seemed to be an eternity.

It was 14 April 1912, and *Titanic*, the largest and most luxurious ship ever built, was on her way from Southampton to New York on her maiden voyage and at full speed; this night was the darkest of nights and she was heading straight for an iceberg.

On board this magnificent liner was a glittering and aristocratic passenger list, the cream of 1912 High Society, all basking in a major social event that nobody with any class could afford to miss: the maiden voyage of the most magnificent liner in the world, a masterpiece of heavy engineering, a floating symbol of the confidence of the Edwardian era.

The bow wouldn't turn.

On the bridge, First Officer Murdoch had already ordered helmsman Hitchens to 'starboard his helm!' (an expression left over from the days of the tiller which, in this case, would turn the ship's head to port) and 'Engines full astern!' and was holding on to the bridge bulwark, staring at this thing, praying for the bloody bow to turn; but the bow wouldn't move.

Deep down in the engine room, everything was as routine as ever. It was the fifth night out. It was a new ship and everything was going smoothly when suddenly the telegraphs clattered 'Stop engines!' and 'Engines full astern!'.

It was nearly midnight. Some die-hard gamblers were playing a last hand or having the last cigar and brandy before retiring to bed.

Slowly the bow began to turn to port.

The lookouts stared at this dark and deadly mass of ice as it slid past them on the starboard side. They must have uttered a 'Thank God' as they watched it pass and begin to disappear into the darkness of night astern. It seemed to have been '...a very close shave'. On the bridge, First Officer Murdoch felt a slight tremble as the iceberg slid past the liner's starboard side, and he hastily operated the switches to close the watertight doors.

'Hard a port!' he ordered, hoping to 'fishtail' around the berg to prevent the stern of the ship from hitting it.

'What was that, Mr Murdoch?'

'An iceberg, sir! I gave a "Hard a starboard" and "Engines full astern", but it was too close!'

'Close watertight doors!'

'Watertight doors have been closed, sir!'

Captain Smith was on the bridge quickly after he had noticed the change in engine rhythm and the slight shudder of impact. He dashed to the starboard bridge wing with First Officer Murdoch, trying to find any indication of what had happened. There was nothing but complete darkness. As they went back inside the wheelhouse the Captain gave: 'Half ahead!'.

Fourth Officer Joseph T. Boxhall was sent below to inspect the damage. He reported to the bridge that everything was fine – but he had not gone down deep enough into the ship. Soon afterwards reports came in that the mailroom was flooding, as were the forward cargo holds and the foremost boiler room. The iceberg had bumped along the starboard side of the ship, beneath the waterline and torn open the hull in several places, mortally wounding the ship. The ship's carpenter and her designer, Thomas Andrews, were ordered onto the bridge and instructed to inspect the ship to see what damage had occurred. They went below, using corridors that were allotted to crew members only so as not to upset the passengers.

Shortly before midnight, Andrews returned to the bridge and reported that the first six watertight compartments had been opened to the sea. *Titanic* was designed to stay afloat with any two adjoining compartments flooded. In addition, any three of her first five compartments could be flooded due to damage caused by a head-on collision and on top of that *Titanic* would still remain afloat with the first four compartments flooded. Andrews saw that the first six of *Titanic*'s watertight compartments were flooding and he knew she could not remain afloat. As the compartments flooded, the weight of the water would push the bow of the ship down. The deeper the bow got, the higher the water level would rise in each compartment. Unfortunately, the watertight bulkheads reached only as high as E deck. Eventually the water level would reach the top of the bulkhead and flow into the next compartment, and then the next, and the next...

'She's going to sink, Captain!'

After a moment of silence:

'How long?'

'About an hour, Sir! If the pumps hold – maybe an hour and a half!'

The order was given to stop engines. Both Andrews and Captain Smith knew that *Titanic* carried lifeboats for barely half of the 2200 people on board. Outdated Board of Trade Regulations stated that all British ships exceeding 10,000 tons must carry 16 lifeboats with a capacity of 5500ft^3. This meant that *Titanic* had to carry boats for only 962 people. Altogether, *Titanic* carried boats for 1178 people, still less than one-third of the liner's capacity of 3320. In fact, the general manager of Harland & Wolff, Alexander Carlisle, who had retired in 1910, even considered installing two boats per davit set, thus up to 40 boats could have been installed on *Titanic*. But as the Board of Trade regulations insisted on only 16 boats, Carlisle was overruled as the boat deck would have been far too cluttered with 40 boats. Captain Smith and Thomas Andrews therefore knew that if no ship was near enough to come to their immediate assistance, most of the 2200 people on board the ship were going to die.

In the meantime, passengers noticed that the engines had stopped and began to leave their cabins to find out what was going on. Nobody could tell them what was happening because nobody knew. One steward thought that the ship had probably only thrown a propeller blade and that they would be underway again very soon. Ice had fallen onto the forward well deck. Some steerage passengers enjoyed a game of soccer using some of the ice-chunks as footballs. Some passengers grabbed a souvenir lump of iceberg and dashed inside with it to show it to their friends.

Boxhall was instructed by Captain Smith to calculate the ship's position. He did so by estimating the ship's speed incorrectly as 22kts. The plotted position was incorrect. Captain Smith took this position to the Marconi operator's room and gave Senior Wireless Operator Phillips the order to send the distress call 'CQD' (Come Quick Danger). It was a cry for help.

Second Officer Lightoller was instructed to prepare the port side boats for launching. The canvas covers were removed amidst the tremendous roar of steam being released from the boilers through the exhausts. Stewards were ordered to advise the passengers to come on deck with warm clothing and their lifebelts on. Small groups of passengers had already gathered on deck but went back inside again very soon afterwards due to the intense cold and the noise. On the starboard side Murdoch was supervising the preparations for lowering the boats and had brought them level with the boat deck. Suddenly the tremendous roar of steam escaping through the exhausts stopped.

At 00.25 the order was given to load the boats with women and children first.

'Come along, this way please, ladies!'

This picture was taken while *Titanic* was leaving Southampton Water. The dark April overcast is symbolic of *Titanic* steaming into her destiny to become the most tragic liner in history.
(Photograph: Günter Bäbler)

Nobody responded. Surely nobody could be expected to exchange the safest liner on earth for a small wooden boat hanging from its davits in the ice-cold night air some 60ft above the black surface of the water. These creaking little boats, swaying from side to side, would have hardly seemed inviting to anyone who paid thousands of (1912) dollars for a seven-day trip on board the most luxurious liner ever built.

At about 00.45, at Boxhall's order, Quartermaster Rowe began to fire rockets off the starboard bridge wing. The lights of a steamer on the horizon had been spotted in the distance, about five or six miles away. From the position of its lights, Boxhall believed the steamer to be heading straight for *Titanic*. Soon afterwards he recognised the red port light and two masthead lights. Together with Quartermaster Rowe he tried to contact the passing steamer by Morse lamp, but to no avail. The steamer passed, turned away and vanished into the darkness.

About 10 miles away the Leyland steamer *Californian* had stopped because she was surrounded by loose ice. At around midnight Ernest Gill, a fireman, came on deck after finishing his 8-12 watch. He noticed a very large steamer passing *Californian* about 10 miles away. He decided to retire and went below deck. Unable to sleep, he was back on deck again at about 00.30. He had been on deck for about 10 minutes when he spotted a white rocket. At first he thought it was a shooting star, but seven or eight minutes later he saw a second one.

Californian's wireless operator, Cyril Evans, had received a severe reprimand earlier that night from *Titanic*'s Wireless Operator Phillips, who had been busy all day sending private messages to shore. First Class passengers were very fond of this little piece of gadgetry with which they could send messages to friends and relatives. Phillips was exhausted. He had been sending signals to Cape Race all day, when suddenly *Californian* broke in.

'I say, Old Man, we're stuck here in ice…'
'KEEP OUT! KEEP OUT! You're jamming me! I am working with Cape Race!'

The rebuke worked. Evans remained in front of his set for a further 25 minutes listening to the conversation between *Titanic* and Cape Race. However, his receiver was not very powerful and he could only hear messages from *Titanic* so he switched his set off and finished his watch. Soon after this *Californian*'s Third Officer Charles Groves entered the wireless operator's cabin. Groves was fascinated by wireless communication, and he had spent many an off-watch hour with Evans listening to the signals. Evans, who had finished his watch at 23.30, told Groves that he had only been in touch with *Titanic*. Groves put the headphones on.

Californian's Marconi apparatus had a magnetic detector which was powered by clockwork. Groves must have known this, and yet he did not wind the set. Why should he? After all they had both finished their watch. He heard nothing. Not even *Titanic*'s frantic distress calls which were being blasted into the ice-cold night air a mere 10 miles away.

At 00.45hrs, the first boat, No 7, was lowered from the starboard side. Built for 64 people, it had only 28 on board. On the port side, boat No 4 was lowered so that passengers could climb into it from the promenade deck. However, the promenade deck windows were closed. The group assembled on the promenade deck would have to wait for nearly an hour before they boarded boat No 4. These were people who were not accustomed to waiting, such as the Thayers from Philadelphia as well as Mr and Mrs John Jacob Astor, probably the wealthiest man on board. His young wife Madeleine was pregnant. She was younger than Astor's son, and the 1912 yellow press had the time of their life with the story.

On the starboard side, Third Officer Pitman was loading the boats. While Pitman was preparing the boats, a passenger approached him and started to instruct him in what he had to do. Pitman had never met J. Bruce Ismay, chairman of the White Star Line, but the description matched. Unsure, Pitman went to the bridge and told Captain Smith that a gentleman looking very much like Bruce Ismay was ordering him to lower the boat.

'Well, do as he says!' Captain Smith replied. Pitman went straight back to boat No 5, jumped in it and called, 'This way, please, ladies!'

Ismay ordered everyone nearby into the boat, no matter whether man or woman.

'Is there anyone else who would like to take a seat in this boat before it is lowered away?'

No response.

'Lower away!'

A shy girl quickly dashed across the deck towards the boat.

A large number of distinguished guests were invited by Harland & Wolff to witness the launch of their greatest ship – Titanic. As usual at Harland & Wolff's there was no naming ceremony. At 12.05 two rockets were fired to warn small craft to stay well clear followed a few minutes later by a third. After the launching triggers had been fired Titanic's hull began to move down the ways under her own weight. Thousands of spectators cheered as she slid backwards into the River Lagan just after midday. After reaching a speed of 12kts and having travelled some 500m, the hull was stopped by six anchors and two 80-ton chains. Workers removed the anchor cables from the hull and tugs towed Titanic to the deep-water wharf to be fitted out. On the same day Olympic was handed over to her owners the White Star Line.
(Photograph: Terrell Wright)

Titanic during fitting out. The shell-plating containing the B deck windows has already been removed as these were in the original Olympic configuration. As Titanic had further staterooms installed in this area, a decision that was made while the ship was under construction, the window arrangement on her was different from that on Olympic.
(Photograph: Terrell Wright)

After midnight on 3 April 1912, at high tide, Titanic reached Southampton, a few hours after Olympic had left for another crossing to New York. Tugs carefully nudged her, stern first, into Berth 44 from where she would depart for her maiden voyage on 10 April. Preparations to make Titanic ready for her journey began straight away. Enormous quantities of china, knives and forks, bedclothes, tablecloths and provisions were taken on board, listed and stored. There were, amongst many other things, 3000 teacups, 1200 teapots, 300 nutcrackers, 6000 teaspoons, 15,000 bottles of mineral water and 20,000 bottles of beer. On 5 April she was dressed overall with flags. There were no tours of the ship as the White Star Line was hard-pressed to get her into service on schedule. The maiden voyage had already been postponed once. The general public would get their chance to visit the ship and its splendid interiors after her return.
(Photograph: Terrell Wright)

Departure was at noon, Wednesday, 10 April 1912. As Titanic steamed passed the American Line steamship New York, the suction of her propellers caused New York to snap her moorings and the ship was drawn towards Titanic as if it were a giant magnet. Only the swift reactions of the officers on board and the foresightedness of the captain of one tug prevented the collision. Many travellers considered this a bad omen. The voyage was delayed for an hour.

Titanic steaming down Southampton Water on her maiden voyage assisted by a tug. The tug shows the size of the liner. The emergency cutter is still swung in as are the Second Class boats at the aft end of the boat deck. These were swung out before she arrived at Cherbourg.
(Photograph: Terrell Wright)

Taken by the same photographer who took the previous photograph. Surprisingly there are hardly any passengers on deck. They are possibly still sorting out their cabins and staterooms or having lunch.
(Photograph: Terrell Wright)

Titanic arriving at Cherbourg before dusk to take further passengers and mail on board. Passengers were ferried out to the ship at anchor outside Cherbourg harbour on two specially-built tenders, the *Nomadic* (First and Second Class) and the *Traffic* (Third Class passengers, baggage and mail). The two First Class gangway ports on D deck are open. The emergency cutter and the Second Class lifeboats are swung out. After all passengers were taken on board, *Titanic* steamed to Queenstown, Ireland, her final stop before her crossing of the Atlantic to New York.
(Photograph: Terrell Wright)

A rare view of the *Titanic* off Queenstown, 11 April 1912. The notice boards attached to the outside of the railings can be seen and also the stream anchor and the bulkhead lamp behind the flagstaff. Note the two docking lamps on the aft mast. The majority of people that can be seen in this photograph had only four more days to live; the deck would not be so crowded again until the night of 14/15 April when passengers of all classes and crew members gathered here, clutching at the few minutes of life they had left.

This part of the ship is now a rusty and twisted heap of steel, broken away from the bow, on which only a few details can be recognised. She is deteriorating rapidly due to micro-organisms and currents and before long both the bow and stern sections will collapse. The visitors and 'expeditions' down to the wreck are taking their toll as well. Photographs of the wreck have answered many questions but there are many others that will probably never be answered.
(Photograph: *Cork Examiner* – Claes-Göran Wetterholm collection)

'Well, get on with it!' ordered Ismay.
'But I'm only a stewardess.' answered the girl.
'GET INTO THAT BOAT!'

Forty people were in boat No 5 (also designed to carry 64) when Pitman jumped back onto *Titanic* and ordered it to be lowered away. Murdoch appeared and gave Pitman command of this boat as well as of the other three in this group. He also instructed Pitman to head for the gangway ports to take up additional passengers from there. Unfortunately, the ports were shut, and Pitman decided to row away from the sinking ship as quickly as possible.

At midnight on board the Cunard liner *Carpathia*, Wireless Operator Harold Cottam was waiting for confirmation of an earlier signal from the Allan Liner *Parisian*. As he had heard nothing from *Parisian* and his watch was over, he tuned into other frequencies to pass the time and heard a number of messages before returning to the frequency on which he awaited the signal from *Parisian*.

While he listened to Cape Race, he noted a number of signals for *Titanic* and planned to forward them first thing in the morning. Then, ready to retire, he called *Titanic*.

'I say, old man, do you know there's a batch of messages coming through for you from Cape Race?'

'Come at once! We have struck an iceberg! It's a CQD, old man, position 41° 46´N, 50° 14´W!'

'Shall I tell my Captain? Do you require assistance?'

'Yes! Come quick!'

Carpathia, on her way from New York to the Mediterranean, was 58 miles away from *Titanic*. Her Captain, Arthur Rostron, was one of the few protagonists of the *Titanic* disaster who showed a considerable amount of far-sightedness. He immediately ordered the doctors to be awakened and the dining saloon to be turned into a surgery. All gangway doors were to be opened and powerful lights installed at the ports. Canvas bags were made ready to haul up children. *Carpathia*'s speed was normally 14kts, so she was literally shaking herself to pieces as she sped her way across the North Atlantic at an unbelievable 17½kts towards the dying *Titanic*.

Boat No 3 was launched at 01.00 with only 32 people on board. Murdoch then prepared to launch boat No. 1. Its capacity was 40, but it was lowered with just 12 people on board, including 7 crew. On deck at this time was an elderly couple, Mr and Mrs Isidor Straus. Mr Straus was one of the founders of Macy's department store in New York. Mrs Straus had been offered a place in a boat but she refused to be separated from her husband. In return, Mr Straus refused to take a place in a boat before the other men did. Later they both sat down on A deck and watched the activity. After persuading their maid to take boat No 8 they were seen going below to meet their fate. Boat No 8 left the *Titanic* at 00.50 with only 28 on board, including the Countess of Rothes who was at the tiller.

Boat No 9, having been lowered to the edge of the boat deck, was nearly filled to capacity. The *Titanic* had a noticeable list to starboard, and Purser Herbert McElroy put three men in the boat to assist women climbing over the wide gap between the boat and the *Titanic*'s side.

By now, wives were becoming increasingly reluctant to separate from their husbands. Rockets had been fired, the forecastle deck was under water. It was becoming clear that something was going seriously wrong. Husbands tried to persuade their wives to get into the boats and that it was only a precautionary measure. They would take the next boat and would be reunited for breakfast. But in most cases it was the last time that they would ever see their husbands.

At 01.10 on board the *Californian*, Second Officer Stone and apprentice Gibson counted five rockets. Stone contacted Captain Lord and Lord asked if they were company signals.

'I don't know,' answered Stone, 'but they seem to be white rockets.'

'Try to contact them with the Morse lamp!' Captain Lord advised him.

Stone handed his binoculars to Gibson.

'Here, take a look at her now. Don't you think her lights look queer?'

Gibson studied the *Titanic* for a while. Stone, standing beside him, noticed that the red port lamp had disappeared.

The *Titanic*'s stern rose out of the water as her bow sank. People in the boats could clearly hear passengers on deck talking, or occasionally shouting, and the *Titanic*'s band played ragtime on deck to cheer up those on board. The ship was lit up brilliantly from stem to stern as the boats rowed away from her. The firing of rockets continued, to no avail.

Boat No 11 was loaded from A deck to beyond its capacity. As it reached the water, it was nearly flooded by a jet of boiling water coming out of the condenser exhaust. At 01.25, boat No 13 was lowered with 64 on board. When it reached the water, the falls could not be unhooked. Moments later boat No 15, filled and lowered immediately after boat No 13, nearly came down and crushed the passengers in boat No 13 directly beneath. The passengers desperately tried to push themselves free from the fully-laden boat No 15, which was right on top of them, and frantic cries to the crew on deck stopped them from lowering the boat any further. Just in time the falls on boat No. 13 were cut with knives and they rowed away.

At 01.30 panic began to break out amongst some of the passengers. Passengers in boats that had been lowered to A deck were fighting others back who tried to force their way into the boats. At boat No 14, Fifth Officer Lowe pulled out his revolver.

'KEEP ORDER! KEEP ORDER! If anyone else tries that – this is what he'll get!' He held his revolver pointed towards the panic-stricken crowd and fired three times down the *Titanic*'s side. Collapsible boat C had been fitted to the davits of boat No 1. A great crowd pushed and shoved, trying to get into the boat. Purser Herbert McElroy fired twice into the air to regain order. Loading continued. Ismay was helping to prepare the boat. It was still women and children first. Most of the passengers had now gone further aft, so the order was given to lower away even though the complement on board was not the boats' loading capacity.

'Well, isn't there anybody else?' Ismay asked.

'Lower away!' ordered Murdoch.

Ismay hesitated a brief second, moved forward, hesitated again and finally stepped into Collapsible C.

'Lower away!' ordered Murdoch.

The ever-increasing list was drawing the lowered boats towards the hull. Hands and oars were used to push Collapsible C away from the *Titanic*'s hull to prevent the hull rivets from damaging the boat. Collapsible C was the last boat to be launched from the starboard side.

On the roof of the officers' quarters, crew members were trying in vain to release Collapsibles A and B. By this time Collapsible D had already been fitted to the davits of boat No 2. Crew members locked arms and formed a ring around the boat to prevent the horror-stricken crowd from rushing it. At 02.05 Collapsible D was lowered into the water.

On the starboard side wooden planks were propped up against the officers' quarters, where Collapsible A was to be lowered onto the boat deck. Crew members managed to bring the boat upright onto the deck, but there was no more time to attach the boat to the davits. The *Titanic*'s bow took a plunge at 02.10, and those who were struggling to release the boat found themselves in the water. Collapsible A was afloat though more than half-full of water. A handful of passengers and crew had found their way into the boat, but, inside the boat, were fighting their way up deck along the officers' quarters as *Titanic*'s deck sank at an ever-increasing speed, constantly fighting off others trying to get into the boat. In addition, the funnel guy-wires had to be avoided and at first the boat was trapped, as if in a cage, and could not get out. On the port side Collapsible B had fallen off the officers' quarters and landed upside down on the boat deck. As *Titanic*'s bow plunged underwater, Collapsible B floated off the deck. People in the ice-cold water swam towards it and clung onto it. Few had the strength to pull themselves onto the upturned boat.

The weight of the water hogged the *Titanic*'s hull. Expansion joints were probably open to a foot. The aft pair of the first funnel's guy-wires ran across the forward expansion joint and were not able to take the strain any longer as the expansion joint opened even further. First the port wire gave way, followed immediately by the starboard. The funnel could no longer support itself and tumbled forward, over the port side, smashing the port bridge wing. With a screeching roar of tearing steel, amidst soot and sparks, it plunged into the sea and onto the unfortunate souls swimming in that area. For people clinging to upturned B, this came as a godsend. The tremendous wave caused by the funnel pushed the boat further away from the sinking ship.

Fifteen hundred people were still on the *Titanic*. All the boats had left. They began to move towards the stern – away from the water. Below deck, engineers were fighting to keep the lights working. A steward making his way through the First Class smoking room saw Thomas Andrews standing forlorn in front of the fireplace, staring at a painting by Norman Wilkinson depicting Plymouth Harbour.

'Aren't you at least going to try for it, Mr Andrews?'

Andrews turned his head slowly and stared right through him. There was no expression at all in Andrews' eyes. His lifebelt lay thrown onto a table beside him.

The propellers now cleared the water as the *Titanic*'s angle increased. People were jumping off the decks and deck chairs, doors and tables; everything that would make a raft was thrown overboard to those swimming in the freezing water. Those in the boats watched as the stream of passengers and crew moved towards the stern of the ship. As the angle increased further, people were unable to stand on their own feet. Holding onto fittings or railings, they struggled towards the stern. Some lost their grip and slid screaming down the decks, crashing into other people on their way up, sending whole clusters of people down the decks into the ice-cold water.

Suddenly the lights went out, flickered on again, and then went out for good. Two thousand two hundred souls cried out in horror as the death-stricken *Titanic* was plunged into complete darkness. The Third Class passengers, locked below deck, suddenly found themselves in complete darkness, inside a sinking ship tilting at an ever-increasing angle, not able to stand on their feet or find their way out – or find their loved ones. They heard the moans and groans of stressed and twisting steel, the cracking of splintering wood, of a sinking ship – in complete darkness.

Passengers in the boats could now make out the *Titanic*'s stern rising high. There was a sudden rumble, like a distant thunder that turned into an increasing roar as the *Titanic* was no longer able to support the tremendous weight of the stern. Her steel shell plating started to tear and rupture, rivets popped as the hull began to split in two at the aft expansion joint. With a thunderous noise, the departed stern nearly settled back down onto an even keel again as the submerged bow separated from the rest of the ship, but very soon the stern began to rise again very quickly until finally it was completely vertical. Those still on the ship were either hanging from fittings and railings or standing on bulkheads, cranes or bollards. *Titanic* remained like a gigantic finger pointing towards the heavens for a few minutes in deadly silence.

Some remaining on board were unable to hold on any longer and dropped into the water or onto the superstructure. Those in the boats could see the hull rotating slowly through 180°. Slowly at first, and then with ever-increasing speed, the stern began to sink. Those clinging onto the ship watched with horror as the sea, speckled with debris and people in lifebelts rose up towards them until, finally, at 02.20, 15 April 1912, *Titanic*'s stern slipped beneath the waves.

What remained were 1500 people swimming in water that was below freezing, so cold that even the fittest and healthiest would not survive for more than a mere 30 minutes. Those in the boats heard the last desperate cries of 1500 passengers and crew. It was the most horrifying sound that any of them had ever heard and none would forget it for the rest of their lives. Yet, although some of the boats were less than half full, they did not row back.

Fifth Officer Harold Lowe had tied some boats together. He had passengers transferred, so one final boat remained empty. With a few volunteers on board boat No 14, Lowe rowed back. By the time they had reached the scene all was quiet. The sea was covered with the dead. For more than an hour boat No 14 chased after shouts in the darkness, never finding those who had shouted. They recovered only four and, of those, one was to die later.

But at least Lowe had rowed back.

After agonising hours afloat in boats on the North Atlantic a rocket, unnoticed by most of the survivors, shot into the sky on the horizon, burst into stars, and then slowly faded away. Most were far too exhausted even to care. A few minutes later a second rocket was fired; The *Carpathia* was about to arrive at the scene. Only 705 persons, though, were to be rescued.

2 Builders' Models

It was common for large shipyards like Harland & Wolff to have their own model shop. Skilled craftsmen built highly-detailed models of the ships that were under construction at the same time a few hundred yards away from them.

Ship models that were built or commissioned by the builder of the real vessel are today known as the 'builders' models'. This type of model seems to have appeared during the mid-nineteenth century, and it is by no means inferior to the famous and much loved Navy Board model of the seventeenth and eighteenth centuries, either with regard to craftsmanship or to its display potential.

There were two reasons why shipbuilders built models of a planned vessel. First, the shipping company often ordered a model of the commissioned ship as part of the deal, to be displayed in the company's office or booking office to attract customers. Secondly, models were used by the builders to study changes in the design concept in a three-dimensional form, though these models were not as detailed as those commissioned by the owner. We therefore have two types of builders' models, those made for the owner (owner's model) and those that were kept and used by the shipbuilder (working or builder's model). Not necessarily only one owner's model was built. There are at least four of RMS *Mauretania* from 1907. The first one is in the Smithsonian Institution, Washington, the second is at the builder's office in Wallsend on Tyne, the third in the Science Museum in South Kensington and the fourth in the National Maritime Museum in Greenwich. I have only seen the model in Greenwich, and it is a most superb example of its kind, but unfortunately, it is currently not on public display.

Owners' models were very detailed, though a certain degree of artistic licence was generally accepted: deck fittings such as anchors, bollards, cargo winches, air vents etc, were, in most cases, made of brass, left unpainted and highly polished. Sometimes the hulls of these models were made by the yard carpenters and then shipped to a modelmaker's shop to be fitted out. Brass fittings were often made by specialist manufacturers in approved scales (1:48; 1:72; 1:96) and purchased by the yard's model shop to be used for their models.

The owners' models were always full hull models and in most cases were fully rigged. The hull was built in the 'bread and butter' system, though hollowed out to reduce weight. Shell plating was never shown. The hull beneath the waterline was painted in the colour of the protective material used on the real ship, but one often sees models with the underwater hull left unpainted and varnished to show the laminates of wood used and to emphasise the shape of the hull (and to show the modelmaker's capabilities too, no doubt!).

Builders' models are, in most cases built to a scale of 1:48, although 1:96 was later also used for models of larger ships. Another characteristic of this type of model is that deck planks were nearly always shown, the plank seams being drawn on with black ink. Other details such as hatches and gratings were also often drawn on. Only very rarely are models seen where the decks are planked with small individual wooden strips. Windows and doors are also often drawn onto the superstructure but on the more detailed models they were made from cast brass items, such as on the owners' model of *Mauretania* and on *Olympic* class liners.

There were at least four models of the *Olympic* class built by Harland & Wolff's model shop, three half-models, two built to $\frac{1}{8}$in = 1ft, or 1:96 scale, and one built to $\frac{1}{4}$in = 1ft, or 1:48 scale, and one very detailed full-hull owners' model, also built to 1:48 scale. This model still exists and is kept at the Merseyside Maritime Museum in Liverpool, although it has been more or less altered to represent *Titanic*.

The oldest known photograph of one of the builders' models is dated 29 October 1908

11

BUILDERS' MODELS

The 1:96 scale half-model, possibly built for the presentation of the design of the *Olympic* class liners that was held in Belfast on 28 July 1908. Undeniably a model of an *Olympic* class liner, it shows many details that still have to be taken care of: the funnels are too high and there is only one mast. The bridge front is rounded and there appears to be an elevator shaft in front of the grand staircase skylight.
(Photograph: Harland & Wolff Claes-Göran Wetterholm collection)

This 1:48 scale half-model was built possibly after the contract was signed and the design tested on this model. This model has two masts and the bridge front is flat. The elevator shaft in front of the grand staircase skylight has been removed.
(Photograph: Harland & Wolff Claes-Göran Wetterholm collection)

and shows the small scale half-model which was most probably built for the presentation of the design of the *Olympic* class liner that was held in Belfast on 28 July 1908. Although the model is clearly recognisable as an *Olympic* class liner, a number of design details were changed before *Olympic* and *Titanic* were put into service. It is interesting to see that the Second Class promenade on C deck is not enclosed with windows and the forward bulkhead of the bridge is rounded. This rounded bridge front can also be seen on many contemporary postcards showing *Olympic* or *Titanic*. The bridge wing cabs are missing, and a square deckhouse can also be seen in front of the skylight above the forward grand stairway. Though this was not added on *Olympic* or *Titanic*, it was included later on *Britannic* as part of an elevator shaft, though not quite as large as it is seen here. The funnels are too high and all the same height. On the ships as built the third funnel was the highest. The height rose from the first to the third funnels at a slight angle, while the fourth funnel was slightly lower than the third. The portholes of the First Class dining saloon are still in a single row, not the double row as on the real ships. A surprising amount of detail is to be found here, such as entry-ports in the hull and coal-chute lids. On the starboard side of *Titanic*'s F deck, the line of coal chutes was interrupted in the swimming pool area.

The large 1:48 scale half-model was possibly built after the contract letter had been signed and alterations in the design included on this model. Its whereabouts are unknown. However, as no photographs of the small scale model seem to have been taken after this date, it can be assumed that further design stages were tested on the large scale model only and that the small scale model was no longer needed and was disposed of.

The large model could be raised and lowered by turning the large wheel in the centre of the base front. It seems that the model was also lowered into its transport case, which also formed its base, by turning this wheel. The seam running across the backing plate was where it folded when being lowered into the case. This kind of mechanism must have been necessary: according to Harland & Wolff´s records, this model weighed some 1.3 tons. The funnels had to be dismantled when the model was stowed in its case. It can be seen in the photographs that the third and fourth funnel are rigged, although there is a noticeable slack in the wires. Some of the funnel wires, called 'guy-wires', do not extend up to the black rim of the funnels. On the third funnel the few wires that have been attached are pinned to the funnel at about half its height, while on the fourth funnel some wires actually are attached to the bottom of the black rim as well as others being pinned at half the funnels' height, such as on funnel No 3. *Olympic*'s funnels had eyebolts at exactly this position – *Titanic*'s did not. The funnels are still too high, as are the masts. The masts were painted onto the backing plate as was some of the rigging, including the shrouds.

The large entrance to the veranda cafe on the promenade deck has already been included. The shell plating has been drawn onto the hull as have some of the entry-ports. The numbers of the frames can just be seen marked on the hull slightly beneath the waterline as well as above the C deck portholes. The bulwark on the forward part of the boat deck is too long, and the bridge wing cabs have yet to be added. The windows on B deck are evenly spaced. The caption on the backing plate reads: 'White Star Steamers *Olympic* & *Titanic*, combined Reciprocating and Turbine'.

The small half-model which can be seen above the stern is said to be a small vessel, *Kitty of Coleraine*, and was probably included to compare of the sizes of the two ships. Some of the differences between the initial design concept and the vessels as built, mentioned above, have now already been taken care of: the promenade on C deck has been enclosed, the front of the bridge is flat and the bridge sides have been opened. The First Class restaurant has the double row of portholes, and the deck house in front of the skylight has been removed.

This large scale half-model was also used by the British inquiry investigating the cause of the disaster. On 24 April the British Receiver of Wrecks wrote to Harland & Wolff asking for a large scale model of *Titanic* that could be dismantled to show the interior of the ship for use during the inquiry. Harland & Wolff offered to convert their large model to *Titanic*'s configuration for the inquiry. This alteration took place within four days. On 28 April Harland & Wolff wrote to the Receiver of Wrecks that arrangements had been made to have the model shipped to the Scottish Hall, Buckingham Gate, where the inquiry was held.

Another very large half-model was built and attached to the facade of the White Star Line office in London's West End in June 1911. Two huge letters 'G' & 'R' were placed above the model. This was to celebrate the coronation of King George V and the maiden voyage of *Olympic*. Some sources say that this was

the 1:48 scale half-model that was later converted to *Titanic* and used during the British inquiry. The fact that the model attached to the White Star Line building was subjected to the vagaries of wind and weather, makes it seem unlikely that a wooden model was displayed. Where this model came from and what eventually became of it is unknown.

The owners' model is now on display in the Merseyside Maritime Museum as *Titanic*. In early photographs it features the rounded bridge front, though the bulwark on the boat deck has been shortened and the emergency boats or cutters (Nos 1 and 2) are in place. The windows on B deck are still evenly spaced, though breaks appear at the ship's expansion joints. The entrance-doors on this deck have yet to be included. On *Titanic* and *Britannic* this deck was no longer a promenade deck, but had additional staterooms along the hull sides. Thus the arrangement of the windows appears to be quite haphazard when compared with those of *Olympic*. This was one of the major differences between *Olympic* and *Titanic*. The wreck lying some 3800m (12,500ft) beneath the ocean also has staterooms on this deck extended to the hull sides, and so the unevenly-spaced windows which can be clearly seen on photographs and videos of the wreck. This proves the ludicrous theory that it was *Olympic* that sank and not *Titanic* to be nonsense. Large cowl vents can be seen on top of the tank room. These were fortunately not adopted on the real ships. The funnels are still too high and the bridge wing cabs are still missing. The skylight walls above the forward First Class grand staircase have round portholes. An additional window can be seen between the entrance ports on the now closed C deck promenade. This window was never fitted on the real ship and, oddly enough, Harland & Wolff's model-

Stern view of the 1:48 scale half-model. The shell plating strakes are drawn onto the hull and the frames are numbered. It is said that the small half-model above the poopdeck was of *Kitty of Coleraine*. It was possibly added to this model for size comparison. The model could be stowed into its base for transport.
(Photograph: Harland & Wolff Claes-Göran Wetterholm collection)

The owners' model of the Olympic class liner in a very early design stage. This model is currently on display in the Merseyside Maritime Museum though it is in a rather sorry state. The restoration of this model destroyed more than it saved.
(Photograph: Harland & Wolff
Claes-Göran Wetterholm collection)

The owners' model in its glass case. Apart from a few minor details this is an exact replica of Olympic in 1911. This model was later converted to Britannic. The White Star Line never had a model of the Titanic, for obvious reasons.
(Photograph: Harland & Wolff
Claes-Göran Wetterholm collection)

makers never got around to removing it – it can still be seen on the model today.

Later photographs show the model in its glass case, prior to delivery to White Star. The large vents on the tank room have been removed, and the portholes on the skylight have been altered. The model in this picture is very close to the appearance of *Olympic* as she was when commissioned, though a number of vents and fittings as installed on the real ship are missing and were never included on the model as some decisions about including fittings built on the ship were made 'on site', and these modifications may never have got through to the model shop. It probably did not seem worthwhile. This model was fitted with interior lighting as one photograph shows it with its lights on. It must have been quite a sight in darkness.

One frequently reads about this model having been altered to represent *Titanic*. This was seemingly never the case. It is understandable that both Harland & Wolff and the White Star Line did not wish to have the memory of the *Titanic* disaster perpetuated, so this model was never converted to an exact replica of *Titanic*. After the *Titanic* disaster, travellers' confidence in the White Star Line had to be restored, so instead of displaying a model of the *Olympic* in their office, the White Star Line considered it wiser to have the model they had on display converted to an even more superior and safer liner – *Britannic*. The model portrays *Britannic* as she would have looked as a passenger liner. Following the loss of *Titanic*, the design of the *Olympic* class liners was radically altered to improve safety. The most obvious external difference between *Britannic* and her sisters was the innovative boat-handling gear. This takes the viewer a while to get used to after being familiar with the yacht-like lines of *Olympic* and *Titanic*.

One year after the Cunard and White Star Lines merged in 1934, *Olympic* was scrapped. It was frequently the case for builders' models to be shipped to the breakers as well, either also to be broken up or sold. The model was also sent to Thomas W. Ward Ltd. of Sheffield to be disposed of, although its whereabouts are not known until the late 1940s, when it was rediscovered in Blackpool, of all places. It is said that it was on display at Blackpool Airport. The model was apparently in a dreadful state when it was handed over to the Liverpool City Museums, one of the predecessor parent bodies of the Merseyside Maritime Museum, in 1951. It had lost its glass case, was very dirty, had received a great deal of rough treatment and was in dire need of extensive repairs and restoration. In 1957 the model was loaned to Pinewood Studios for a year for use as a study model for the making of the film 'A Night to Remember', though it cannot be seen

After the loss of *Titanic* the owners' model was converted to represent *Britannic*, the third of a trio of liners, which, like her sister *Titanic*, would never complete a commercial voyage. The innovative new boat-handling gear is obvious.
(Photograph: Harland & Wolff Claes-Göran Wetterholm collection)

in the film as another model was built and used for filming in the studio water tank. Photographs taken after filming exist showing this model in a very damaged and dirty condition.

The model did not represent *Britannic* at this time. A photograph showing Joseph Boxhall standing behind the model clearly shows that the innovative boat-handling gear had been removed and replaced with a row of boats running the entire length of the boat deck as on *Olympic*. However, the enclosed aft well deck and the *Britannic*-type enclosure of the A deck promenade walls remained.

Not until the late 1970s was the museum in the position to undertake major restoration, which included a new display case. In 1978 the model underwent a four-year restoration programme by Scale Models International of Crosby. While refurbishing the model, Scale Models found 'Yard No. 401', ie *Titanic*'s yard number, pencilled onto many internal sections. Due to the huge interest in *Titanic*, the model had been restored to represent her, and the name was painted onto the bows and stern even though the model is more or less a hybrid of all three *Olympic* class ships, though many of the details of the model in its *Britannic* period remain. The most obvious of these are the promenade deck and B deck windows and the three expansion joints – *Olympic* and *Titanic* had only two. The deck above the aft well deck was also removed whilst the model was being refurbished.

The model was put on display for the first time in 1982 at the Merseyside Maritime Museum. In 1990 it was loaned to the Ulster Folk and Transport Museum, and is now on display again at the Merseyside Maritime Museum. Unfortunately, the rigging is incorrect and the majority of fittings such as bench seats, vents etc, are missing. The most striking mishap that occurred during restoration is that the funnels were misplaced. The third funnel is the lowest and not the first! Many people, seeing this model, may well believe that it is the original builders' model of *Titanic*. But, as we now know, no such model was ever built.

The *Britannic* model on display, possibly during the 1913 World Trade Fair in Belgium.
(Photograph: Author's collection)

A large half-model of *Olympic*, most probably in 1:48 scale, was attached to the White Star Line office building to celebrate the coronation of King Goorgo V and tho maidon voyage of *Olympic*, both in June 1911.
(Photograph: Paul Louden-Brown)

3 The Hull, Propellers and Display Base

Depending on the scale of the proposed model, there are several ways of building the hull of a model ship. Two methods will be described here. First, the so-called 'bread and butter' system, and secondly the 'plank on frame' system which was used for the Orlando model. For a smaller scale model the 'bread and butter' method is the more appropriate. Wood is the best material to use for both methods.

'Bread and butter'

I usually work with hard wood such as pear or cherry, which is quite a waste really as it is expensive and not visible once the models are completed. However, these woods are a delight to carve to shape and that is why I like working with them. The novice modelmaker would probably prefer a soft wood, such as yellow pine or hard balsa wood. Jelutong is also easy to handle, but is unfortunately also quite expensive.

The planks used should be slightly larger than the model (viewed from above) and the thickness the same as the distance between the waterlines shown in the profile. I have these planks cut to shape by my local timber merchant. I always start by drawing the centreline and the position of the frames on the planks. Once this has been completed, the planks are firmly secured to one another by small blobs of white glue to form a block of wood, but so that they can be separated again without difficulty later on. I secure them with glue in the areas of the planks that will be sawn off at a later stage, *ie* the corners, so that I do not have to remove the remains of the glue and if the planks are damaged whilst separating them, the damage is restricted to areas of wood that are not needed in the future.

Once the planks have been attached to each other, three vertical holes are drilled through the block at the centreline into which brass tubes are inserted. They are not secured as they will be removed again at a later stage. I use a drill in a stand to ensure that the holes are drilled exactly vertically through the block. The brass tubes should have the same diameter as these holes because they will act as guides to ensure that the planks line up precisely when they are glued together permanently. The block of wood can now be taken apart again and the waterlines transferred from the plan onto the planks. I do this using cardboard templates. However, the location of the guide-holes drilled into the planks has to be transferred to the plans first. I photocopy the waterlines onto cardboard but they can be drawn on the cardboard instead using carbon paper – not forgetting the centreline, the frames and guide holes. A cardboard template is needed for each waterline. The cardboard waterlines are then cut out. Cutting out the guide-holes of the cardboard template has to be done with precision. I use a home-made punch made from a sharpened steel tube. However, similar results can be achieved by careful use of a sharp modeller's knife.

The shape of the waterlines of the hull can now be drawn onto each plank. The brass tubes are inserted into the holes, the cardboard template placed on the plank using the tubes as guides and the waterline pencilled on both sides of the plank. For instance, if we take the plank between waterlines 6 and 7, waterline number 7 is drawn on the upper side of the plank and waterline number 6 on the lower side (always using the brass tubes as guides). The plank between waterlines 5 and 6 has waterline number 6 drawn on the upper side, and number 5 on the lower side and so on. I mark each plank to indicate which is the upper and which the lower side. Once the waterlines have all been drawn onto the wood, I cut out the laminates of the hull using a belt-saw. The cut is not made exactly along the drawn line, but about 0.5mm (0.02in) outside the hull. Always use the drawn lines of the upper side of each plank as a guide to cutting out the laminates. This has its reasons: the hull of a ship usually tapers inwards towards the keel. By cutting out the laminate on the upper side, it becomes obvious that the required cut of the hull on the lower side is narrower. The slope between the upper and the lower side can be carved with a knife. However, I always leave a distance of approximately 0.5mm (0.02in) of wood outside the drawn line. It is easier to remove excess wood than to fill and sand dents in the hull resulting from too much wood having been carved from it.

On each plank the position of the frames will have to be sawn in slightly on the outer edge of the hull. These slots will leave the position of the frames visible once the laminates have been fastened to one another and have been sanded. Later we shall use cardboard templates of the frames to determine the final shape of the hull, especially around the keel, where it would be very difficult to determine the shape of the hull without these templates.

I would recommend building the complete hull up to B deck in this method. The promenade deck walls on A deck stand proud of the hull, and to me it seems easier to build the promenade deck as a complete unit by itself and install it after completion at a much later stage. The sheer of the hull and the angle of the well decks have to be taken into account at this stage. I plank the well decks at this stage using a very thin sheet of maple veneer. The thickness of the deck planking has to be taken off the topside of the hull, as otherwise the decks would eventually end up being too high in this area.

The forecastle and poop deck should also be installed at this stage. However, the Third Class entrances of the well decks have to be considered and cut out of the planks for the forecastle and afterdeck. The thickness of the deck planking should also be taken off the planks used for the forecastle and poop deck. A number of modelmakers like to draw the seams of the deck planking onto the decks with a sharp pencil. This can look striking when it has been done with care, as on builders' models of ocean liners or modern warships. We did it on the Orlando model too but I would not do it on a model smaller than 1:200 scale, though the technique of doing so will be described at a later stage.

The planks can now be glued together, also using the brass tubes as guides. The complete construction should be held together using G-clamps and left overnight to cure. Once dry, the brass tubes can be removed and the hull sanded, using templates of the frames to constantly check and recheck the shape of the hull.

The centre propeller was installed in a large oval-shaped cut-out in the aft end of the hull. This can be seen in the plans. The bossing for the central propeller was cut out of the hull, in a V-shape, and a wooden rod of the required diameter glued to the cut-out. The hawse pipe at the bow was added the same way. Though all pictures of *Titanic* show the hawse pipe without its cover, I believe that the cover was added once the ship was at sea so I usually add the cover on my models. The propeller bossings were added with thin wood and rods. Finally, dents and the cut-outs for the frame locations in the hull can be filled and the complete unit sanded.

Plank on frame

This is the system we used in building the hull of the Orlando model, and I can recommend it for models larger than 1:200 scale. Using the Harland & Wolff lines plan the centre- or keel-plate was constructed and cut out from 10mm (0.39in) MDF boards. A board large enough to take the keel-plate as a whole was not obtainable so we had to produce the forward and aft half of the hull separately and the joint was placed between frames 13 and 14. The Harland & Wolff plans are nearly 100 years old and have been stored rolled-up, so on the copies that we had the keel was not a straight line as it should be, so we could not cut out a cardboard copy and use it as a template. We drew a straight line for the keel along the bottom edge of each board, onto which the location of the frames was marked. The frames were then drawn as vertical lines, up to the top of B deck (the height measured from the plans) and lines were added connecting the top of each frame. However, 5mm (0.19in) had to be taken off the top along the hull's entire length to give space for the plywood decking. Once this was completed we had a silhouette of the hull drawn on the MDF boards. Before sawing out the keel-plates the waterline was added and also slots for the frames.

The same material, 10mm MDF, was used for the frames and as frame 13 is the centre-frame, the edges of the slot for frame 13 were placed 5mm (0.19in) in front if and 5mm

THE HULL, PROPELLERS AND DISPLAY BASE

The keel-plate held firmly onto the box by triangular wooden boards that were glued to the box-top. In the centre of the keel-plate we can see where the two halves were mated with boards and additionally secured with nuts and bolts. Handles along the top edge for lifting the plate can also be seen. The frames are leaning against the wall behind the model.

behind the frame-line drawn on the keel-plate. The aft edges for the slots for frames 1–12 were drawn 10mm (0.39in) behind the frame-line, their forward edges were these frame lines. This was to ensure that a sufficient amount of wood was given for the frames when the hull was being planed and sanded, otherwise too much material could be taken off and this would result in a dented and distorted hull. The slots for frames 14–21½ were vice versa: the aft edges of the slots were the frame-lines drawn on the keel-plate; the forward edges were drawn 10mm (0.39in) in front of the frame-line. The slots lead from the keel-plate top down and ended at the waterline. After this had been completed the keel-plate was sawn out. Openings, to act as handles for lifting the construction, were also sawn out slightly beneath the top edge of the keel-plate.

To stiffen the hull we planned to insert two huge alloy-beams into openings in each frame along almost the entire length of the hull. The section of these beams was 100/200mm (3.9/7.8in). The two keel-plate halves were mated with two boards on each side glued across the joint, in the entire length of the distance between frames 13 and 14. A gap was left between these boards to give room for the alloy beams to be pushed past them. The joint was then additionally strengthened with about two dozen large nuts and bolts. We then had the complete, 5.50m (18ft) long keel-plate for the *Titanic* model.

The box upon which the model would later be displayed had already been built and it was also used to carry the model while it was under construction. We drew a centre-line on the top of the box and also cross-lines at the half distance between each frame. These were the locations for the triangular boards that firmly supported the keel-plate on both sides while the frames were being inserted.

Now it was time to prepare the frames. Templates were made of one half of each frame from cardboard, again using the builders' plans. With all the cardboard templates cut out, we drew the frames onto MDF boards, one half first, and then flipped the template at the keel-line and drew the other half. The loaded waterline was also added to the frames on both sides (fore and aft side). The openings to accommodate the alloy beams were also drawn onto the frames and with all the preparation drawing complete, 5mm (0.19in) also had to be subtracted from the hull top for the decks and the slots for the keel-plate drawn, this time leading from the keel up to the waterline, the frames were sawn out using a belt-saw. Before the frames were inserted into the keel-plate, wooden ledges were attached to both sides of each frame, with 12mm (0.47in) distance from the hull sides and bottom. These would support the wooden hull planking that would be applied later. A thin slot was sawn into the sides of each frame at the waterline to ensure that the waterline would still remain visible after the hull had been planed and sanded. The next step was to insert all frames onto the keel-plate.

Elwyn Davies inserting the frames. Note the opening for the aluminium beams, one of which is lying on top of the box.

THE HULL, PROPELLERS AND DISPLAY BASE

The whole construction was then left overnight for the glue to cure and the two alloy beams were then driven into the hull, one on each side of the keel-plate the following day. We started at the stern and pushed each beam slowly through the openings. Passing through about the first seven or eight frames, the beams could be pushed in by hand. However, the further forward we proceeded, the more difficult it became to move the beams. In the end a mallet and a wooden block were called for to drive the beams into the hull.

Each triangular support that had been glued onto the box had to be removed one by one, as the beams were being driven forward. Towards the end of this process we had only a few supports remaining and these did not act sufficiently to hold the hull, nor to withstand the force of the beams being hammered into the hull. Four large wooden blocks were then screwed to the top of the box, two in front of and two behind frame 13, to stop the hull from moving while the beams were being forced into it. In the end it was worthwhile: when we lifted the hull at one end there was no cracking or noise or any sign of movement whatsoever. The beams secure the whole model against any warping or movement.

The hull was then inverted and the gaps between the frames filled with 12mm (0.47in) thick pine planks. The ledges that had been applied to the frames held these planks in position as they were glued and nailed to the frames and ledges. At the centre of the hull this was quite straightforward as we had no complicated shapes of the hull to deal with, but at the stern, around the propeller bossings, it turned out to be quite tricky. Numerous wooden strips of various shapes and sizes were designed and constructed to ensure that the hull turned out satisfactorily with no dents and no oversized gaps between the planks that needed to be filled. The extreme bow and stern were built up of laminates of wood. These were designed and constructed using the builders' plans and attached to the hull once completed.

It was then decided to remove part of the keel-plate between the stern-post and the propeller bossings under the stern counter and to build this part of the hull separately also using laminates of wood, as had been done for the counter and the bow. A new keel-plate was made for this part of thinner MDF, 8mm (0.31in), and the whole area built up of 10mm (0.39in) thick wooden layers and later bolted onto the hull as a complete unit. With the planking complete we had a very strong hull shell that could take a surprising amount of movement and handling without suffering any damage. It was very much like a real boat.

Filler was applied to the hull at every frame, and then sanding and planing could begin. This was without doubt one of the most laborious tasks of the whole project. It was exhausting and also very dirty. The hull was constantly primed, filled and sanded to prevent any blemishes that could show up after the shell plating had been applied.

Inserting the beams into the hull. Pushing these beams through the first seven or eight frames could be done by hand. However, the further we progressed, the more and more difficult they became to move. A block of wood and a mallet were needed to drive them into the hull.

The hull is now inverted and 12mm (0.47in) thick planks were used to fill the gaps between the frames. Along the bilge narrow strips of wood were needed making it easier to fill the round shape of this part of the hull.

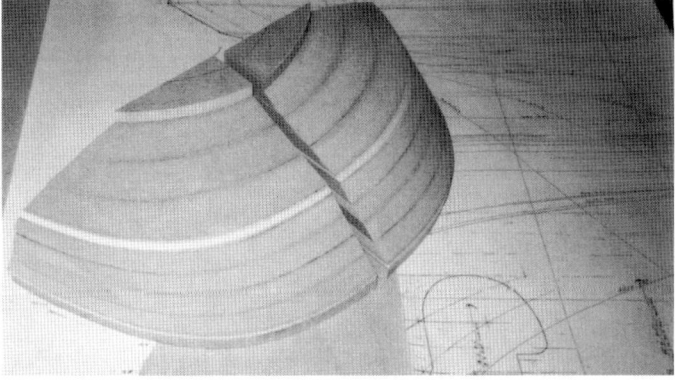

The counter built up of 10mm (0.39in) wood laminates. Thinner layers of plywood were needed to get the correct height between the knuckles. The counter would later be attached to the hull as a complete unit. Note the slot for the keel-plate.

THE HULL, PROPELLERS AND DISPLAY BASE

(Right & far right) The hull being treated with yet another layer of primer to ensure that no dents or blemishes would show up later. The amount of dust that planing and sanding the hull creates can be seen on the workshop floor.

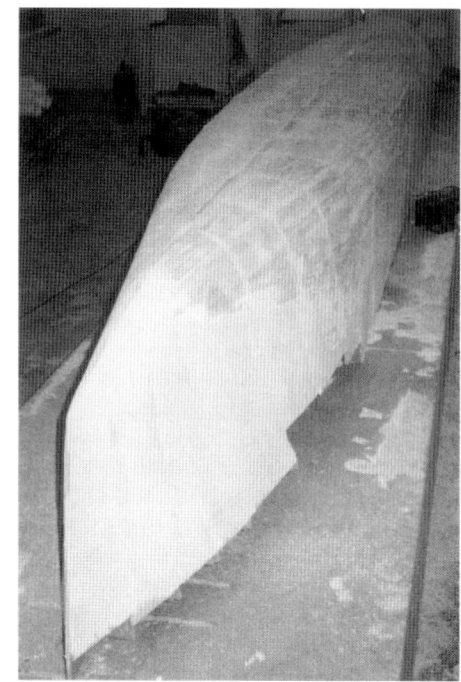

From the start I had been in constant anxiety of any inaccuracy or even carelessness marring the whole work or being obvious when looking at the completed model. Every process had to be well thought-out in advance and great care had to be taken following the builders' plans. I suppose that my education as a civil engineer helped me to spot difficulties in advance and find solutions and ensure a sensible progression of work for the whole project. If anything went wrong whilst building the hull with regard to its anatomy or dimensions, we would have to do it again. It took us three months to build the hull before shell plating even began. Very soon we would know if we had got it right.

The aft ends of the propeller wings were sanded to shape. At first it appeared to me that they were rounded, but after studying photographs and plans of the real ship we noticed that they were actually pointed. This is pretty obvious, as they have to allow for the flow of water to pass them easily while the ship is

(Right) Using paper strips the position of the strakes was taken from the framing plan and transferred onto the hull.

(Far right) The primed hull with all strakes drawn on and ready for shell-plating.

THE HULL, PROPELLERS AND DISPLAY BASE

underway. At this stage the periphery of the centre propeller's cut-out was also sanded and filed to shape. The rudder was made of a single sheet of 8mm (0.31in) MDF and the stiffeners and hinges added.

One of the last measures prior to shell plating was to give the hull a final coat of primer.

Decks of 5mm (0.19in) plywood were also added, but at this stage they were only nailed to the hull in case they had to be removed again later. The stem was added next using 2mm (0.07in) sheet-styrene, the shape taken from the builders' plans. We designed the stem for the model about 20mm (0.78in) deep, so the same depth was removed from the bow accordingly. A slot also had to be sawn into the hull to accommodate the stem where it meets the keel.

For the shell plating we had two builders' plans: the shell plating plan and the framing plan, both in 1:48 scale. Two plans are necessary as in plan view the exact dimensions of most of the shell plates are not given due to the curvature of the hull. We took the length of each plate from the shell plating plan while the heights were measured from the framing plan which turned out to be one of the most important plans we had even though it appeared pretty unspectacular to us at first sight. From this plan we marked the location of each strake at each frame on thin strips of paper, placed onto the plan, starting from the centre of the keel and working our way up to the hull top. Using these strips of paper as guides, one for each frame, the strakes were transferred onto the hull. Thus placing these paper strips onto the inverted hull, at the marked centre of the keel, the hull top marked on these strips should end exactly at the top of the model's hull. They did – every single one of them! This showed us that we were going the right way.

Each strake was then drawn onto the hull following the markings that were transferred using the paper strips. Flexible rulers were called for to tackle the complicated curved areas at the bow and stern. With the hull primed and the strakes and waterline added, the shell plating could begin. However, we felt it would be better to leave the wooden hull as it was for a period of six weeks to allow the wood to work and settle. We continued with the fittings on the forecastle deck but this will be dealt with in Chapter 7.

Titanic's centre propeller in the background and the wing propeller bosses at Harland & Wolff, 31 May, 1911. The letters TC can be just made out on one of the centre propeller's blades. Their meaning is unknown – possibly 'Turbine Centre'. (Photograph: Terrell Wright)

Propellers

Titanic's centre screw propeller and the blades of the wing propellers were cast in manganese bronze, which is a relatively soft metal. The idea was that the blades would distort if they hit a submerged object while the ship was underway. If the propeller blades had been also made of steel, the impact of the rotating propellers hitting an object would also have caused serious damage to the propeller shaft. Replacing a propeller blade involved far less labour than replacing a complete shaft. This, however, also had one disadvantage: the blades on the wing propellers were bolted onto the boss. *Olympic* lost a propeller blade in March 1912 and had to be returned to Harland & Wolff for repairs. The propeller bosses were cast in steel.

On wreck footage one can still see the yard number 401 on one of the propeller blades. This number was applied to all wing propeller blades on both sides. Each blade had its own number at the base, *ie* S1 for Starboard 1, P1 for port 1 etc. In addition to this it seems that the centre propeller also had the letters 'T C' stamped into it. What this means is not known; perhaps 'Turbine Centre'?

All propellers for the model were cast in resin. For the centre propeller I carved a quarter-propeller in wood. This included one blade and a quarter hub. Four quarter-propellers were cast in resin and then joined together. The advantage of this approach was that all blades of the completed propeller had the same pitch and angle. The complete propeller would have been very difficult to carve in a single piece. After the quarters had been cemented together, the seams needed a little tidying up and the hub was cut off as it had not turned out as well as I had hoped. A new hub was turned from wood, a resin item cast and this was added to the propeller. After the

Display Base

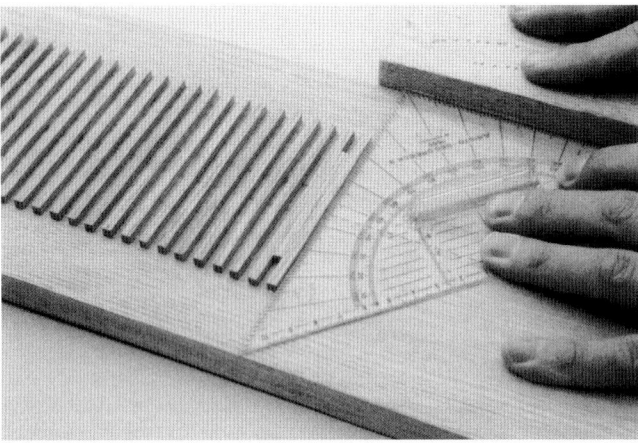

(Above) Attaching wooden strips to the base using a block of wood and a triangle to ensure that all strips are at a perfect 90° angle to the base's sides. A small wooden strip as a spacer is placed between an already-attached strip and the next strip to ensure that all strips have the same distance.

(Below) After the glue has cured the spacer is removed and the next strip can be applied.

I believe the most suitable base for a model of a large ship, no matter in which scale, is one representing a dry-dock floor using thin wooden strips acting as the blocks on which the hull rests. For smaller models I prefer an oak plank about 1cm (0.4in) thick which I usually get from my timber merchant already cut to shape.

The first step is to draw the centerline onto the board. I then use the hull of the model as a template to draw the outline of one half of the hull bottom onto a piece of cardboard. This outline is transferred onto the base using the cardboard template. Due to the complex shapes of the hull it is, of course, not easy to draw an exact outline of the whole hull on the cardboard. The hull sides or halves would definitely not match. This is why only one half of the hull is drawn on the cardboard and then cut out and transferred onto the base. This template is then flipped over at the centerline and the other side is drawn on the base to ensure that both hull sides have the same outline.

Of course, the outer edges of the wooden strips do not have to follow the sides of the hull exactly, but I like to get it pretty close. With the outline of the hull bottom in place the lengths of the wooden strips can be determined. Once these have been cut their centres are marked with a pencil. This is where the strips will be attached to the base at the centerline.

These thin square strips of oak are attached using a block of wood placed alongside the base and a triangle held against this block as a guide to ensure that all strips are at a 90° angle to the centerline. Between an attached strip and a new strip a shorter strip of wood is placed which acts as a spacer to ensure that all wooden strips have the same distance. Once the glue has set the spacer is pushed out and placed between the affixed and the successive strips; this is continued until all strips have been applied. Two small wedges are attached to the middle of the base, one on each side, to prevent the model from rocking. When a glass case is required I put the oak board onto another board about 1cm (0.4in) larger on each side, so the bottom board forms a step around the outer edges onto which the glass case's framework is placed.

For the Orlando model the base was a completely different matter, even though the appearance of the base is generally the same. A whole box was built which would have to support the model's weight as well as its own and which would also have to be as warp-free as possible to prevent the base or box ends from sagging while being lifted. A base was designed some 6m (20ft) long, 60cm (2.3ft) high and 1.20m (4.7ft) wide.

This box was also built using the plank-on-frame system. Three identical longitudinal plates were designed; two side plates and one centre plate. Slots were cut into these halfway down the top to the centerline, spaced at one foot. Thus 21 transverse plates with slots from the bottom up to the centreline were required which would then be inserted in the longitudinal plates and secured with white glue and screws. Before the top or lid was attached this basic box structure was still very flimsy.

Wooden beams about 5/5cm (2/2in) were then screwed to the inside of each corner of the box, thus to every joint in the plates. The top was added, and once this had been nailed onto the sides and frames the whole box was inverted, and wooden beams were fixed to the inner joints between the box top and the sides and frames.

Two layers of MDF boards, which were slightly smaller than the box top, were attached to the bottom of the box. This gave the whole construction considerable strength, and the box was now more or less warp-free but extremely heavy.

How the triangular supports were attached to the top of the base to support the keel plate while the hull was being built was described above. When these were no longer needed they were removed from the base and the base surface was sanded until smooth. Later, the top was covered with oak veneer boards onto which the wooden strips were attached. At first, these boards were slightly larger than the base top. Later, their outer edges were cut off flush to the sides before the black boards covering the sides of the base were attached. The wooden strips of the dry-dock floor had a

The completed base for a 76cm (30in) long model of the *Titanic*.

cross-section of 4/4cm (1.6/1.6in). This was done in the same way as described above, only in a much larger scale. There was no need to include a step at the edges of the base top to accommodate the glass case as the framework was screwed directly onto the base.

Finally, after the model had been completed, the sides of the base were covered with black plywood.

The base for the Orlando model under construction. The same technique as described for smaller models was used. Here the beams had a cross section of 4/4cm (1.6/1.6in). The sides of the base were later covered with black plywood.

THE HULL, PROPELLERS AND DISPLAY BASE

The propellers on the model. The starboard propeller has already received the yard numbers in white decals.

(Top right) Building the centre propeller for the model. The wooden master is at the top left. The four quarter propellers were joined together to form the one-piece centre propeller.

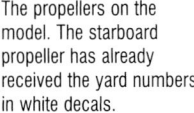

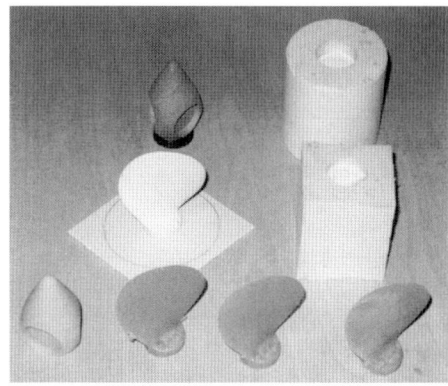

(Right) The wing propellers. The blades were handed, as these propellers rotated in opposite directions, so a master blade for the port and starboard propellers had to be carved from wood. Here the master blade can be seen primed in white. Holes were drilled into the blade mount and small nuts and screws added to the master as the bolts. The resulting gaps between the screws and the mounting plate were filled with diluted putty: any excess was wiped of with a damp cloth.

seams had all been filled and sanded, the propeller was given a coat of primer to reveal any further blemishes; there were none so the propeller was painted in bronze. After the paint had dried the numbers and letters were applied with white decals and the propeller was given a final coat of gloss varnish. Water-dilutable varnish was used so as not to attack the bronze enamel which had been applied earlier. I now think matt varnish, rather than gloss, would have given the propeller a more authentic appearance. Holes were drilled into the rear of the propeller and into the propeller shaft and the propeller was attached to the bossing with a large screw.

The wing propellers were built up more or less like the real thing. First the master blade was carved from wood and bolts from small screws and nuts added into pre-drilled holes. Three blades were cast from resin and attached to the resin-cast boss. The completed propellers were painted to match the centre propeller and numbers and letters added with white decals.

Smaller propeller blades can be cut out of thin brass sheet, bent to the required pitch and inserted into slots cut into a wooden or styrene hub.

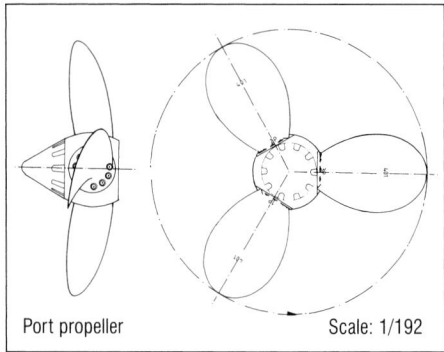

Port propeller   Scale: 1/192

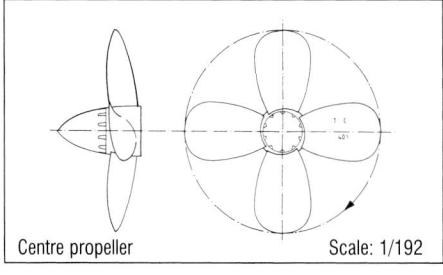

Centre propeller   Scale: 1/192

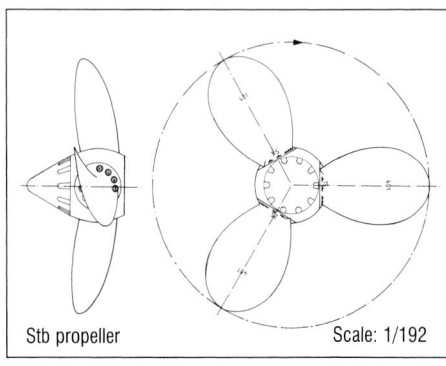

Stb propeller   Scale: 1/192

4 Shell Plating and Rudder

The hulls of these great liners from the early twentieth century were covered with steel plates, which were riveted to the frames in rows or 'strakes'. They formed the outer skin of the ship but they also added to the structural strength. They were massively engineered, the largest plates on the *Olympic* class liners being some 6ft wide and 36ft long and weighing approximately 4 tons. These shell plates were both riveted to the frames and to each other on the outer edges. The edge of a plate was placed over the edge of an attached plate, and these plates were then riveted together. The vertical joint between two plates is known as the 'butt lap', the horizontal joint as the 'landing'.

The hull bottom was clinker-plated, *ie* the edge of each plate facing the keel overlapped the edges of the plates facing the hull side of the preceding strake (like the hull planks on a Viking ship). The hull sides, however, were plated with 'inner' and 'outer' strakes so a pair of inner strakes had to be applied before an outer strake could be riveted onto them.

The hull of *Titanic* taken from the tender in Queenstown. Details of the hull are shown to advantage here such as shell plating, coal chutes, mooring cleats and riveting. A canvas cover has been half-lowered forward of the aft expansion joint on the promenade deck. If it was still like this or even fully lowered during the sinking is unknown. (Photograph: With kind permission of Jeremy Nightingale)

SHELL PLATING AND RUDDER

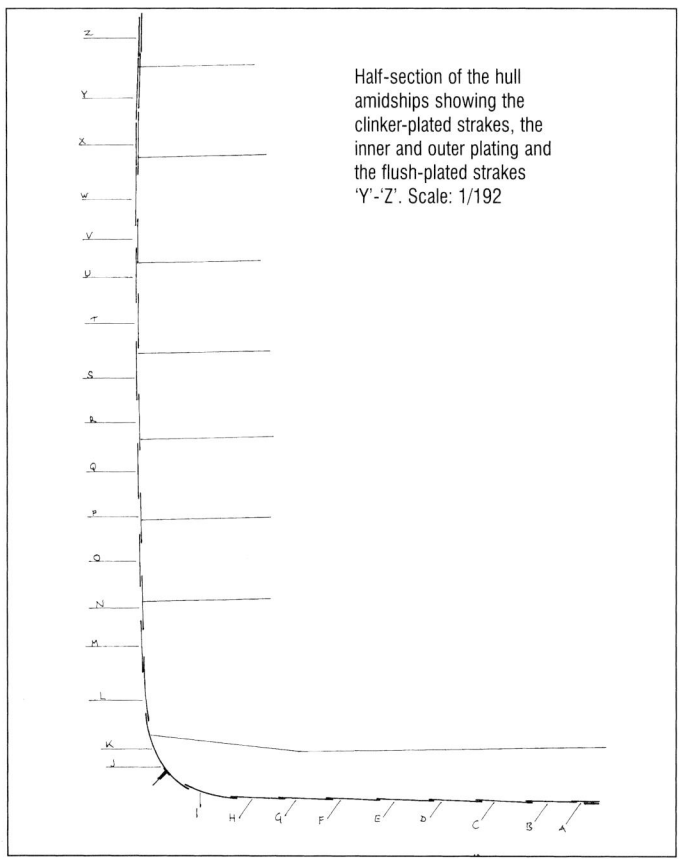

Half-section of the hull amidships showing the clinker-plated strakes, the inner and outer plating and the flush-plated strakes 'Y'-'Z'. Scale: 1/192.

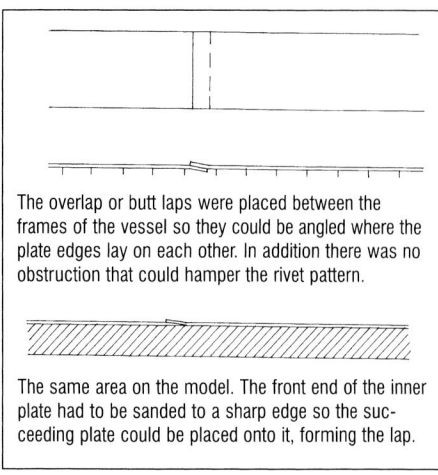

The overlap or butt laps were placed between the frames of the vessel so they could be angled where the plate edges lay on each other. In addition there was no obstruction that could hamper the rivet pattern.

The same area on the model. The front end of the inner plate had to be sanded to a sharp edge so the succeeding plate could be placed onto it, forming the lap.

Each strake was lettered, starting with strake 'A' next to the keel and ending – according to the plans – with strake 'Z' at C deck. From strake 'W' upwards to strake 'Z' the hull was flush-plated, *ie* apart from stiffeners or butt straps the hull was perfectly flat with no visible inner or outer strakes and laps or landings. Here the hull was double-plated for added strength against movement and flexing in heavy seas. This part of the hull was heavily riveted with round-headed rivets that were also added on the model. There was no need to include flush rivets on the model as they were hardly visible on the painted hull of the real ship, so they most certainly would not be visible at 1:48 scale.

The shell plates were numbered, No 1 plate being the first plate at the bow, although plating commenced at the stern, so No 1 plate would be the last plate of each strake to be riveted to the hull. The average strake consisted of some 32 plates. Each plate that was applied to the model had the number written onto it to avoid confusion. The first strake, strake 'A', had flush joints, *ie* the shell plate ends did not overlap. From strake 'B' onwards the overlaps had to be included. The length of each overlap was taken from the shell plating plan and varied between 3 and 6mm (0.11 and 0.23in) at 1:48 scale. The laps were always in the gap between two frames. There was a simple reason for this: the ends of these plates were bent in the area where the plate ends were positioned

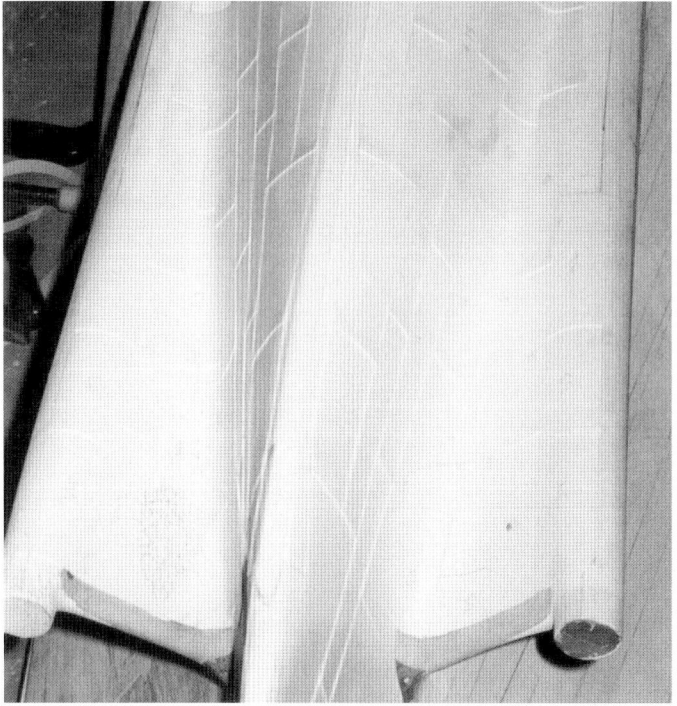

(Left) The shell plating began at the stern next to the keel. At the top of the picture can be seen where a single strake is converted into two strakes.

SHELL PLATING AND RUDDER

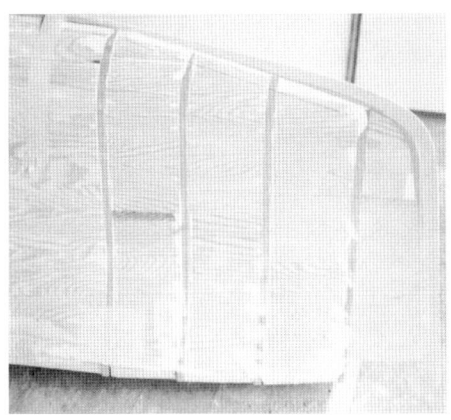

(Far left) The stem was made of 1.5mm (0.05in) sheet-styrene and attached to the hull in a slot which had been cut into the hull in front of the keel.

(Left) The keel plate tapered towards the bow to meet the stem. A small slot was cut into the keel plate to give access to the stem. This was later sanded smooth.

on top of each other. The forward end of a preceding plate would be bent slightly inwards, while the aft end of the successive plate would be bent slightly outwards so that both laps would fit perfectly in the overlapping area. As we were applying the sheet-styrene shell plates to a wooden hull, there was no room for us to bend the end of the preceding plate inwards. This end had to be sanded to a sharp edge with a sanding block. The aft edge of the following plate was then bent slightly outwards as on the real ship.

As on the original ship, shell plating commenced at the stern next to the keel and progressed towards the bow. We first attached strake 'A' on both sides, then applied the keel bar to this strake when it had been completed. The outer edges of strake 'A' were left approximately 3mm (0.11in) wider than drawn on the hull, so the inner edge of the following strake (in this case strake 'B') could be attached to it to form the landing.

The keel bar was a steel strip of 19½/3in, which equates to 10.3/1.6mm (0.4/0.06in) at 1:48 scale. It was made from lengths of sheet styrene, and after it was completed the stem was added to the bow. A vertical slot was cut into the extreme bow to accommodate the stem which was made from 15/1.5mm (0.59/0.06in) sheet styrene. The stem was then secured in this slot with epoxy resin. This was followed by all of the strakes on both sides of the keel. We used white sheet styrene for the shell plating, which was glued to the hull using cyanoacrylate superglue. The advantage

Olympic in dry dock. The transition from the keel bar into the stem can be seen.
(Photograph: Harland & Wolff – Claes-Göran Wetterholm collection)

SHELL PLATING AND RUDDER

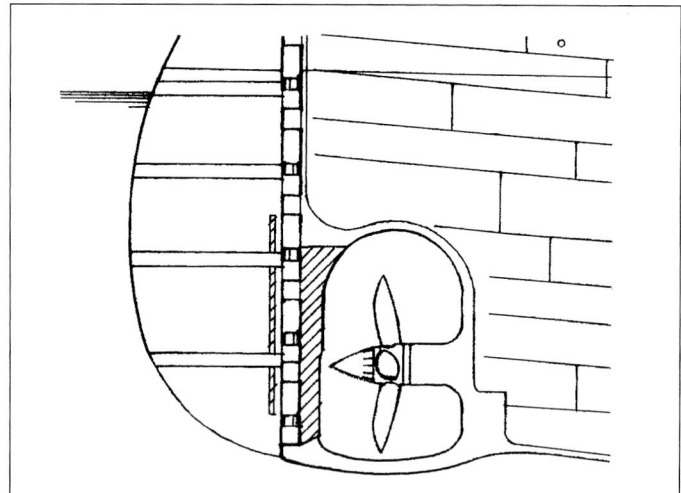

The zinc sheathing can be seen in the shaded area. The manganese bronze propeller caused electrolytic reactions which resulted in pitting of the stern post. The pitting of *Olympic*'s stern post became so severe that it broke more than once.

The zinc sheathing heat-moulded over a wooden master. The mould was cut from styrene sheet and attached to the hull.

of these thin white sheets was that the strake lines drawn on the white hull remained visible through the styrene plates after they had been attached, and could be easily transferred as a guide for positioning the plates of the following strake.

The sternpost was one weakness in the design of the *Olympic* class. The four-blade manganese bronze centre propeller rotating in front of it caused electrolytic reactions which resulted in pitting on the stern post. On *Olympic* this continuous pitting became so severe that the stern post was unable to cope with the pressure and broke more than once. Harland & Wolff were already aware of this problem while the ships were being designed. To counteract it, the stern post was sheathed with zinc and thin zinc strips were added to the forward edge of the rudder.

The sheathing for the sternpost was heat-moulded in an oven over a wooden master and attached to the hull.

A number of people who saw the model at this stage believed that we could produce endless amounts of plates all the same size and simply attach them to the hull. But this was not the case, as nearly every shell plate had its own dimensions. At the bottom of the hull in particular, the strakes get wider as they approach the centre frame, where they reach their greatest width before becoming narrower again towards the bow. In some cases a single strake continued at one point with two strakes of narrower plates to prevent the plates from becoming too wide. These double strakes reduced to single strakes again as they approached the bow. The widths of the strakes on the hull sides were more or less constant. The result of this was that nearly every single shell plate had to be made, cut out and attached to the hull individually. We never calculated exactly how many plates there are on the hull, but I am sure we got pretty close to 2000.

Plating the hull bottom was quite straightforward as no further details had to be added. Around the bilge keels, however, the hull was flush-plated to accommodate the double plating

(Above) The plating of the hull bottom getting well under way. Every shell plate has its own dimensions and had to be designed and cut out individually. Here too can be seen where single strakes were continued as double strakes.

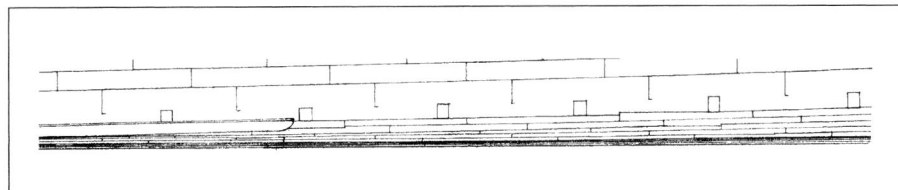

The hull around the bilge keels was flush plated, *ie* there were no laps at the plate ends, these being covered with butt straps.

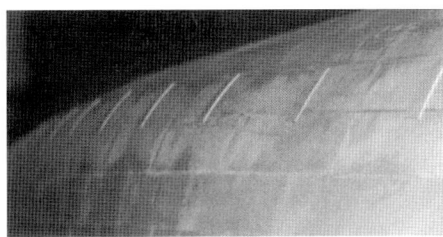

inside the hull behind the bilge keels. Here the vertical joints between the plates were covered with narrow stiffeners or 'butt straps'. The laps and joints were all just filled with liquid poly to ensure that the fully-plated hull was completely sealed. This was done very carefully, as too much poly would have melted the sheet styrene and the plating could have buckled. The plating around the propeller bossings was tricky. These plates were long and narrow and had to be pre-formed around a wooden dowel. The result, however, speaks for itself. In strake 'K' the two injections on each side were added. These were also heat-moulded in an oven over a wooden master. The exact size and location of the doublings around the injections was taken from the shell plating plan. Their cross-sections were found in an old issue of *The Engineer*.

The bilge keels were made of two layers of 1.5mm (0.05in) sheet styrene. The arrangement of the bilge keel strips and fastenings to the hull with L-beams can be seen in the drawing.

The inner and outer shell plating commenced at strake 'L' which was the first inner strake to be applied. As mentioned above, two inner strakes had to be applied before an outer strake could be applied to them. Unlike in real shipbuilding practice, the inner strakes on the model were wide enough to meet at the centreline of the outer strake that would later be attached to it. This meant that the sides of the whole wooden hull were completely covered with inner strakes. Here too the lines drawn onto the hull were visible through the thin sheet styrene and were transferred. However, the laps of the inner plating in the area to which an outer strake was to be applied had to be cut out first. These were simply cut out with a sharp scalpel and then removed from the hull with a small chisel.

Soon after we began the shell plating above the waterline, we added the first plates with portholes, including the rims of the actual portholes. These were small squares of sheet styrene with holes drilled into them which were slightly smaller than the adjacent holes that had been drilled into the shell plating. These squares were then glued onto the inside of the shell plates, and here too the area on

(Above left) The butt straps attached to the hull.

(Above) The same area after the bilge keel was attached.

(Below) Shell plating around the propeller bossings. This was one of the most difficult areas during the whole shell-plating process and the first major hurdle which had to be tackled soon after shell-plating began.

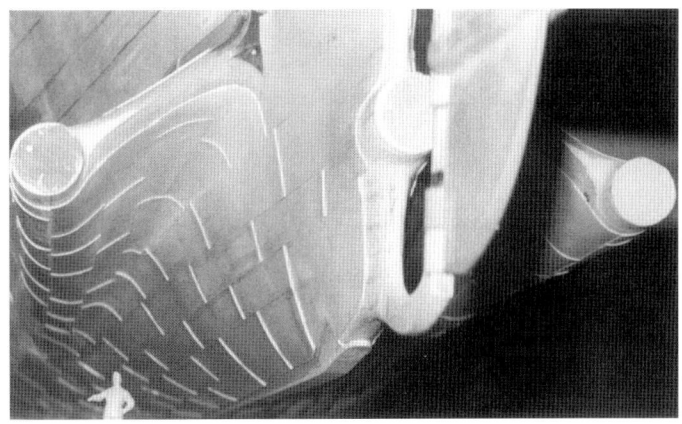

The two injections were heat-moulded in an oven.

SHELL PLATING AND RUDDER

A: The sheer lines drawn on the hull.

B: Two strakes of inner plating attached to the hull. The shaded areas show where part of the laps have to be removed to give room for the outer strake which will be attached to it.

C: The outer strake attached to the inner strakes.

D: Section through the hull side showing shell plating and a porthole.

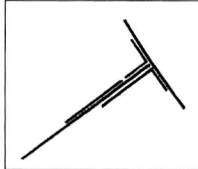

(Above) Section through the bilge keel showing different steel strips building up the keel, and also L-beams which fastened the keels to the hull.

(Below) Portion of *Titanic*'s starboard side hull beneath the waterline before launching.
(Photograph: *Cork Examiner*, Claes-Göran Wetterholm collection)

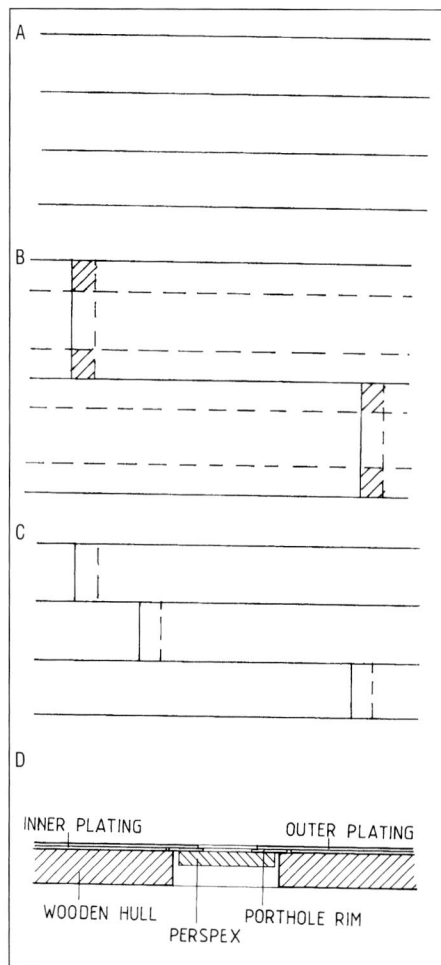

the inner strakes on which these squares would lie had to be removed from the inner strakes to give access to the rims. As if this was not enough, the portholes were glazed in 3mm (0.11in) perspex, which was also attached to the inside of the plate. This area had to be drilled out of the wooden hull to give access to the glazing. As the porthole glazing had to be masked prior to the hull being painted, the rims were painted black before the glazing was applied. This meant the portholes could be filled with generous amounts of masking fluid. Excessive paint on the shell plate had to be removed; we simply wiped it off with a fingertip.

The completed shell plates (*sans* glazing) were placed on the hull and the portholes drawn on the hull using the portholes in the shell plating as templates. The next step was to cut out the area in the inner strakes where the porthole rims would fit. After these had been cut out, holes were drilled into the hull to make room for the porthole glazing. At first the sides of these holes were then painted black so that they would not be visible when looking at the model. This turned out to be a mistake, as they can be seen in photographs taken with a flash. It would have been better to paint the inside of the glazing black instead. When all this was finished, the plates were attached to the hull with superglue and liquid poly along the laps and landings.

We came across the first flaw in the Harland & Wolff shell plating plan whilst producing plate 28 in strake 'S' (beneath the aft well deck). According to the plans we had, this plate had eight portholes on the starboard side and only one on the port side. Eight portholes in a shell plate of this size looked spectacular, to say the least. I had draughted my own set of

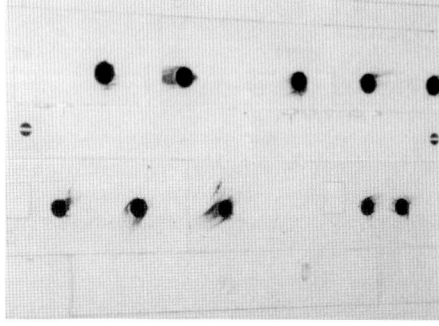

(Above) Details of the hull side showing coal chute doors, mooring clamps, ash ejectors and coaling clamps.

SHELL PLATING AND RUDDER

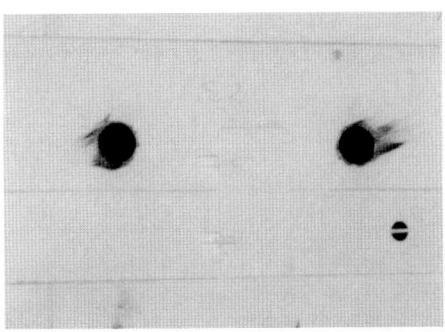

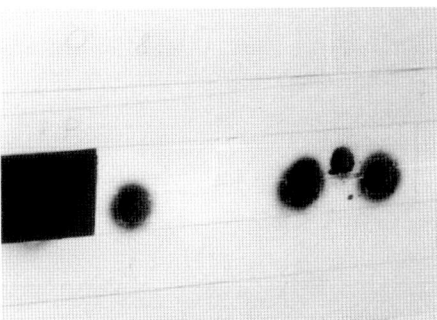

(Left) Holes had to be drilled into the hull side to give room for the porthole glazing. The sides of these holes were blackened to avoid their being visible when looking at the model.

(Below) Watertight portholes with brackets at 12, 6, 3 and 9 o'clock.

(Above) Ash door on the starboard side. The top half of the door was flush with the shell plating, the lower half was placed on the inner strake. Door hinges were made from styrene strip filed to shape.

Titanic plans several years before I built this model without the aid of the Harland & Wolff plans. But even my plans had no shell plate with eight portholes in this area. Nevertheless, as this was what the Harland & Wolff plans said, we made the plate accordingly. But the plate kept staring at me whenever I went past it, and I soon I started to get a little concerned about it. We got out all the photographs we had and compared every porthole in the plans with those that could be seen in photographs. My concern proved to be well founded, as plate 28 in strake 'S' only had four portholes on each side. Once this had been clarified, my concern grew. If there was a mistake here, where else would we find them? So we went through the plans, checking and comparing every porthole with the pictures we have. In addition to plate 28 we had to close six more portholes on the model and add five. We know how this happened: on-site alterations were made while the ships were under construction. Unfortunately, these alterations were never recorded in any of the plans. So we learned that we can never take plans for granted – even the builders' plans for *Titanic*.

The exact location of the ash ejectors was taken from the shell plating plan in strake 'R'. These were drilled into the hull after the shell plating had been completed. Great care was taken to ensure that the inside of each plate was completely covered with glue before it was fixed to the hull, otherwise sawdust and wooden splinters would have accumulated between the shell plating and the wooden hull as we drilled holes in the hull, through the shell plating and the wood, resulting in lumps which would have been very difficult to remove. The ash ejectors were the only holes that were drilled into the hull after completion of the shell plating.

For the mooring cleats, a hole was drilled into the shell plate; the plate was then placed on the hull and the location of the mooring cleat pencilled on. Here a small 'bowl' was drilled into the hull to form the back of the mooring cleat. This was also painted black before the shell plate was added. A horizontal bar was later added across each hole in the shell plates made from plastic rod.

Some of the portholes on the real ship in the bow could be covered with waterproof 'plugs'. These were attached to small triangular brackets which were fastened to the inside of the shell plate. These brackets were located at 12, 6, 3, and 9 o'clock inside the porthole rim and extended into the porthole. We shaped

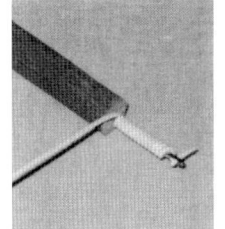

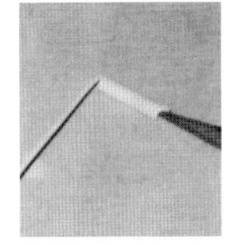

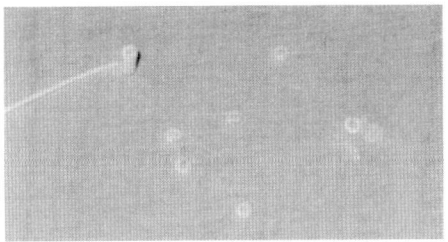

Producing small eyelets over steam. Styrene rod was inserted into the eye of a sewing needle and was wound up over boiling water. This was cut into small eyelets with a sharp scalpel.

31

SHELL PLATING AND RUDDER

(Right) The knuckle for the stern counter was made from 2mm (0.07in) sheet-styrene. The outer edges were rounded.

(Below) A slot was cut into the hull, into which the knuckle was inserted before the shell plating in this area was applied.

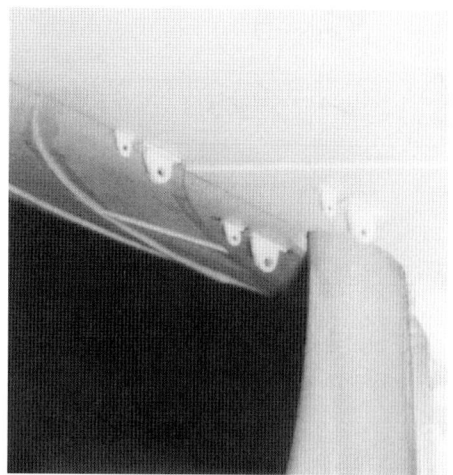

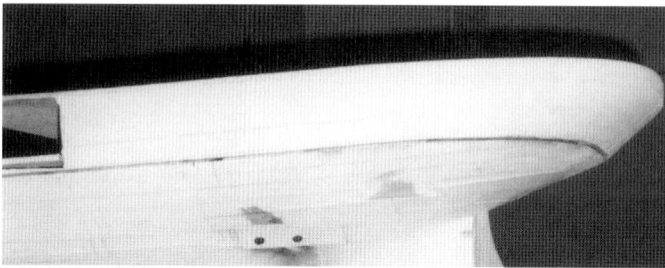

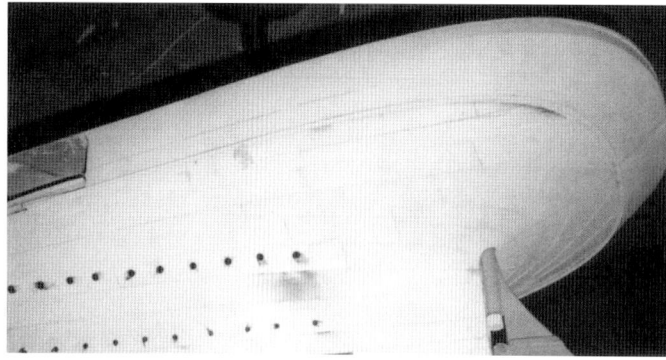

(Top right) Brackets for raising and lowering the rudder for maintenance. Note the backing plates. These brackets also appeared above the propellers. Their locations were not in any of the Harland & Wolff plans – we located them using photographs.

(Above) The knuckle attached to the hull and shell plating of the counter begun.

(Right) The positions of the rivets were drawn on the inside of the plates. Each cross indicates a spot where a rivet is to be punched into the plate.

them from styrene strip. Further portholes had steel rods over them. These were made from styrene rod.

In strake 'S' coaling doors had to be added. Strake 'S' was an outer strake, so the door openings were cut out and the door, which was slightly smaller than the opening, simply glued to the inner strake behind it. To ensure that the rounded corners of the door openings were uniform, holes were drilled in each corner and the remaining sides cut out with a sharp knife. Gangway doors for passengers were cut out of the shell plates in the same way as the coaling doors. The door hinges were all on the forward edge of the doors apart from one: this was the third door from the stern in strakes 'T' and 'U' (underneath No 4 funnel) on the port side, which had the hinges aft. These hinges were made from styrene strips and rod.

Small eyelets were added to the hull slightly above these doors from which the gangways were suspended when the ship was in harbour. A small sewing needle was driven into the end of a wooden dowel which served as a handle for rotating the needle. A strip of very thin styrene rod (or stretched sprue) was pushed into the eye of the needle and heated over steam. After the rod had become soft the needle was slowly rotated, still holding it over steam and with the other end of the rod in the other hand. Thus the styrene rod wound around the needle. When enough rod had been wound for the amount of eyelets required, it was plunged in boiling water for a few seconds, then taken out and left to dry. When the rod had been removed from the needle we had a spring which was cut into small eyelets by pushing a sharp scalpel into

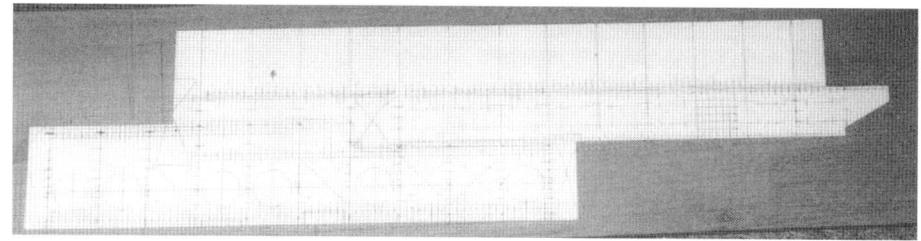

the hole at either end and cutting off small rings of styrene rod. These small rings can be made in any size required, and many were used for the model.

Coaling clamps were small, very flat triangles which were attached to the bottom edge of strake 'U'. They had a small hole drilled slightly beneath the peak from which working platforms for coaling the ships were suspended. These coaling clamps cannot be found in any of the Harland & Wolff plans, but the basic guide that we had indicated that they appear in pairs above each coal chute. Using archive photographs we located them as best we could and attached them to the hull.

The knuckles beneath the stern counter were produced in the same way as the stem: a slot was cut into the hull into which the knuckles, which were made of 2mm (0.07in) sheet-styrene with the outer edges sanded round, were inserted before the shell plates joining the knuckle were attached. The hooks for attaching tackles for dismantling the propellers and the rudder for maintenance were also applied. They are also in none of the Harland & Wolff plans, but their positions can be seen in photographs. These hooks appeared in pairs, with one small and one large bracket.

The first shell plates that also featured round-headed rivets appeared in strake 'U'. I had been experimenting in riveting with the smallest brass brads by nailing them into a wooden board, but the results were never satisfactory. It was very difficult to nail the rivets into the board in a straight line, so a different approach had to be found. The shell plates that required round-headed rivets were attached to a hard wooden board with double-sided tape with the inside facing up. Using the Harland & Wolff rivet pattern plan, the rivets were drawn onto the plate. A small nail was then held to the position where a rivet was marked and given a gentle tap with a small hammer. After the rivets had all been punched in, the plate was removed from the board and the rivets inspected. The rivet lines were still not perfectly straight, so I decided to use a ruler to guide the nail. I taped the ruler to the board to ensure that it would not move while I punched the rivets in. This meant I had to move the ruler and re-tape it to the board for each row of rivets and also to follow the strake. It was a very time-consuming process, but the end results were excellent. After a lit-

tle trial and error, we got the feel for it and ended up with row after row of perfectly true-to-scale rivets. But there was one snag: the riveting caused the shell plates to buckle, which made it very difficult to glue them to the hull absolutely flat, especially when working with superglue which does not allow much time for adjusting the plates. We decided to use two large steel plates that were heated with a blow-lamp to iron the styrene plates out again.

The first steel plate was heated and once we were satisfied with the temperature, we put several sheets of newspaper on it. In the meantime, the second steel plate was also

(Left) Every rivet is precisely where it should be. The buckling of the plates was taken out by 'ironing' them between two hot steel plates.

(Above) The author tapping the rivets into the plate using a steel ruler, taped to the board as a guide. The ruler had to be removed and replaced every now and then to follow the sheer of the hull.

(Below) Rivet pattern between frames 6 and 16 on the starboard side. Flush rivets and flush joints have been omitted for clarity.

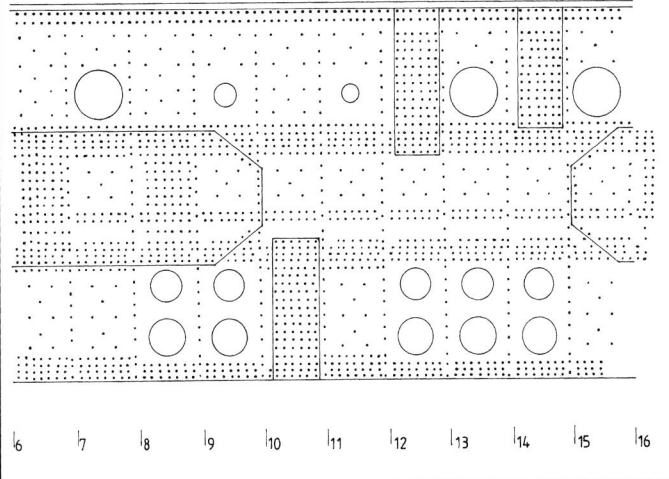

SHELL PLATING AND RUDDER

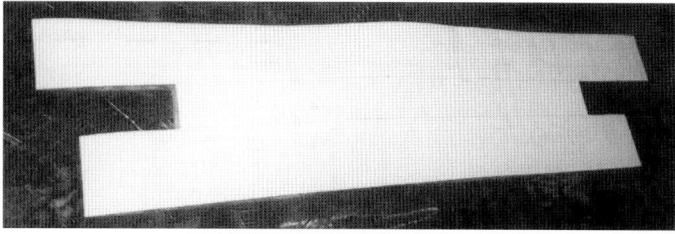

(Above) One of the large plates after ironing it flat.

(Right) Large portholes with flat sides were made from 2mm (0.07in) styrene. If I were to build a model like this again, I would make one master for these portholes and cast the items required from resin.

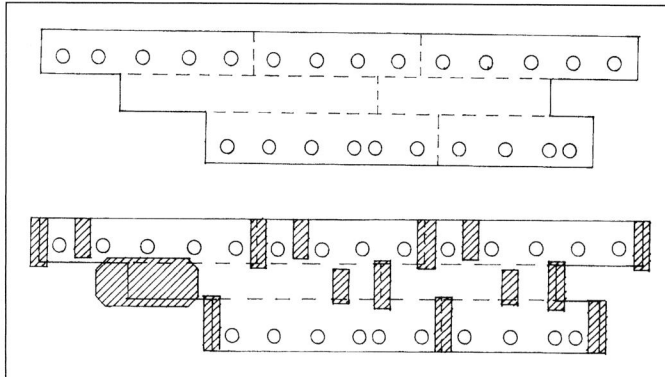

being heated and once it had reached the required temperature we placed the styrene shell plate on the newspaper on the first steel plate. We then put several layers of newspaper on the shell plate, followed by the second heated steel plate on top. The results were excellent: when we removed the styrene shell plate, most of the buckling had been ironed out. The newspapers acted as a sort of cushion so that the hot steel plate did not melt the rivets and push them back in.

I recall reading about the 1:22 scale model of *Titanic* that was used in James Cameron's 1997 movie. This article stated that some 20,000 rivets were driven into the hull of this model. I have no idea how many round-headed rivets there actually were on *Titanic*'s hull, so I used the figure of 20,000 as an indication of the amount. Every single rivet was punched into the hull by hand. I found I became accustomed to it after the first several hundred rivets. I could even tell from the sound of the hammer tapping against the nail if I had got it right or not. Occasionally the nail went through the sheet styrene and punched a hole in it. This appeared to be

(Left) In the flush-plated part of the hull large styrene plates were made covering the area of several shell plates. The seams between these plates were later covered with butt straps.

(Below) The shell plating completed up to C deck. The riveting can be seen clearly, as well as butt straps, strengthening plates and doubles between two outer strakes.

disastrous at first, but when it did happen the cure was simple: we applied filler to the hole from the inside of the shell plate. We rubbed it in with a finger, and the filler came out through the hole in the rivet on the other side, closing the hole. When it was dry we gently rubbed a finger over it – and once again had a perfect rivet.

When we had completed the riveting, I did some sums and calculated that it took us 22 days of working 8 hours a day to punch the rivets into the shell plates. By then I knew that the figure of 20,000 did not add up. I counted the rivets in the area of seven frames (approximately 12/12cm or 3.6/3.6in) and found this area contained 904 rivets. Multiplied by the completely riveted part of the hull, this resulted in 61,000 rivets in the entire hull. The rivet pattern changes slightly underneath the well decks so the figure of 61,000 might not be entirely accurate, but I am sure it is pretty close.

The largest portholes on the *Olympic* class had flat sides. This was so the porthole rims would not protrude into the frames of the hull, even though the holes in the shell plating for these portholes were circular. The porthole rims were produced by drilling holes in 2mm (0.07in) sheet-styrene, slicing off the outer edge of the portholes and adding a straight strip of 3mm (0.11in) styrene to the sliced-off sides. The rims were then cut into squares and attached to the inside of the shell plating.

As mentioned before, the hull above strake 'W' was completely flat, safe for the stiffeners and butt straps but with no inner or outer strakes. Thus it was not necessary here to produce each plate individually and attach it to the hull. Large sheet styrene plates were designed and cut out which covered strakes 'W'-'Y' about 60cm (2ft) in length. The vertical seams in these plates all received 'butt straps' and 'stiffeners' which would conceal the joint between these large plates.

While we were drilling open the portholes in C deck we came across another flaw in the shell plating plan. First the rivets were punched into the plates according to the rivet pattern plan, then the portholes were drilled into the plate according to the shell plating plan. We noticed that two rivets above the portholes of C deck were ominously close to the portholes. As we worked our way forward, these two rivets suddenly vanished into the drilled-out portholes. Something was wrong.

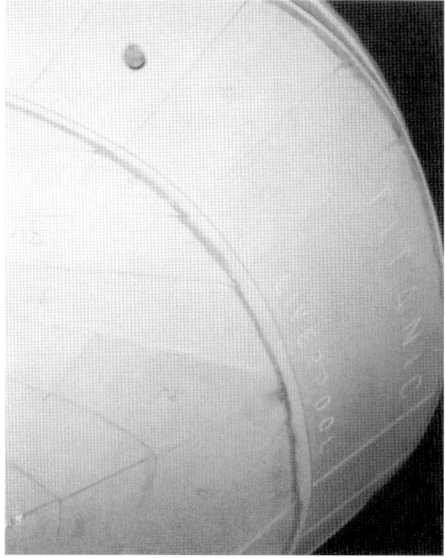

(Above) The ship's name cut into the shell plate. This was highlighted with yellow paint.

(Left) The stern counter showing the 'inverted V'-shaped plates underneath the counter and the name and the homeport cut into the shell plating.

We stopped work and got out the plans. Comparing the rivet pattern plan with the shell plating plan, we realised that the portholes in C deck in the shell plating plan had all been drawn 4mm (0.15in) too high. By this time the first of these large styrene plates had been attached to the hull. We couldn't just say, 'Oh well – no one will notice!'; we wanted to do the job properly. The only solution was to remove the plates that had been attached to the hull and do it again. I think that the shell plating plan was not the plan that gave the exact location of the portholes. It just indicated the amount of portholes in each plate and roughly where they would have to be drilled into the plate. The distance between the deck level and the portholes must have been specified elsewhere. I blame no one at Harland & Wolff for inaccurate drawing.

The names '*Titanic*' on the stern and bows were cut into the shell plating. The names of the ship at the bow and stern were 18in high, her homeport 'Liverpool' was 12in high. These were later painted yellow after the hull had been painted.

To give access to the knuckles underneath the forecastle deck a gap of approximately

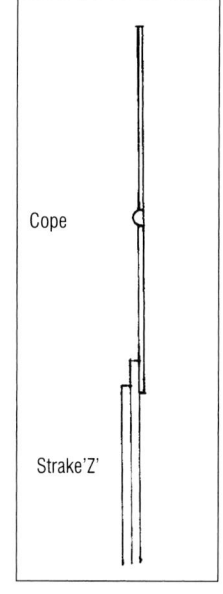

Section of the hull showing the transition from strake 'Z' to the final inner strakes above it. Note the cope between the two inner strakes.

SHELL PLATING AND RUDDER

(Right) The bow showing the hawse-pipe which was fabricated from a *Titanic* model kit funnel. The seams to the hull were filled with Milliput and sanded smooth. The paper strips in the portholes are for removing the masking fluid after the hull is painted.

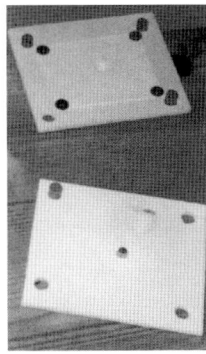

(Above) Heat-moulding mooring ports over a wooden master. The first board has already been covered with sheet styrene. The hole in the centre of this board is faintly visible in the middle of the styrene sheet. After it had been heated in an oven, the board with the wooden master was placed on top of it, pushing the master through the sheet styrene, into the hole in the first board, forming the item required. It was then trimmed off the backing and attached to the hull. The wooden dowels ensure that both boards are placed exactly on top of each other.

2mm (0.07in) was left between the plates of strakes 'Y' and 'Z' on the outer plates only. This gap was later filled with styrene strips attached between the strakes onto the inner plating. We noticed that the knuckle between strakes 'Y' and 'Z' were actually square in profile with slightly rounded corners. The knuckle on the top edge of strake 'Z' was half-round. The same applied to the knuckles beneath the poop deck.

Above strake 'Z' are two further strakes which are not lettered but numbered. These plates were not riveted apart from the rivets of the sliding windows that were attached to the inner sides. Here too a small horizontal gap approximately 2mm (0.07in) wide was left between the lower and upper strakes for the cope, the half-round profile connecting the two strakes. This was later added with half-round styrene rod.

The large B deck stateroom windows were cut out in the same manner as the coal ports: we first drilled the corners and then cut the sides with a sharp knife. The large windows

SHELL PLATING AND RUDDER

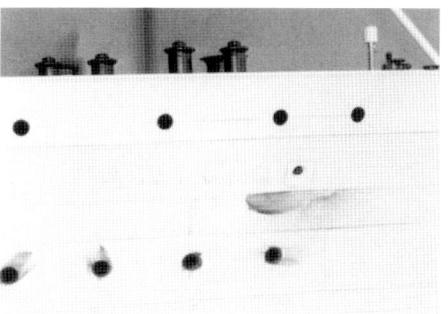

(Far left) A mooring port attached to the model. The stiffening ring was made from rod which was moulded over steam.

(Left) A mooring port attached to the hull with the seams filled and sanded.

had small rims which stood proud of the shell plating. These were produced from stretched sprue, just like the small eyelets. A wooden master was made which had the same cross-section as these windows. A length of stretched sprue was then wound around it over steam. This was then plunged in boiling water for a few seconds and left to dry. These window 'frames' were attached to the outside of the shell plating.

The hawse-pipe on the stem was made from a *Titanic* kit's funnel which happened to be the correct diameter and shape. The joint to the hull was filled with generous amounts of filler and sanded smooth. As our model shows the ship 'at sea' we elected to add the lid to the pipe. No pictures of *Titanic* show the hawse pipe with the lid in place, though once at sea the lid was most probably closed.

The last items to be added to the fully plated hull were the mooring ports. These are where the mooring ropes went through the hull to be tied to bollards when the ship was in harbour. They had a section like a funnel so that the ropes would not be damaged when they rubbed against their sides. They were also heat moulded, and I will describe the process here. I made a wooden master of the item required and mounted it to wooden board. I then made a cut-out in the middle of a second wooden board that followed the outline of the item required. I secured a thin sheet of styrene to this board with drawing pins, which I put in a pre-heated oven; I usually work at 200-220°C. It only takes about 30 seconds for the sheet styrene to soften. I then took it out of the oven and placed the wooden master on top of it, pushing it through the cut-out. I used this technique throughout the building stages of the model for items such as cowl vents, sky-lights and the No 1 cargo hatch lid. These moulded mooring ports were cut into small squares. Small squares the same size were cut out of the outer plating to which the ports had to be applied. The seams were filled and sanded.

Painting the hull

Before the hull was painted all portholes were masked with white glue. Small strips of paper

The shell plating took four months to complete, but it was well worth the effort. Every detail was included.

SHELL PLATING AND RUDDER

(Top) The hull beneath the waterline was primed in red and then painted.

(Above) Klaus Thyssen painting the white on the hull with an aerosol can.

were placed into the glue before it dried which helped us to remove the masking after the painting was complete.

First, the hull beneath the waterline was primed in red. Once this had dried repairs and corrections were carried out. Then the final coating of 'red hand' was applied. The exact shade of this is also unclear today, but looking at models in museums and also Ken Marschall's famous paintings we decided to use RAL 3016 'Korallenrot' which appeared to be close enough. The complete hull was painted in satin colours.

After the red had dried the hull beneath the waterline was masked and the black applied. The waterline is not in a straight line, but rises towards the bow and the stern. The shell-plates were a great help here to give the waterline the slight curvature, as the position of the waterline could be seen in contemporary pictures in the shellplates it crossed. Painting the hull black appeared to be a massive step forward in the progress of the model, but it was only a matter of about half-an-hour. After the black had dried this part of the hull was masked and the white applied.

One of the final measures in building the model was the application of the yellow trimline. It was impossible to mask the edges of this line with masking tape due to the rivets in the hull.

The hull painted black.

SHELL PLATING AND RUDDER

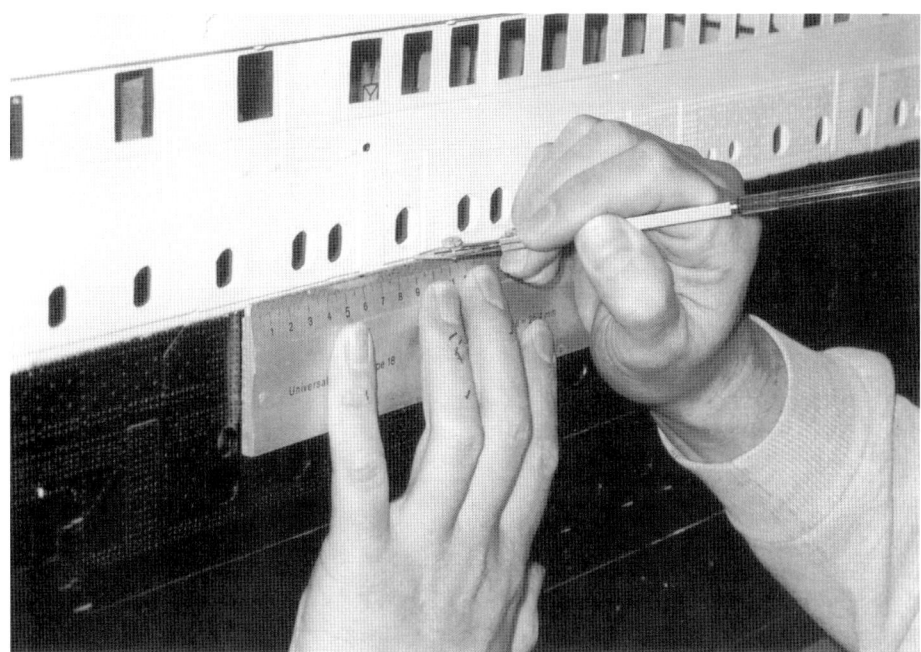

Adding the yellow trim-line with a draughtsman's ruling pen.

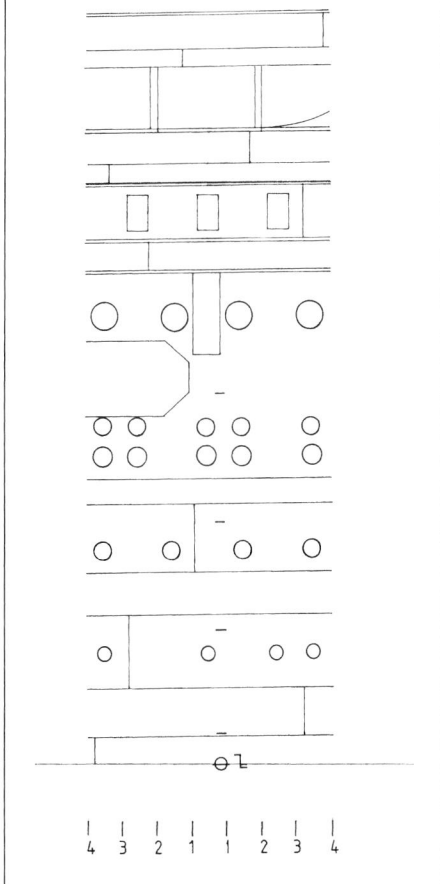

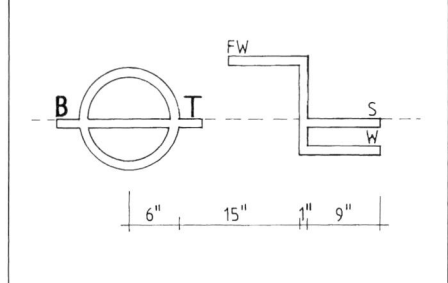

(Far left) The freeboard deck lines on C, D, E and F decks. This was a white line, at least 1in thick and 1ft long.

(Left) The load mark indicating that it has been assigned by the Board of Trade.
FW = Fresh Water
S = Summer
W = Winter

Needless to say the exact colour isn't known either but the specification booklet mentions 'gold-yellow' for the trim line which, is by today standards, a very dark yellow so this is what we went for. We applied the outer edges of the trimline with a draughtsman's ruling pen. This took a little practice on scrap shell plates before we were able to apply it to the hull of the model, but the result looked marvellous. The gap between the upper and lower yellow line was filled with a brush. We used Model Master insignia yellow. The name *Titanic* on the hull was painted in the same colour.

The draught numbers were available as decals in the right shape and size. They numbered at the bow 13-42 with 40 being at the waterline (30 at the LWL); at the stem 17-40 with 37 being at the waterline. The Load mark and freeboard lines were also made up from decal strips circles and letters.

SHELL PLATING AND RUDDER

Detail of *Olympic*'s rudder showing sheathing and stoppers. The load draught markings on *Titanic* were from 17–40ft while on *Olympic* only from 23–40ft. The numbers were stamped into the hull and highlighted with white paint. On *Titanic* the numbers were also stamped into the zinc sheathing (17–22) while on *Olympic* they were not. (Photograph: Harland & Wolff, Claes-Göran Wetterholm collection)

The rudder was made of one sheet of 6mm (0.23in) MDF and sanded to shape. The rudder tapered towards its rear edge.

The stiffeners were made of wooden strips and attached to the rudder slightly longer than the rudder itself. The rear ends were then sanded to shape. The post can be seen at the top of the rudder made from a 13mm (0.51in) thick wooden dowel.

Rudder

The model's rudder was built from one sheet of 6mm (0.23in) MDF. The outline was taken from the frames and waterlines plan and the rudder was drawn on the wood using a cardboard template. After cutting it out it was sanded to shape. The rudder tapers towards the end so that its aftmost edge is very thin. The area of the post was cut out of the rudder and a large wooden dowel of 13mm (0.51in) diameter attached, long enough to protrude into the hull beneath the counter. The seams between the rudder and the post were then filled and sanded smooth.

The stiffeners were made from strips of wood which were sanded to shape according

SHELL PLATING AND RUDDER

Titanic just prior to her launch on 31 May 1911. The rudder was secured to the hull with steel beams to prevent it from moving and changing the course of the hull while the ship was being launched.
(Photograph: Harland & Wolff, Claes-Göran Wetterholm collection)

to the plans and then glued to the rudder. They extended across the rudder's rear edge and were sanded to their final shape after they had been attached. The rudder's hinges were made of wooden rods 13mm (0.51in) in diameter and 11mm (0.43in) high. A hole was drilled into the centre of the hinges to accommodate the bolts which would later secure the rudder to the sternpost. At this stage, the hinges were also added to the sternpost. Then a small triangular eyelet was attached to the rear edge of the rudder, slightly beneath the second stiffener from the top. First, its reinforcement plates from thin sheet styrene were added. The eyelet was formed from a brass rod and fed into a hole drilled into the rear edge of the rudder. Stoppers cut out of an 11mm (0.43in) thick wooden block were then glued to the hinges (see plan). The corresponding stoppers at the stern post were cut from triangular styrene strip and attached to the sternpost.

Bolts of a sufficient size including washers were found in a DIY store. They needed to be shortened and were cut to the required length with an angle-grinder. The rudder also featured similar zinc sheathing as the stern post. This sheathing was made of thin strips of styrene which were also riveted in same manner as the shell plating. I found it easier to draw the strips onto the styrene sheet, mark the position of the rivets and cut the sheet into the required strips after the rivets had been punched in. The completed strips were then attached to the rudder with cyano.

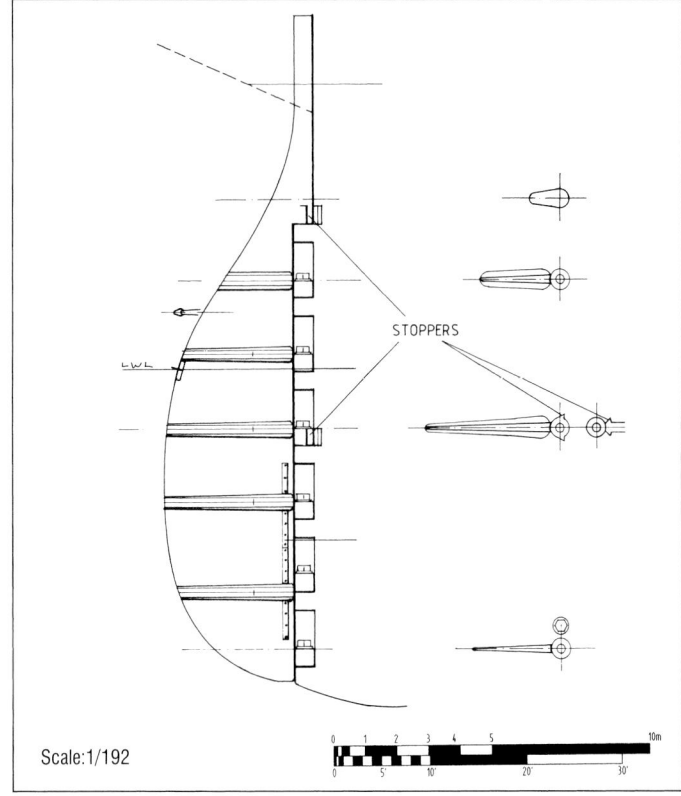

5 Well Decks

Titanic's well decks were a Third Class area. Unmarried male passengers had their accommodation at the bow of the ship while married couples and unmarried female passengers were accommodated at the stern. The White Star Line made sure that there were no parties below decks – unlike in the movies!

The decks

The decks were covered with 0.8mm (0.03in)

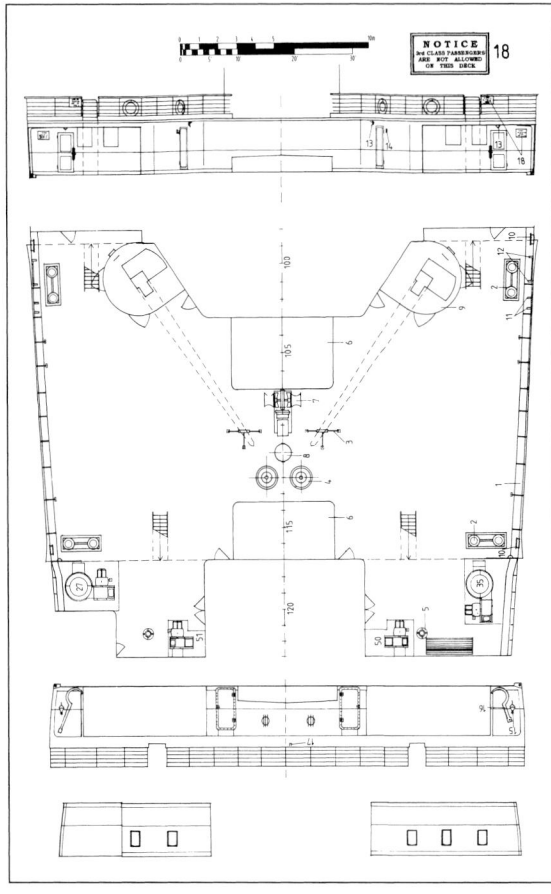

The aft well deck. (Scale: 1/384)

1. Waterway.
2. Bollard.
3. Jib crutch.
4. Low roller.
5. Poop deck crane support bedplate.
6. Cargo hatch.
7. Electric winch.
8. Ventilator.
9. 2½-ton electric crane.
10. Mooring ports.
11. Rigging bracket.
12. Shroud bracket.
13. Bulkhead lamp.
14. Electrical outlet.
15. Drinking fountain.
16. Propeller shaft spanner.
17. Rain tent bracket.
18. Notice board.
50; 51. Cowl-vent motor.
27; 35. Thermotank.

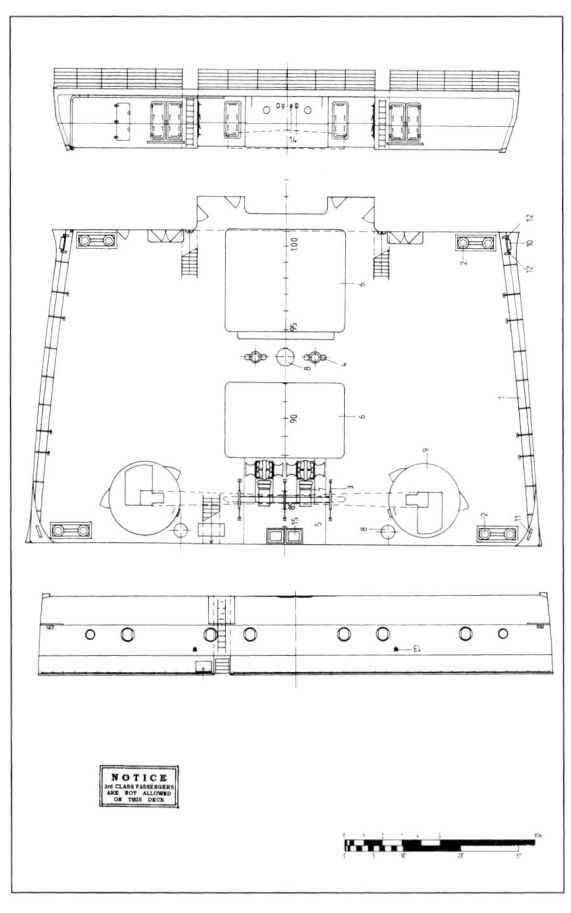

The forward well deck. (Scale: 1/384)

1. Waterway.
2. Bollard.
3. Jib crutch.
4. Roller.
5. Reinforced deck-planks.
6. Cargo hatch.
7. Electric winch.
8. Ventilator.
9. 2½-ton electric crane.
10. Mooring ports.
11. Rigging bracket.
12. Shroud bracket.
13. Bulkhead lamp (*Lusitania* style).
14. Electrical outlet.
15. Squash court light- and air shaft.

maple veneer. At first I intended to use pearwood veneer but when I went to my timber merchant, I saw several sheets of maple lying on a shelf. This had exactly the colour I had hoped for and was nearly entirely free of grain. However, these sheets were only about 30cm (11.8in) wide. I bought them anyway and took them to a local furniture factory and explained them what I needed them for. They came up with the superb solution that they could sew three of these sheets together alongside each other. This would give me veneer sheets wide enough for all decks. As the maple sheets were slightly too thin, we agreed upon having an additional layer of birch-veneer glued crosswise to the underside of the maple, which would also give the veneer adequate strength. The result was awesome: there were no visible seams, only an occasional slight variation in colour which was acceptable. Once the deck planks had been drawn on, this was hardly noticeable anyway.

A template was made of the complete aft well deck and this was transferred onto the veneer and the deck cut out in one piece. The biggest task lay ahead: drawing the plank seams on the deck. The actual well-deck planks were 6in wide. The plank ends were not drawn on, firstly because they were not tarred and would not be visible anyway, secondly their exact location is not known even if the lengths of the planks are, and most of all, the shipbuilders did not do it on their models either, even though the Orlando model is not in builders' model style. First, all fittings were drawn onto the template that was used for cutting out the deck. The fittings were then cut out of the template and these were also transferred onto the deck. The bulkheads, cargo hatches and cranes were also added. The first planks to be drawn were the margin planks along the waterways. We did all margin planks 1½ times wider than the deck planks save for those surrounding smaller fitting such as bollards and vents, which had the same width as the deck planks. I had two thin long strips of paper onto which lines were added each at 6in distance. These were drawn using a computer to ensure that all widths were equal and at 6in at 1:48 scale. The plank seams at the centreline were drawn on the deck first. Then the paper strips were placed at the forward and aft edge of the deck and secured with drafting tape. Great care had to be taken to ensure that one of the lines on these strips was placed exactly on the centreline which was drawn onto the deck. The next step was to add the margin planks in front of and behind the fittings. At the corners of items with round corners protruding through the deck surface, like the superstructure, cargo hatches etc., the margins were angled at 45°. The length of this angle followed the width of two planks (see Drawing H).

I started to draw the plank seams at the centreline, using the markings on the paper strips as a guide. When we neared one of the deck fittings, the planks seam getting nearest to 1½ times the width of the 6in deck planks was the edge of the margin planks (Drawings I to K). After all planks were finished the deck was cleaned with compressed air and matt varnish was applied with an air-brush.

The deck was then glued to the hull with contact cement, applied to the deck on the hull and the bottom side of the veneer. Weights were used to press the veneer down onto the hull deck while the glue was setting.

I have seen a number of *Titanic* models that were built from kits and some of them were extremely good. Using after-market items and scratch-built improvements they were true masterpieces. However, some of these had one fundamental flaw: plastic decks. Some modellers using plastic model kits as a basis seem to be fascinated by this material and would not substitute it for any other. There are decal sheets available with a wooden deck-like print on them, to which the same applies as to painted plastic decks: it is not wood and that is clear to anyone who sees it. On the other hand, I have also seen plastic

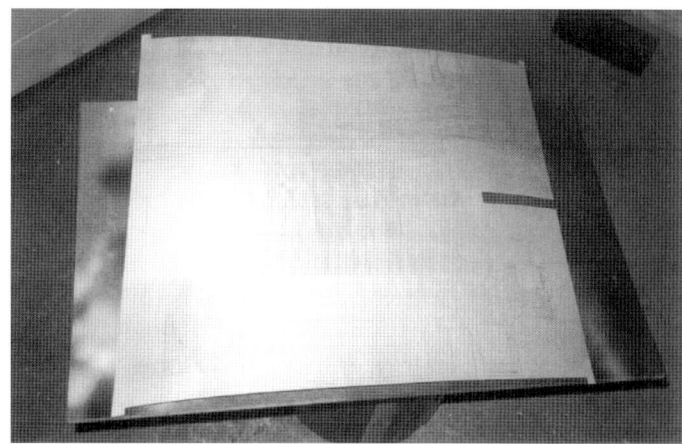

The veneer aft well deck with plank seams drawn on. The cut-out area at the deck sides is to accommodate the waterways. This complete sheet was glued to the 'underdeck' on the hull with contact cement.

Drawing the deck planks.

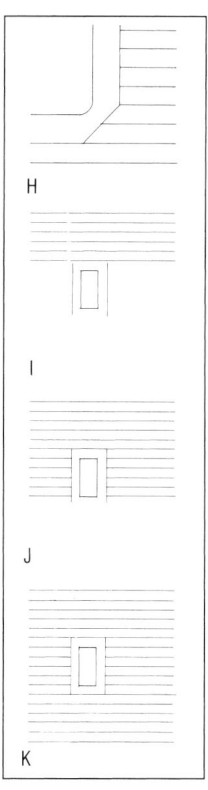

WELL DECKS

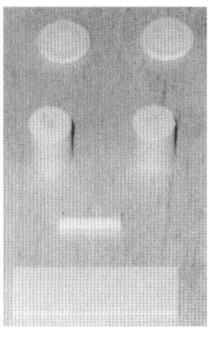

(Above) The master bollard under construction. The two cylinders were built up of several layers of discs. The large plate at the bottom is the base plate. This later proved to be too thin to cast in resin, so it was later added separately to the resin-cast items.

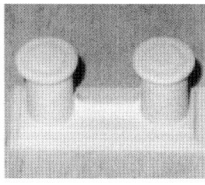

(Above) The finished master bollard.

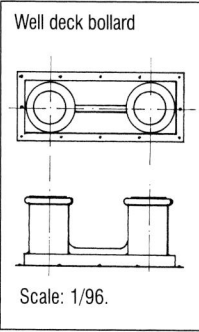

Scale: 1/96.

The bollard base plates, riveted and ready to be attached to the resin-cast bollards.

models on which the decks were made from wood. The difficulty is, of course, finding wood with hardly any grain which would give some scale-like appearance. For any model of an ocean liner with wooden decks I can highly recommend maple veneer. It is suitable for any scale. If some slightly overscale grain should be visible, it is by no means as disturbing as painted plastic decks. The decks included with the kit can be used as templates for cutting out wooden decks.

The waterways in the well decks were 15½in wide – this results in 8.2mm (0.32in) at 1:48 scale. They were made of styrene strips and attached to the hull 'under deck' before the veneer was attached. It is difficult to determine their colour from black and white photographs, but we used a statement by the famous maritime photographer Everett Viez, who said that *Olympic*'s waterways were black. The waterways in the well decks were covered with limber boards, so that passengers could stand at deck level. Waterpipes ran along these waterways on both sides in the aft welldeck, and on the port side only in the forward well deck. Perhaps these covers also served as some protective measure for the pipes inside them. What these limber boards were made of is unclear. Some historians say they were made of steel, while others state they were made of wood and were removed while the ship was under way. They are not on the wreck and were probably lost while the ship was going down. I made these covers from styrene strip and painted them light grey. Small openings had to be cut out at the sides to give access to the gooseneck vents and the bulwark struts.

Bollards

I started to build various fittings of the model before I started to build the hull, and even before I got the commission. Among these were the bollards of the forecastle deck, the forward and aft well decks and the poop deck.

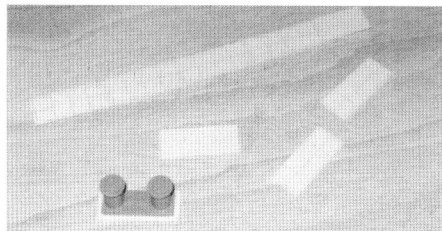

The bollards of the well decks had flat tops while those of the forecastle and poop deck had round tops. A master bollard was made up using from small discs of thick sheet-styrene with 11mm (0.43in) diameter for the cylinders, fixed onto a base of 3mm (0.11in) styrene. The tops or caps were also made from 3mm styrene and these were glued to the tops of the cylinders. A strengthener was added to the base between the cylinders, again made from 3mm styrene. All the seams were then filled with putty and once dry were filed with a round file and a grinding bitt for areas which the file could not reach. Bollards for smaller models can be built in the same way, but rod can be used for the cylinders instead of styrene discs.

I built only one master of each item required and none of these masters were used on the model. The items required were cast in resin using a silicon rubber mould. Once the master bollard was finished I made a small box (*sans* lid) for it, also from thick sheet styrene. The bollard was then glued to the bottom of the box using liquid poly to fill the mating edges between the bollard and the box floor. Silicon rubber was then prepaired and the item painted with it using a hard brush to ensure that no air bubbles were trapped on the item. The remaining silicon was then poured into the box, covering the item. I have come across a number of different qualities of silicon rubber and as usual the more expensive compound is the best. Usually between 3 and 6 per cent of vulcaniser has to be added. The more vulcaniser that is added, the quicker the rubber will cure. This has one major disadvantage: air bubbles do not have sufficient time to escape out of the mould. For items with complicated shapes a mixture with less vulcaniser was used to give bubbles inside the silicon enough time to rise to the surface and escape. Once the silicon has set, the styrene box is broken up and the master taken out of the mould. Before the silicon rubber mould is used for casting resin items I leave it to 'breathe' for about 24 hours, as otherwise the resin will attack the surfaces of the mould and after a few items are cast, the mould becomes more and more useless; *ie* parts of the mould will stick to the resin while the cast item is being removed from the mould and thus damage it. If this breathing period is allowed for, a large number of items can be cast from a single mould.

For casting items in resin, I usually use

polyurethane resin which is mixed with a hardener in equal amounts. Great care had to be taken that the two components were mixed in the same amount, as otherwise it would not harden. The hardening process is supported by the heat the resin develops while it is setting. Thus larger amounts will set considerably faster than smaller. Amounts beyond 60–80g of resin have to be cast within 20–30 seconds. Once the curing process has begun, the resin thickens rapidly; work with this mixture has to be completed quickly, as otherwise the oil inside the resin will bleed out of the finished item after it has hardened. Although this bleeding begins more or less immediately after the resin has hardened, it can take weeks or even months before it becomes noticeable. The disastrous results could be oil stains creeping out on deck underneath the item.

Once the resin has been stirred and is ready for use, the mould of the item is painted generously with resin using a hard brush, particularly in areas where in which air is likely to be trapped. At first I was very careful in doing this, as I did not want to damage the mould. However, these silicon rubber moulds can take a great deal of pressure and stress without being damaged. The early items that were cast in resin still needed the odd bubble to be filled and sanded. Today, when filling moulds with resin I really make sure that no air is trapped inside and literally press resin into the mould with a paintbrush no matter how much the mould is distorted while I am doing so. The mould can take it and the item will be usable.

Back to the bollards: after the eight items required (four for each well deck) had been cast, the thin bedplates attaching the bollards to the deck were added. These were not included on the master item because they were too thin to be cast in resin. They were made of 0.3mm styrene and the rivets were punched into them using the same method described in the shell-plating chapter. Here too the mating edges between the resin bollard and the styrene base plates were filled with liquid poly. The bollards were then primed and painted in semi-gloss black.

Vents

The next fitting that was built was the 'French' vent located between the cargo hatches. This was simply made up using styrene tube in two different diameters, 9mm (0.35in) for the shaft and 18mm (0.70in) for the head. The openings on one end of the head was closed by simply fixing the head to a small square of sheet styrene with liquid poly, and after the poly had set the excess styrene was cut off with a sharp knife. The rims along the top and bottom edges of the vent head were added using thin styrene strips. The trunk was then attached to the head by pushing it into the open end and cementing it to the inside of the closed head.

Cargo hatches

The cargo hatches were also built up from 3mm (0.11in) sheet-styrene also. First a floor was was made, onto which the cargo-hatch walls or coamings were glued. After this had set, the corners were rounded with a sanding disc and the seams cleaned up with fine sandpaper. The canvas hatch covers on the real ship were fastenend with iron bars that were pushed through battening cleats that were attached to the hatch walls.

The complete hatch covers of the model were also made from 3mm styrene with their edges and corners rounded with a file and sandpaper. To represent the canvas cover pulled halfway down the side, a very thin strip of 4mm (0.15in) wide styrene was attached to the upper edge of the coaming. After this the hatch cover was attached. The battening cleats were made of styrene U-beams, cut in slices and were attached to the hatch sides. A thin styrene rod was pushed through the cleats representing the iron bars.

The exact colour of the hatch covers (this applies to the lifeboat covers as well) is unknown today. In photographs they look off-white or a very light grey. I certainly do not believe that they were canvas colour, as one sees on models.

I chose white, as this seemed to me to be the closest colour to the real covers. The hatch covers were not airbrushed – the paint was applied with a brush stroking each layer of paint in different directions. Once the first layer had dried the second layer was applied but this time stroking in the other direction. This was repeated about four or five times. Applying the paint in this criss-cross manner leaves one with a canvas-like texture. When this is given a VERY SLIGHT wash with dirty brown, the result is extremely convincing.

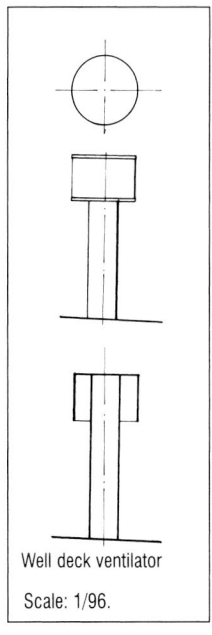

Well deck ventilator

Scale: 1/96.

WELL DECKS

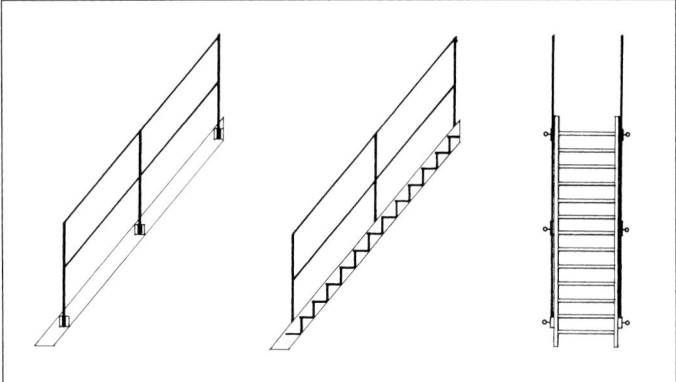

(Above) Stairway leading to the aft well deck. (Scale: 1/96.)

(Far right) The stairs leading from the aft well deck up to B deck. The fastening of the railings into tubes on the side of the stairs can be seen. The railings were secured with eyelet screws. This is also *Olympic* in her prime, the 1920s. (Photograph: Author's collection)

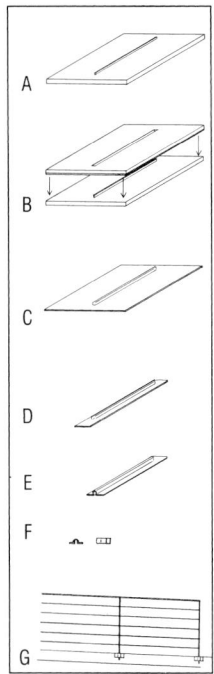

Producing brackets for mounting railing stanchions onto the bulwarks.

The stairs

The stairs were made up entirely from 1mm (0.03in) styrene. Those leading to B deck had 13 steps while the stairs leading to the poop deck had 14. There was no riser under the bottom step so water did not accumulate in corners causing the wood to rot.

The handrails of these stairs were detachable. The rail stanchions were pushed into tubes that were attached to the sides of the stairs and were fastened with round-headed screws. The items representing these tubes were heat-moulded. In fact, on the model they were not even really tubes, but the end result was very convincing.

The drawings illustrate how this was done: a long thin long strip of wood approximately 1 by 2mm in section was attached to the centreline of a plywood board with the 2mm-high side standing upright (Drawing A). A second plywood board was produced with a slot cut along the centreline slightly larger than the wooden strip attached to the preceding board onto which a thin sheet of styrene was attached with drawing pins. This was heated in an oven, and after about 30 seconds at 220° C the styrene had become soft enough to be moulded. The first board was then pressed onto it and after the material had cooled down it was removed again. This left me with a styrene sheet with a 'ridge' moulded into it (Drawings B and C). This sheet was then cut into a thin strip approximately 5mm (0.19in) wide with the ridge at the centre (Drawing D). From this strip small 'brackets' approximately 3mm (0.11in) high were cut (Drawings E and F). These small brackets were used throughout the ship to attach railing stanchions to the inside of the bulwarks (Drawing G) and to the stairs. The eyelet screw can be added by attaching a small sprue-eyelet as described in Chapter 4.

Railings and handrails were built using items supplied by Display Models. Their stanchions are produced as very thin half-round brass rods, which are pre-folded to shape to form the stanchion with holes into which the bars can be fed. The result looks like the real thing once the railings have been painted. The major advantage of this system is that the rods are actually fed into the stanchions just like on the real ship. These are available from Display Models in various scales.

Modellers building smaller models might want to use the etched-brass after-market items that are available from sources noted elsewhere. I have seen models on which the builder went through the tedious task of producings railings from stretched sprue. If it is well done, it can look pretty tidy but it is never really convincing as the rails can only be attached to one side of a stanchion and it is of course very difficult to get the railings in a straight line. I remember seeing a model of *Titanic* on which the builder made the railings from thin clear sheet styrene onto which the railings were scored. The result was stunning. As the rails were inscribed using a ruler as a guide, they were arrow-straight. The only drawback was that when looking at this model from certain angles, the light reflected on the clear styrene and made some areas look somewhat odd, but I would still recommend this approach to modelmakers building small scale models.

Cranes

Each one of these could be seen as a model in its own right. There are no plans available of the originals so I had to start from scratch using basic Harland & Wolff plans and photographs. Wreck footage was little help, as rusticles now hanging down from the cranes obscure a lot of detail.

The base or cylinder was designed by counting the amount of deck planks in front of one of these cranes (the width of the planks is known) and then the height calculated in relationship to the width of the base using the dimensions taken from a head-on photograph. The result is the plans of the cranes published here. I was fortunate enough to find some plumbing tubes which had the correct diameter (77mm [3.03in]). To these the outer shell plating was added and other details such as doors, their handles and hinges. A thin rim was added to the top edge using a very thin strip of styrene. The door handles were made from rod.

One master crane column was built from sheet-styrene. Using the plans I drew as a guide, I first cut out the sides of the crane and rivets were punched into them from the inside. The forward and rear walls were also cut out, riveted and these jointed together. It started to look like a crane. The next job was to add a vast amount of L-beams, inspection and manufacturer's plates, fuse boxes and handles. At first the flanges of the L-beams were drawn onto stryrene and riveted BEFORE these strips were cut out, as it would have been impossible to do so afterwards. Using photographs, I placed every rivet where it should be. The round base was cut out of three 3mm (0.11in) styrene, joined to the bottom of the column and small triangular gussets added to the sides and the base.

The boxes attached to one side of the cranes were built separately. These were made of blocks of several layers of thick styrene and detail added, such as stiffeners with thin strips of styrene. Small doors were added from thin sheet. Silicon rubber moulds were made and all items required were cast in resin. The operators' platforms had to be made individually from styrene, but this was not too much trouble.

The jibs, however, were a different matter: I didn't want to run the risk of resin-casting these items only to be told in a few years or so that these had started to sag or distort. So I decided to do it the hard, but tried and tested, way, and made each one separately, and it was a lot of work. The dimensions of the jibs

I was lucky enough to find plumbing pipes in the correct diameter for the crane bases or cylinders. The shell plating and details such as doors etc, needed to be added.

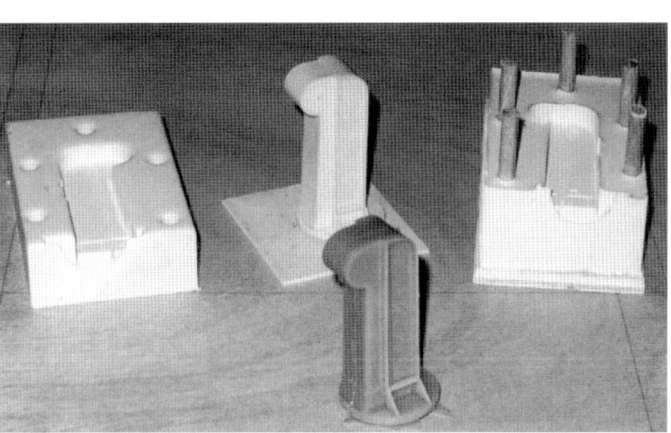

The master crane (in white) and the silicon rubber mould. A resin-cast crane stands in the foreground. Resin-casting these items was obviously far quicker than building each crane individually. All eight cranes were cast in one afternoon. The resin-cast item is an exact replica of the master. Corners and edges are equally as crisp.

The jibs were drawn on sheet styrene and cut out individually. I found it easier to cut out the area within the braces, and once this was completed the jib was cut out.

WELL DECKS

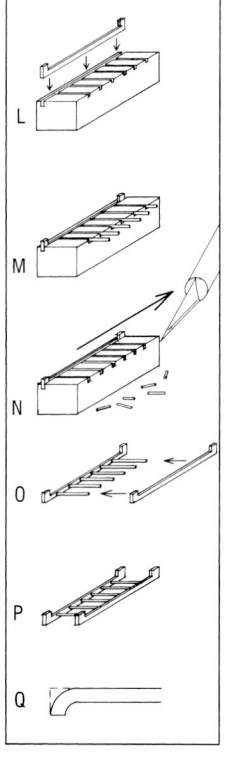

Making ladders

(Right) Aft well deck jib crutch. (Scale: 1/48.)

(Below) Forward well deck jib crutches. (Scale: 1/96.)

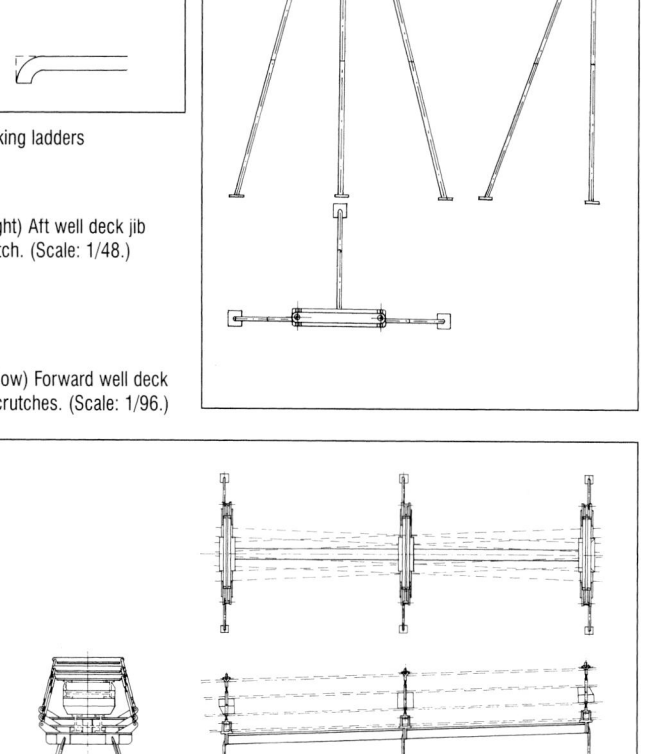

were transferred onto sheet-styrene and each one was cut out carefully with a sharp scalpel. The side beams were designed, riveted, cut out and added. All the stiffeners were added to the braces with thin strips. Then the tops of the side beams were added. There were two wheels at the ends of the jibs, one vertical and a horizontal wheel. These were made of numerous discs, plates and strips of styrene. The axles were made of rod.

The wires for the cranes were made of fine steel wire. As the columns were massive solid resin, I drilled a tiny hole into where the wire was to lead into the column to give it adequate strength. On the other end the hook was made of thick steel wire which was bent to shape and weights of thin styrene tube were added which had been filed to shape. These were hooked into the loops at the opposite end of the jib. While these cranes were in operation, they also had two lines attached to their sides. These were removed from the column whilst at sea, although they can be seen still leading around the horizontal wheel. It is not known exactly where the loose ends of these wires were stored, but it is likely that they left lying on the jibs. This is how we did it on the model, and they are pretty safe where they are.

The signs on the sides of the jibs reading 'Load not to exceed 2½ Tons' were produced on a Word programme, printed out and attached to small styrene plates with double-sided tape and glued to the jibs.

Ladders

All of the ladders that were needed for the model were built using a wooden jig. Slots were cut into a square wooden strip, into which the steps would later be pushed when the ladder was under construction. Another slot was cut in at one side in the entire length of the ladder required. One side of the ladder was cut out and placed into the slot (Drawing L). Then the bars could be attached using the horizontal slots as a guide. The bars were left slightly too long to make them easier to handle (Drawing M). After everything had been attached the excess rod was cut of with a knife (Drawing N). The ladder was removed from the jig and the other side attached (Drawings O and P). The last step was to file the corners round (Drawing Q).

Jib crutches

The jib crutches were made from styrene rod and strips. It was at a later stage during construction that I noticed that the lower halves of the crutches were also painted in reddish brown like the dadoes.

Bulwarks

The inside of the bulwarks proved to be difficult to reconstruct, as no detailed plans exist of this particular area either. However, in the shell-plating plan the location of doors, washports and L-beams is shown, so this was a basis I could start from. The L-beams were made by cutting off a strip of approximately

WELL DECKS

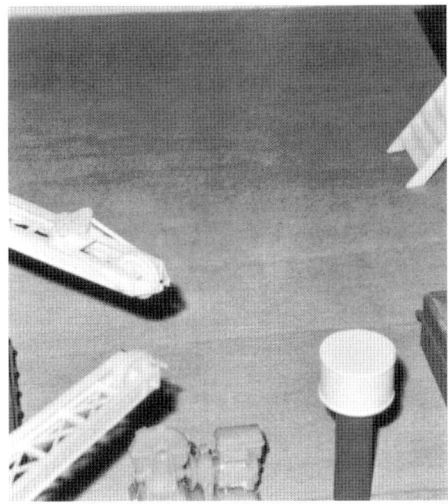

1mm (0.03in) wire from 0.3mm styrene. This strip was then glued to the top edge of the sheet at an angle. After this had dried, it was cut from the sheet at also approximately 1mm (0.03in) distance from the strip that had been attached, giving me an L-beam about 20–30cm (7.8in–11.8in) long. From this strip, stiffenersin the required length were cut off and their ends rounded slightly with sandpaper. It can be seen in the shell-plating plan that the flanges face aft. The stiffeners for the folding doors were cut out using these doors as templates. Their flanges were then attached with thin strip-styrene. The wash-ports also had a horizontal bar on the inside which were added from rod. These were attached to triangular plates which themselves were attached to the doors or bulwarks, depending on their location. The top edge of the bulwarks received a half-round profile in its entire length between the forward and aft bulkheads.

Gooseneck vents were made from brass wire, bent to shape and attached to the bulkhead with superglue. A small hole was drilled into the waterway into which the end of these vents was pushed to give them added support.

The final details that needed to be added

(Above) The two cranes in the forward well deck showing the storage of the wires within the jib. The lower halves of the jib crutches were painted like the dadoes. The casings of the electric winches were painted dark green.

(Above left) The ends of the jibs showing the horizontal and vertical wheels. The mushroom vent with its 'French' head is to the right.

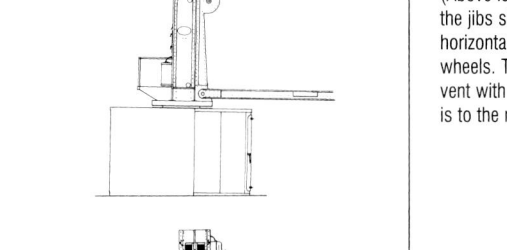

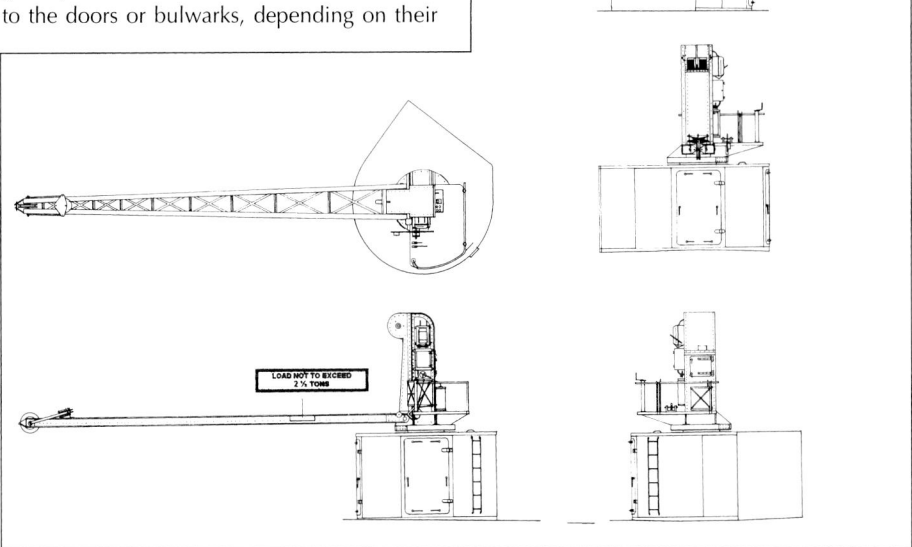

Aft well deck starboard Stothart and Pitt 2½-ton electric crane. (Scale: 1/192)

WELL DECKS

A finished aft well deck crane.

were the rigging and loading line brackets. Contrary to common opinion, the shrouds etc. were not attached to the deck, but to the inside of the bulwarks. At first holes, 2mm (0.07in) in diameter, were drilled into 2mm styrene. Then small plates were cut out with these holes at their centres. Two corners were rounded with a file and sandpaper and the flat end attached to the inside of the bulwark. The two brackets for the shrouds received an additional backing plate connecting them. The small brackets for the loading lines were built the same way, only being much smaller.

Bulkheads

The bulkheads were made of 1mm (0.03in) styrene. The corners of nearly all the bulkheads were rounded so to acchieve a joint-free construction, and where possible the bulkheads and the superstructure were cut out of styrene in one piece which then had to be folded to the required shape. Of course the sloping decks had to be taken into account on deckhouse walls, which were parallel to the keel. I thought this was going to be very tricky at first until I got started on it. To transfer the angle of the decks, I placed a sheet of paper on the shell-plating plan so that the right edge was positioned exactly along the frame located at the forward edge of this particular deckhouse wall. The top left-hand corner of this sheet was placed at deck level. Following the deck level to the right edge of the sheet of paper, the deck level would protrude several millimetres lower than on the left edge. Working at the bow it was the other way round: the top right edge of the sheet was placed at deck level, while the left edge was at the frame. This gave me the angle of the deck. This angle was then transferred onto the sheet-styrene in longitudinal

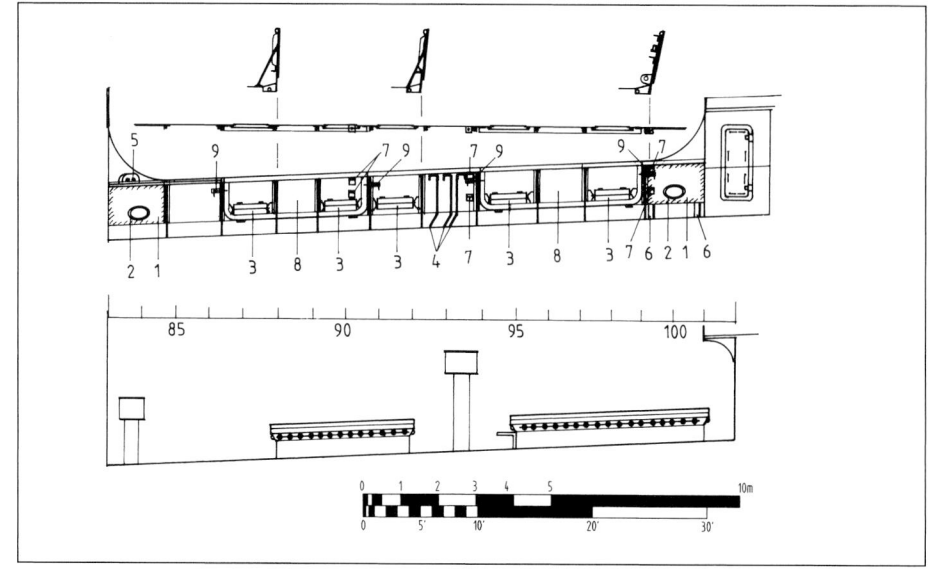

Side elevation of the inside of the forward well deck bulwark and the cargo hatches. (Scale: 1/192.)

1. Doubler.
2. Mooring port.
3. Washport.
4. Gooseneck airpipe.
5. Rigging bracket.
6. Shroud bracket.
7. Loading tackle bracket.
8. Loading port.
9. Loading port locking

WELL DECKS

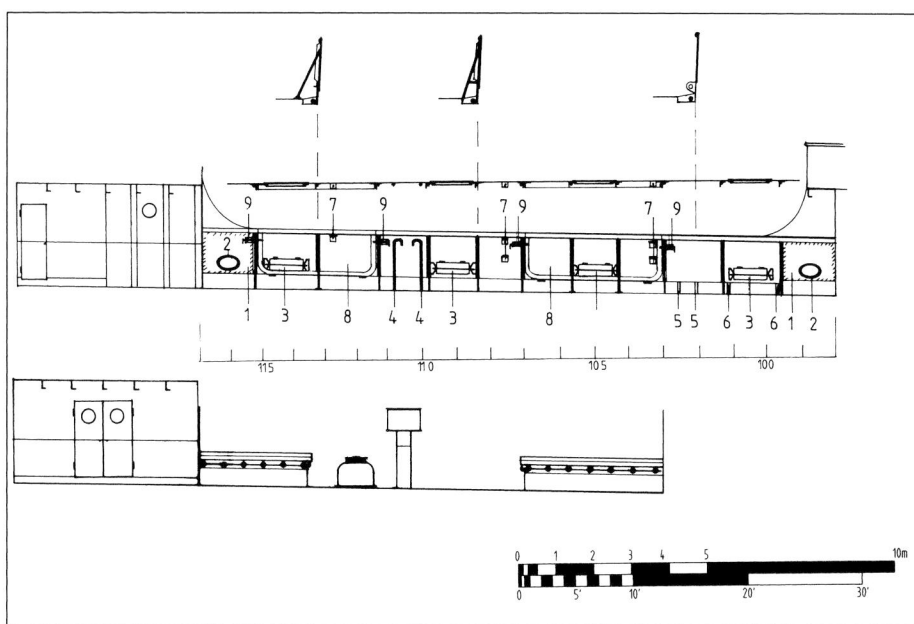

Side elevation of the inside of the aft well deck bulwarks and the cargo hatches. (Scale: 1/192.)

1. Doubler.
2. Mooring port.
3. Washport.
4. Gooseneck airpipe.
5. Rigging bracket.
6. Shroud bracket.
7. Loading tackle bracket.
8. Loading port.
9. Loading port locking mechanism.

(Far left) The inside of the aft well deck port bulwark. L-beams, rods over the washports and gooseneck valves can be seen. The locking mechanism and door hinges were added from styrene rod. The waterway was added at a later stage.

Aft well deck of *Olympic* in the 1920s, showing good detail of the inside of the bulwark. (Photograph: Author's collection)

deckhouse walls. If this had not been taken care of, the cross-bulkheads would have ended up at a slight angle, ruining the whole appearance of the model. After this had been done a few times it became pretty straight forward.

A wooden jig was built of strips of wood which were attached to the inside of the walls to ensure that they remained in the required shape.

Electric winches

Titanic had eight electric winches in two different sizes. They were all supplied by the Sunderland Forge and Manufacturing Company. Needless to say, no plans of these have survived either but there is a very detailed side-view of one of the small boat-deck winches in the Souvenir edition of *The Shipbuilder – Olympic* and *Titanic* from 1911. A further edition of *The Shipbuilder* contains a photograph of the factory that produced these winches, and a large number of both types can be seen in various stages of completion. These winches are also included in the Harland & Wolff general arrangement plans of *Olympic*, but unfortunately the sizes

51

WELL DECKS

(Right and below, far right) Aft well deck bulkheads. These were all cut out in one piece and folded into shape. A wooden jig was built behind them to ensure that they remain in the required shape. The levers on the watertight doors in the forward well deck were made of rod. The 'boxes' above the portholes on the forward well deck bulkhead were wall sockets or electrical outlets with watertight covers. They were found all over the ship.

(Right) The rubbing plates behind doorknobs were drawn on a computer and printed on decal sheet. The notice board next to the door can be seen. These were also written on a computer and printed out on coloured cardboard. The exact colour of these boards in unknown. We opted for 'White Star Line' colours, ie black and buff.

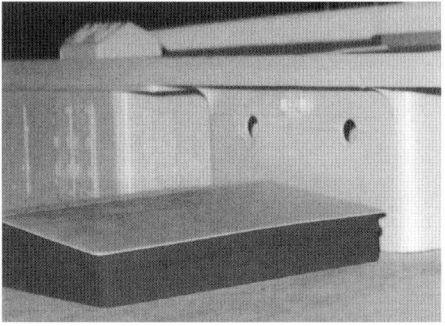

(Below) Well deck and poop deck Sunderland Forge and Engineering Co. Ltd 3-ton electric cargo winch. (Scale: 1/48.)

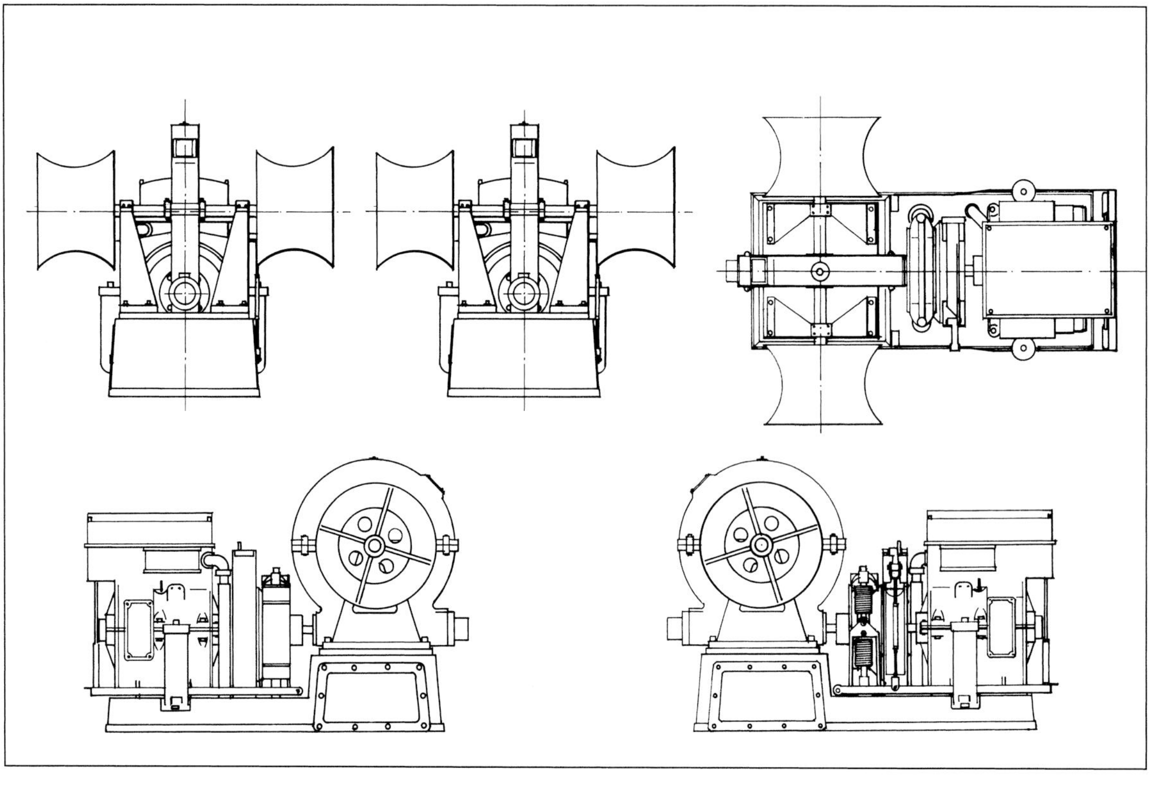

WELL DECKS

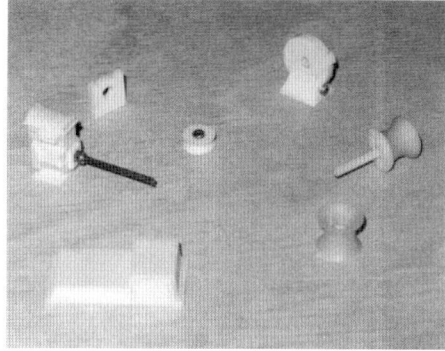

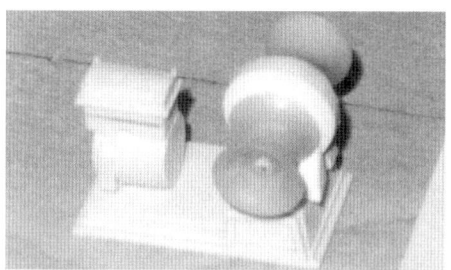

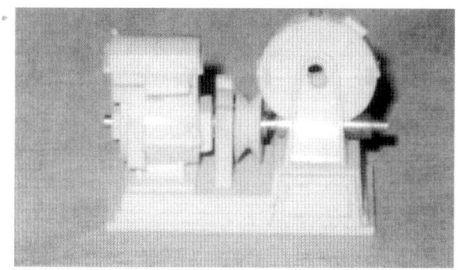

(Top, far left) The basic parts of a small electric winch. The base was made of layers of thick sheet styrene. The motor casing is of plastic tube. The gear housing was also cut out of thick styrene and filed to shape.
(Centre, far left) The basic items filed to shape and placed together. The drums are cast in resin.
(Bottom, far left) The engine casing of the electric winch. Details have been added from thin styrene strips and rods.
(Top left) The items required for the electric winch engine casing. Brass rod and tubes were used for the axles.
(Left) The completed master winch. Once the items have been cast, further details such as brake levers and their cylinders and also a small eyelet on top of the gear housing needed to be added.

of these vary enormously in these plans. The two large winches, used for loading the ship with cargo, were placed on the poopdeck and on both well decks. From a photograph of *Olympic* under construction we were able to determine the width of one of these large vents by counting the deck planks leading up to it.

The base was built up of several layers of sheet styrene. The electric motor casing was made from tube and further details added with strip and rod. The axle was made from brass rod which was pushed through a brass tube in the gear housing. The drums were made of styrene tube to which small discs were added to the ends. After the glue had dried the drums were filed to shape. A small tube was inserted inside the drum and glued to the backing

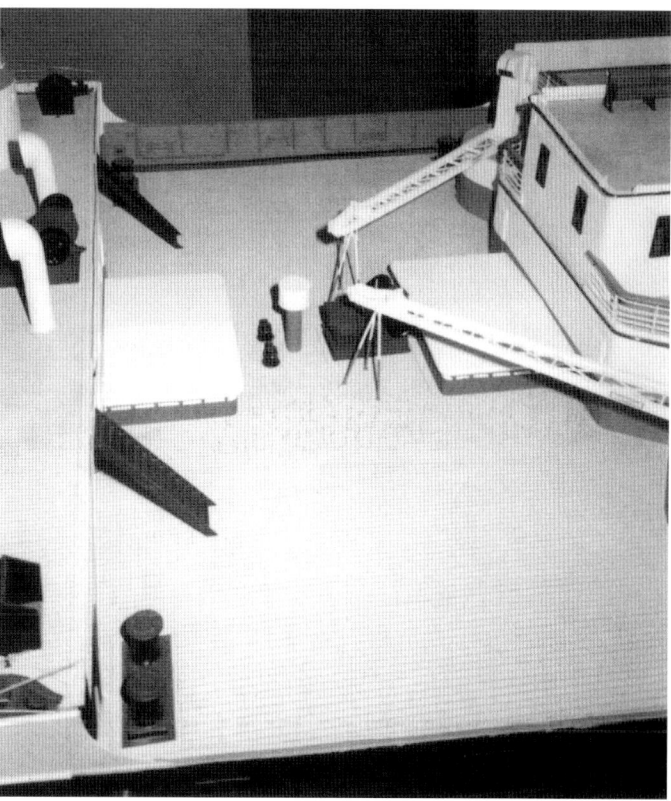

(Right) The nearly-complete aft well deck. Struts inside the bulwark still have to be added, as well as the covers on the waterways.

53

WELL DECKS

plate; stiffeners were added from thin styrene.

Before the winches were painted, the brake levers were added and also the small eyelets at the top of the gear-housings were added. The bodies of these winches were painted in dark green, the drums in satin black.

Low rollers

The low rollers used to aid the ropes while cargo was being lowered down into the holds were substantially different on both well decks. Those on the aft well decks were at deck level, while the two on the forward well deck were on columns. These too were built up of thick discs of sheet styrene and filed to shape.

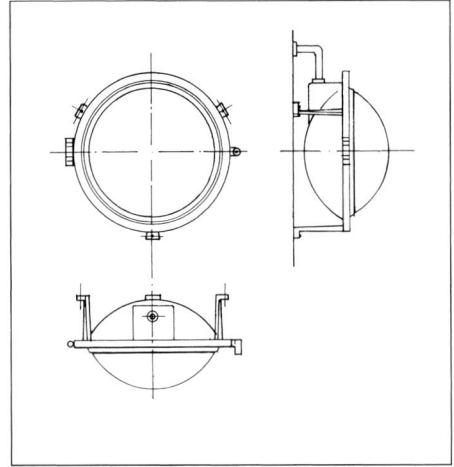

Bulkhead lamp. (Scale: 1/12.)

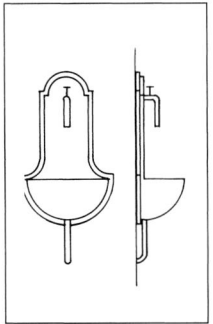

The drinking fountains which were found on the aft bulkhead of the aft well deck. These were attached to a thin wooden backing plate. The bowl was heat-moulded. The tap and pipe were added from rod. (Scale: 1/24.)

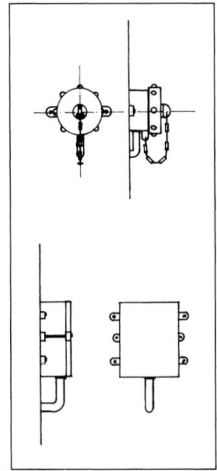

Electrical outlets. (Scale: 1/12.)

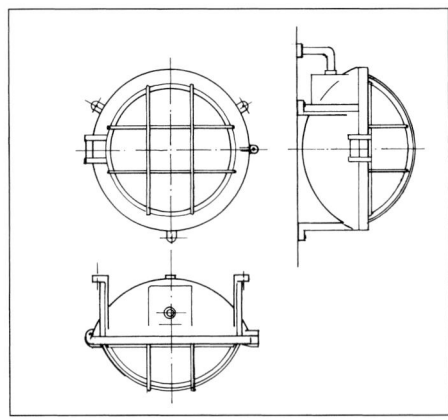

'Lusitania Style' bulkhead lamp. It is believed that only two of these were used on Titanic, on the forward well deck aft bulkhead. (Scale: 1/12.)

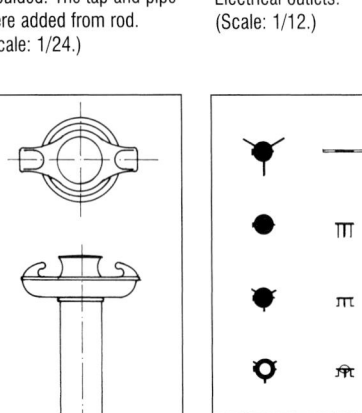

The 'Rollers' on the forward well deck. (Scale: 1/48.)

Building bulkhead lamps from etched brass. A whole fret was photo-etched with small discs (top) that were connected to each other with three small arms. After removing one of these discs the arms were folded to form the arms (middle). Two resin-cast shells were then added, one on each side (bottom). The outward facing shell was painted silver to represent the glass. The rest of the lamp was painted white with a black rim surrounding the glass. (Scale: 1/96.)

(Left) The model is not displayed inside a glass case. Dubious chemical reactions resulting from different materials used for the model can wreak havoc to a model locked inside a confined atmosphere. Instead the model is cleaned once a week. Here she can breathe and settle freely.
(Photo: Lee Everitt and Andy Wright)

(Below) The model is on display in the museum in Orlando, Florida.
(Photo: Lee Everitt and Andy Wright)

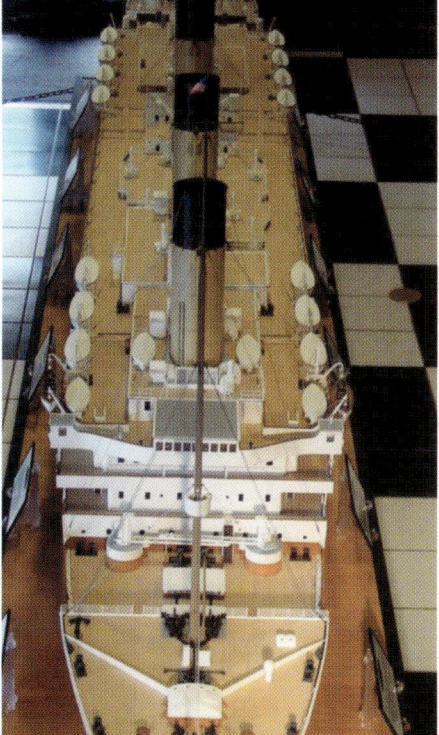

(Above) The colour of the maple veneer used for the decks clearly comes to advantage in this image. There was no need to add any weathering to the model. The construction time of nearly two-and-a-half years took care of that - the weathering came by itself and looks most realistic.
(Photo: Lee Everitt and Andy Wright)

(Right) The model was built in Germany which has an entirely different atmosphere than Florida. Even though the museum is air conditioned, the museum staff kept an eye open for any movement or warping of parts of the model which might occur in its first months on display.
(Photo: Lee Everitt and Andy Wright)

(Below) One of the few photographs taken with the model in direct sunlight. Here the model is being unpacked before going on display at the British *Titanic* Society's annual convention 2004 though when this picture was taken the model was still in its crate.
(Photograph: Axel Breest)

(Top) Taken on the same occasion, showing First and Second Class deck spaces. (Photograph: Axel Breest)

(Left) The poop deck and docking bridge. Here the remaining passengers gathered before *Titanic* sank.
(Photograph: Robert Hahn)

(Above) The roof of the First Class lounge. Note the shuffleboards.
(Photograph: Axel Breest)

(Above) The navigating bridge. The bridge roof on the model has been changed from natural wood to grey.
(Photograph: Axel Breest)

(Right) First Class promenade deck. Note the leaded windows of the First Class smoking room.
(Photograph: Axel Breest)

(Left) Second Class entrance and First Class smoking room roof.
(Photograph: John McFadyen)

(Below) No 4 funnel deckhouse.
(Photograph: John McFadyen)

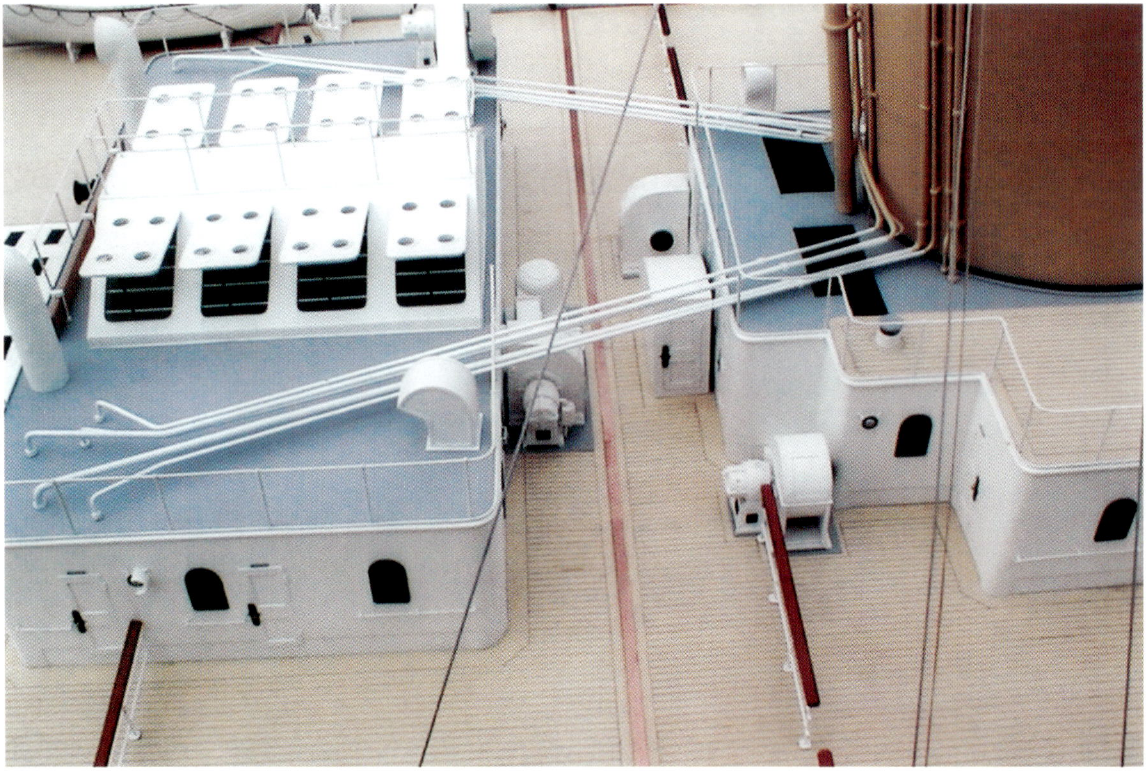

(Above) Tank room and No 3 funnel deckhouse.
(Photograph: John McFadyen)

(Right) First Class lounge roof with the compass platform.
(Photograph: John McFadyen)

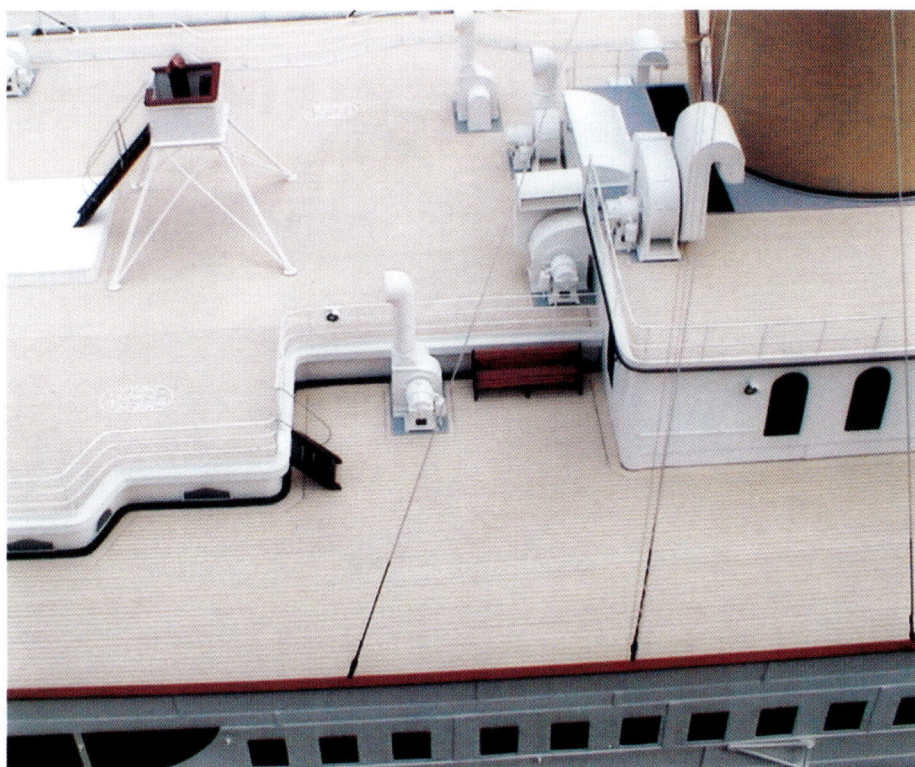

(Left) Lounge roof and gymnasium.
(Photograph: John McFadyen)

(Below) Officers' quarters.
(Photograph: John McFadyen)

Two views of *Titanic* as if they were taken in Southampton harbour, looking at the real ship.
(Photographs: John McFadyen)

6 Poop Deck

During the final stages of the sinking, the remaining passengers on board *Titanic* made their way to the stern, away from the freezing water. The poop deck must have been filled with people clinging to their last hopes of survival. After the sinking ship had broken in two some actually believed that the stern was staying afloat. The chief baker Charles Joughin said at the British inquiry: 'I kept out of the crush as much as I possibly could, and followed down – followed down getting towards the well of the deck, and just as I got down towards the well she gave a great list over to port and threw everybody in a bunch except myself. I did not see anybody else outside this bunch apart from myself. . . . I was not exactly in the well, I was on the side, practically on the side then. She threw them over. At last I clambered on the side when she chucked them. . . . It was not going up but the other side was going down. I eventually got on the starboard side of the poop.'

The deck

The poop deck planks on the real *Titanic* were 5in wide, and on the model they were drawn onto the veneer in the same way as the well decks. It seems that there were two margin planks along the side of the hull, but they only led up to the aft fairleads behind which was only a single margin plank.

Some fittings that did not protrude through the deck planking, such as capstans, did not have margin planks, nor did other items that were bolted to the surface of the deck such as rope reels or drums.

Titanic's poop deck taken in Queenstown by the *Cork Examiner*'s photographer Thomas Barker on 11 April 1912. Taken from the aft end of the boat deck it is looking down onto the First Class promenade deck. The two ladies sitting on the bench in the centre of the picture would have a near 100 per cent chance of survival. Five female First Class passengers were lost in the disaster. The aft welldeck and poopdeck were the Third Class area. The little child standing on the far left of the picture in the aft well deck would have a 30 per cent chance of survival: 53 children travelling Third Class were lost, 23 survived. Married couples and unmarried women travelling Third Class were accommodated in the stern, unmarried men in the bow. (Photograph: *Cork Examiner*, Claes-Göran Wetterholm collection)

55

POOP DECK

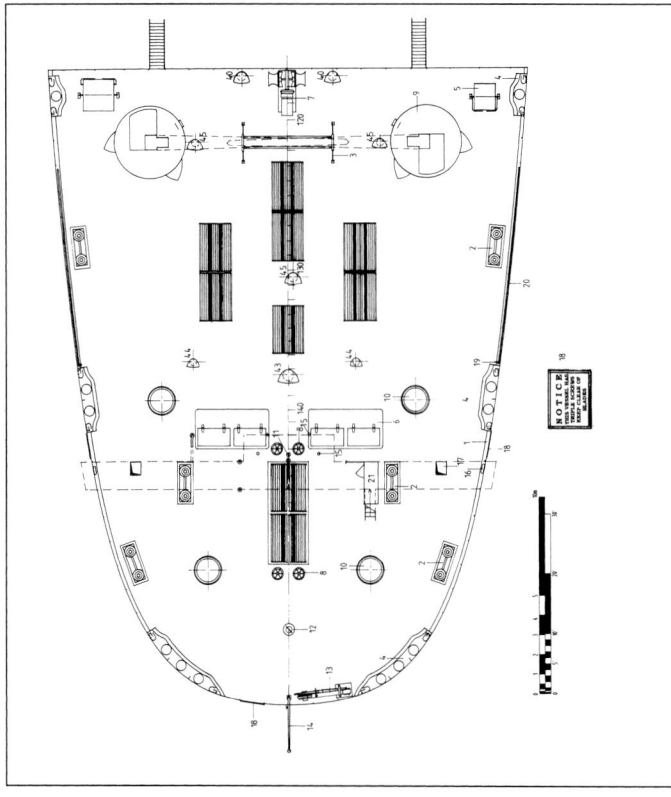

Poop deck. (Scale: 1/384.)
Key:
1. Waterway.
2. Bollard.
3. Jib crutch.
4. Fairlead.
5. Rope reel.
6. Steering engine room skylight.
7. 3-ton Sunderland Forge and Engineering Co. Ltd electric winch.
8. Capstan steam supply valve.
9. 2½-ton Stothard and Pitt electric crane.
10. Napier Brothers Ltd capstan.
11. Rigging bracket.
12. Rope scuttle.
13. Stream anchor.
14. Flagstaff.
15. Docking bridge strut.
16. Air vent.
17. Ventilation shaft.
18. Notice board.
19. High-pressure water valve.
20. Water supply pipe.
21. Storage locker.

Cowl vents

A wooden master was made for each cowl vent by joining together two wooden dowels of different sizes, one forming the cowl opening and the other the trunk. It seems that on the poop deck the cowl opening was twice the diameter of the trunk it served. The seam was then filled and the vent sanded to shape. The master cowl was cut into two halves down the centreline and thin pieces of wood glued to the cut area on both halves. This would give enough material on the moulded cowls to work with when the heat-moulded vents were cut from the backing sheet.

Both halves were then attached to a wooden board, one on each side of the board, and the cowl number written onto the board to avoid confusion. Then the outline of the vent was cut out on a small piece of plywood and the two halves of each vent were heat-moulded, as can be seen in the photograph. The vent halves were then cut from the backing sheet at the line where the wooden cowl half joined the thin piece of wood which was glued behind it. The mating edge was then sanded flat on a sanding board. Cementing the two halves to each other was quite straightforward. As both were actually taken from the same master, they fitted perfectly. After I had joined the two halves together, I sanded the seams and the cowl opening on both ends, which I had cut out with a sharp scalpel after the glue had dried. The handles for turning the cowl were made from stretched sprue, shaped over boiling water and attached one to each side of the cowls. The insides of the cowls were painted white.

Capstans

Like many other fittings on the model, the capstans were made of several layers of thick sheet-styrene discs. They did not have to be perfectly round when they were joined together, as once

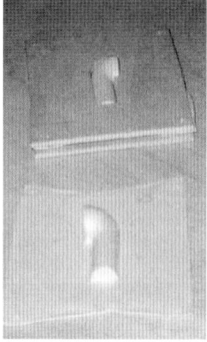

Heat-moulding cowl vents.

(Left) Cowl vents in place on the poop deck.

POOP DECK

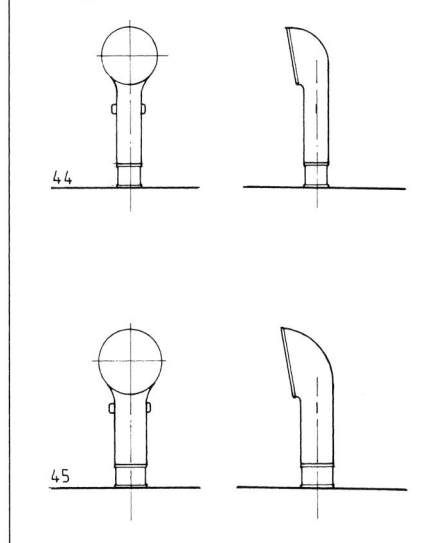

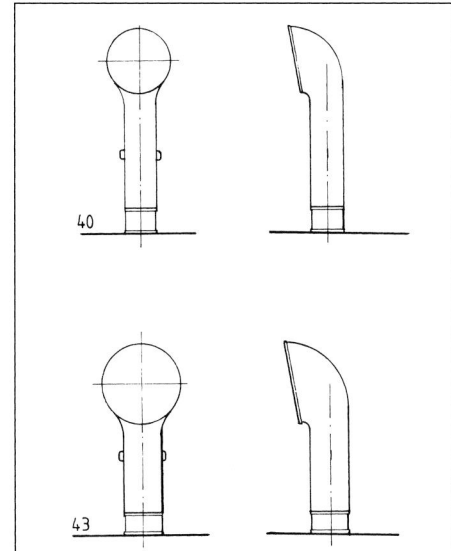

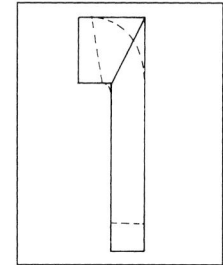

Cowl vents. (Scale: 1/96.)

Wooden dowels attached to each other for the cowl vent former. This is also a very effective method of building small-scale cowl vents. If wood is used, it would have to be treated with a grain-filler before painting.

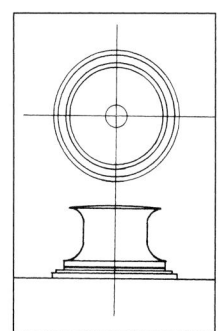

Poop deck and forecastle deck capstan. (Scale: 1/96.)

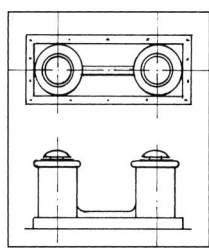

Poop deck and forecastle deck bollard. (Scale: 1/96.)

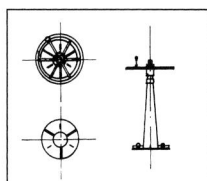

Capstan operating valve. (Scale: 1/96.)

the basic capstan was finished, it was attached to a lathe and filed to shape. The capstans of the real ship were produced and delivered by Napier Brothers Engineers Ltd, Glasgow, and they all featured the manufacturer's plate on the centre of the cap. These were photo-etched for the model. They were drawn in life-size on computer by an architectural student I know, along with other photo-etched pieces such as lifeboat nameplates, the Harland & Wolff builders' plaque etc. The drawings were printed out at 1:48 scale and sent to a company that does photo etchings, who returned them after a long wait – but the results were well worth waiting for. Some plaques are legible even at that scale. The plaques for the capstans were then attached to the resin-cast items. In the meantime I had made a silicon rubber mould of a capstan to which the plaque had been attached, so these photo-etched pieces will not be needed for future models.

Steam valves

There were four steam valves to operate the capstans. To make these, first a wooden dowel was sanded to a conical shape, using a disc sander, to form the pillar. The round baseplate was made from styrene, and small ring-bolts were made from heat-moulded styrene rod. Thin stiffeners were attached from styrene strip. The wheels were also made from rod. First I drew a complete wheel onto a wooden board. The centre of the wheel was cut from a piece of small-diameter styrene tube and was then tacked to the board with a thin nail through the centre. The spokes were made from styrene rod and added using liquid poly. They were left a little longer than they needed to be, as I found it easier to cut them to the required length after they had been attached to the centre. The wheel rim was moulded over steam around a wooden dowel and after the spokes had been cut to the required length – using the drawing on the wooden board as a guide – the rim was glued to the spokes. A small handle was added, made from a brass belaying-pin of which the bottom half had been cut off.

Fairleads

The fairleads were placed over the waterways, so the ends were open to form a tunnel through which water could pass unhindered. They were also heat-moulded. Before the heat-moulded fairleads were cut from the backing sheet, rivets were punched into them from the rear side. The masters for the rollers and clamps were made from styrene and the required items cast in resin.

Steering gear skylights

These were flat, box-like deckhouses mounted to the poop deck, slightly forward of the docking bridge. I began by cutting the rounded corners from a styrene tube. I then cut out the inner

POOP DECK

One of the capstan steamwheels. After this assembly had dried the spokes were cut to the required length and the ring attached to them.

(Right) A completed fairlead before painting.

Poop deck and forecastle deck fairlead. (Scale: 1/24.)

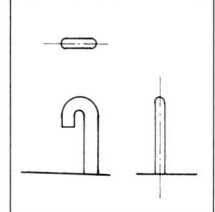

Air vent attached in waterways underneath the docking bridge. (Scale: 1/48.)

plating and drilled portholes into them. These too received porthole rims as described in Chapter 4. The glazing was also made from 3mm (0.11in) perspex and the inner side of the perspex was painted black. Then the walls were attached to the corners. The top was made from 2mm (0.07in) styrene and the lids from 0.5mm (0.01in) styrene. The hinges were made from strip and rod.

Air pipes

There were two air pipes mounted in the waterways on the port and starboard sides underneath the docking bridge. They were cut out from 3mm (0.11in) styrene with a belt saw and filed to shape.

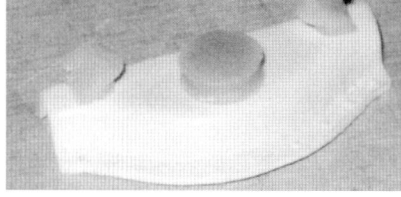

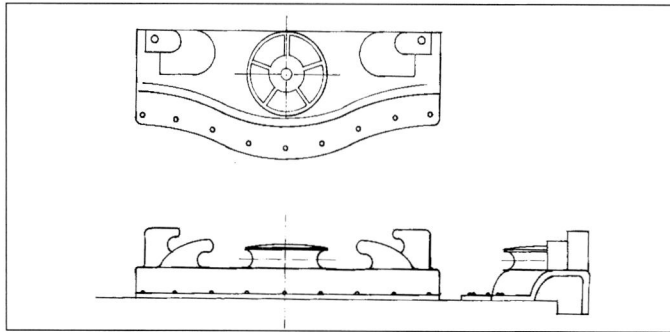

Cranes

The cranes were constructed in basically the same way as those on the well decks (see Chapter 5).

Bench seats

All cast-iron bench seat-end and centrepieces were cast in resin. First I photocopied a photograph of a side view of one of the benches, reducing it to a scale of 1:48. It was then transferred onto 0.5mm (0.01in) sheet-styrene and cut out. The details were added with stretched sprue on both sides. Using this master I made a two-piece silicon rubber mould. First I made

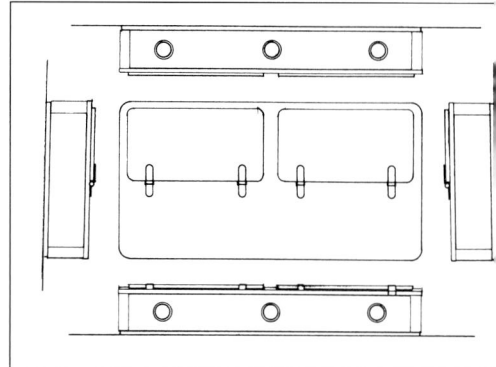

Steering engine skylight. (Scale: 1/96.)

a small box and half-filled this with plaster of Paris. Before it dried I dropped the master onto it, and it floated on top of the plaster. When this had cured I poured silicon rubber on top of it. After the silicon had set, I turned the box over and removed the floor and the plaster of Paris. The master bench seat end was still firmly in the silicon rubber half. I gave this a coating of release agent to ensure that the two halves of the mould could be separated.

Then I poured silicon rubber for the second half of the mould into the box. After this had set, I dismantled the box, separated the two

Close-up view of the port-side poop deck crane.

58

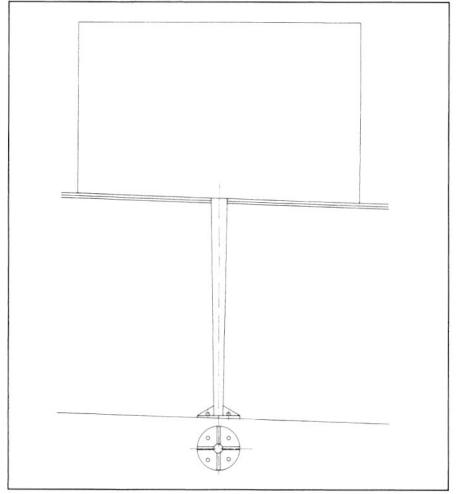
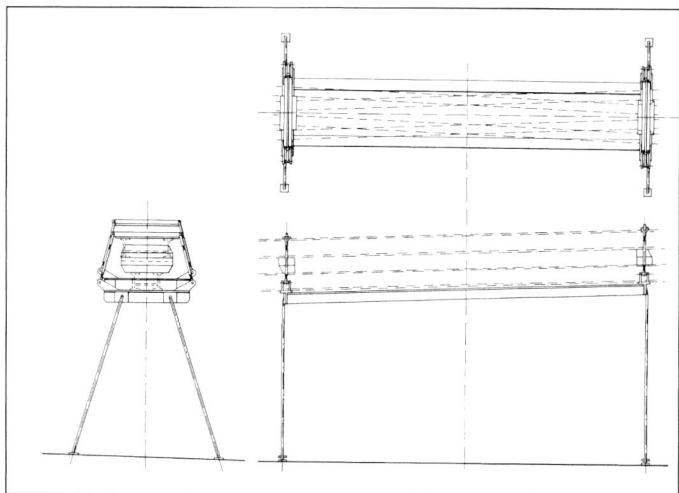

halves and removed the master. I made several more moulds, as I needed more than 140 of these items. After the two halves of the mould had had a day to breathe, I could cast the first items. I gave both halves of the mould a generous coating of resin and mated the mould halves. Excess material was forced out of the mould as the two halves were pressed together. After about an hour the item could be removed. There was some flash which had to be removed with a sharp scalpel, but apart from that the item was superb and ready to be painted in satin black.

For the centrepiece an end piece was cast and the upper half removed with a sharp knife. Occasionally an item was cast with air bubbles trapped inside, and some of these items were unusable. But I sorted out any end pieces with bubbles in the top area and used them as centrepieces after the upper half had been cut off.

For adding the wooden slats we made a jig from aluminium. This was basically the outline of the centrepiece, into which we cut small slots so that the slats could be pushed into them and remained there securely while the end pieces were joined to them. The slats were made from pear-wood. These were cut to the required length and sanded smooth, then pressed into the jig and once they were all in line the end pieces were added. We then removed the bench seat from the jig and added the centrepiece to the bottom of the seat. The completed benches were given a coating of satin varnish and were ready to be attached to the decks.

The stream anchor

To build the stream anchor, I began by cutting out the arms from 3mm (0.11in) styrene with a belt saw, cleaned it up and rounded the edges with a file. The flukes, which were made from thinner styrene and sanded to a conical shape, were attached to the arms. The shank was made from 4mm (0.15in) styrene and two strengthening plates were added to the sides of the crown. This formed a fork which held the arms. The stock was made from styrene rod which was sanded to a conical shape with a disc sander set at the slowest speed to prevent the material from melting during the

(Above) Poop deck jib stanchions. (Scale: 1/96.)

(Above left) Crane cylinder support. The supports were made from wooden rod, the mount from styrene discs with bolts added from styrene rod. (Scale: 1/96.)

The master bench seat end piece. Carved from sheet styrene details were added from sprue.

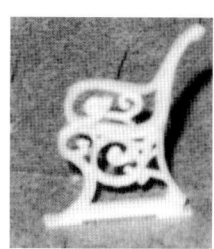

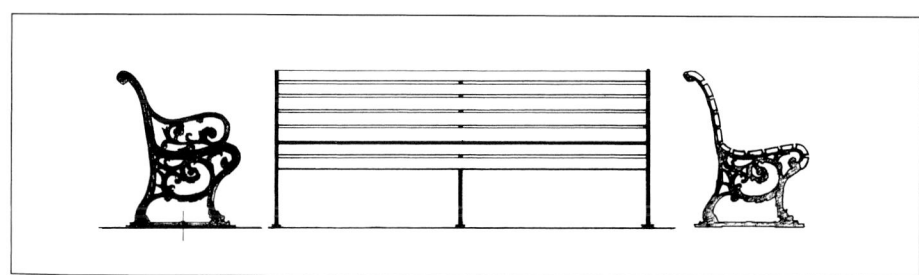

Bench seat. (Scale:1/48.)

POOP DECK

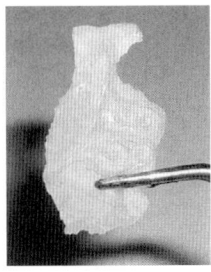

One of the bench seat ends before removing the flash...
(Jörg Graffe)

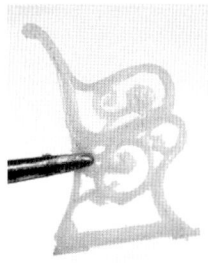

... and after.
(Jörg Graffe)

The jig for holding the slats, while the bench is being assembled.
(Jörg Graffe)

(Top far right) All pieces required for a bench seat. The slats were cut from pear wood.
(Jörg Graffe)

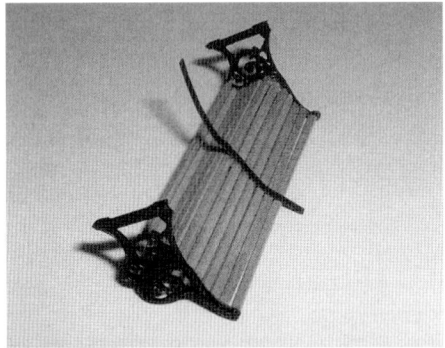

(Far right) A bench seat under construction.
(Jörg Graffe)

(Right) A strip of black sheet-styrene forming part of the centre support.
(Jörg Graffe)

(Right) A completed bench seat viewed from underneath.
(Jörg Graffe)

(Far right) Fully-assembled benches ready for installation. Though I cast the end pieces and cut the slats myself all benches were assembled by a fellow modelmaker Jörg Graffe. The quality of his workmanship deserves the highest praise.
(Jörg Graffe)

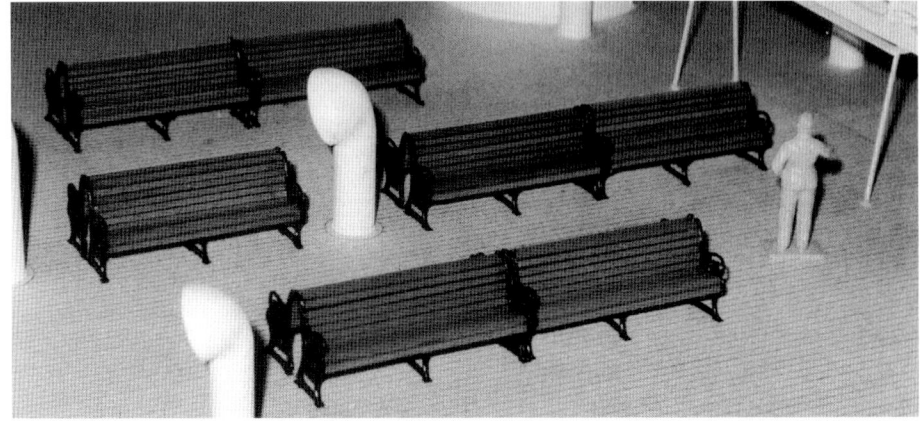

Groups of bench seats on the aft well deck.

process. Both halves were made separately and joined to two small thick discs forming the bands which were also joined to a small piece of rod forming the centre. The openings for the ring and the stock at the end of the shank were cut from rod and attached to the shank. The joints of these were given a generous filling of putty and filed to shape after the putty had hardened. The ring was cut from styrene, the edges rounded with a file and formed around a wooden dowel. Straps and gravity bands were added from strip and sprue.

The flagstaff

The flagstaff on the real ship was 24ft high. It was attached to the deck on a swivel, possibly so that it could be folded forwards when the flag was removed while the ship was at sea. The flagstaff rested on the railings behind it when it was raised, to which it was secured with a band.

The flagstaff on my model was made from a wooden dowel. Having fixed it in a hand drill, I sanded it to shape by slightly pressing it against a sanding disc with a wooden block. I drilled a small slot into the top of the pole for the pulley and made the truck from a small disc of styrene. A small hole was drilled into the bottom of the pole to give access to the swivel which was made from thin brass wire. One end of this wire was pushed into the hole and the centre of the wire bent slightly to represent the swivel. The base plate was made from two squares of thin styrene, which also needed holes drilled into them through which the wire would pass. Another hole was drilled into the deck and the other end of the wire pushed into it. This strong construction was essential as the flagstaff was prone to damage when people walked past the model, and even more so when the model was in transit to the USA. The band was added from styrene strip and secured to the railings with a small blob of resin.

High-pressure water valves

The high-pressure water valves were used for cleaning the ship, and possibly even as fire extinguishers, and they are all over the ship. About 25 of them were needed. Even in 1:48 scale they are tiny, so we chose to simplify them. The body was made from a small wooden

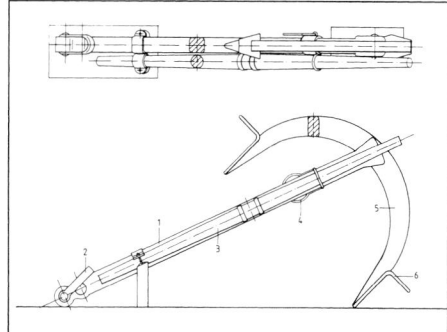

Poop deck stream anchor. (Scale: 1/48.)
Key:
1. Shank.
2. Ring.
3. Stock.
4. Gravity bands.
5. Fluke.

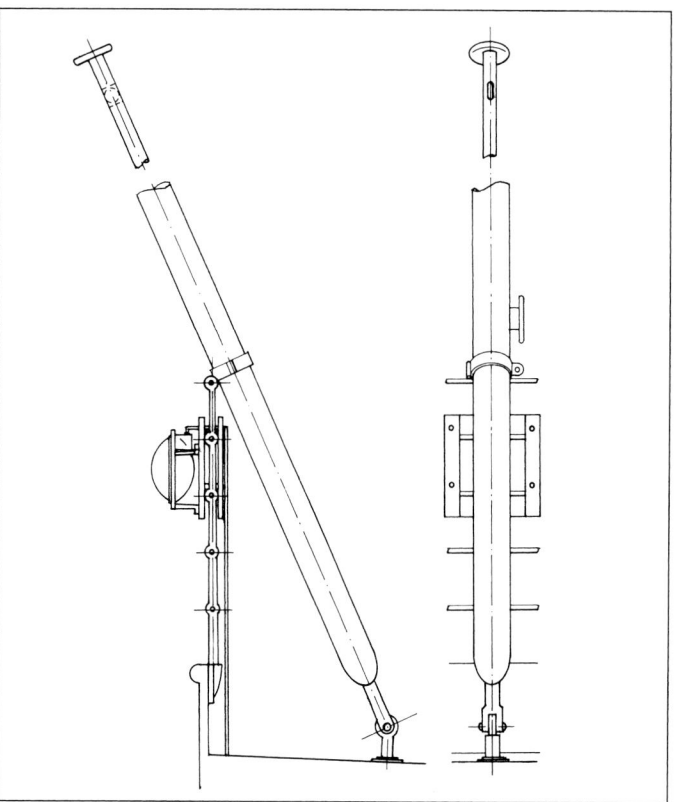

pellet approximately 3mm (0.11in) in diameter. The hose mount was attached to it with rod and a base of sheet-styrene. The handle was made from thin rod. Here again we made a master and cast the required water valves in resin. We used several two-part moulds as described above for the bench seats.

Flagstaff and bulkhead lamp at aft end of poop deck railing. (Scale: 1/24.)

Rope reels

Titanic had three rope reels, which were used for loading cargo. There were two on the poop deck and one on the forecastle. The two on the

POOP DECK

(Right) The flagstaff and stream anchor at the end of the poop deck. The rear side of one of the red notice boards can also be seen. There was no waterway between the aft fairleads.

(Far right) *Olympic*'s flag being lowered while the ship was out at sea. The swivel mount on the deck can be seen to advantage.
(Photograph: Author's collection)

poop deck were of different sizes, the port reel being larger than the starboard reel. When not in use they were covered with canvas so there was no need for us to build a detailed interior.

We built the side walls attached to a base. The supports on each side were made from rod. The canvas covers were heat-moulded using wooden block formers and looked extremely convincing once they had been painted and a wash applied. The sides of the canvas covers were cut to give access to the rods. The crank handles were made from brass wire.

The docking bridge

We cut out the docking bridge from 1mm (0.03in) styrene and added the L-beams to the bottom side with thin strips. Two square shafts – which also acted as supports for the docking bridge – were attached near the outer edges. They were also made from styrene, but in one piece. As the edges were slightly rounded, they were carefully folded over a steel ruler. The joint where the two outer edges of the one-piece support mated was placed in the middle where filling and sanding the seam was easier than it would have been if I had placed the joint at a corner. The angle of the poop deck had to be taken into account at the bottom edge of the supports. This was done the same way as described in the well decks' superstructure (Chapter 4), by placing a sheet of paper onto one of the frames, drawing the

(Right) High-pressure water valve. (Scale: 1/8.)

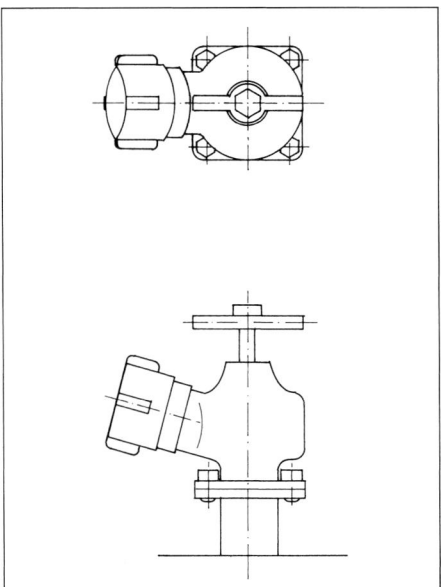

(Far right) Rope reels port side (top) and starboard side (bottom). (Scale: 1/48.)

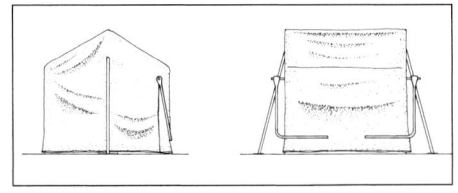

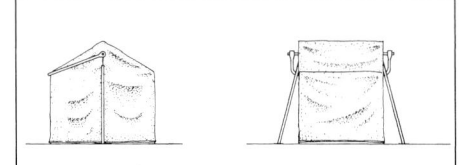

POOP DECK

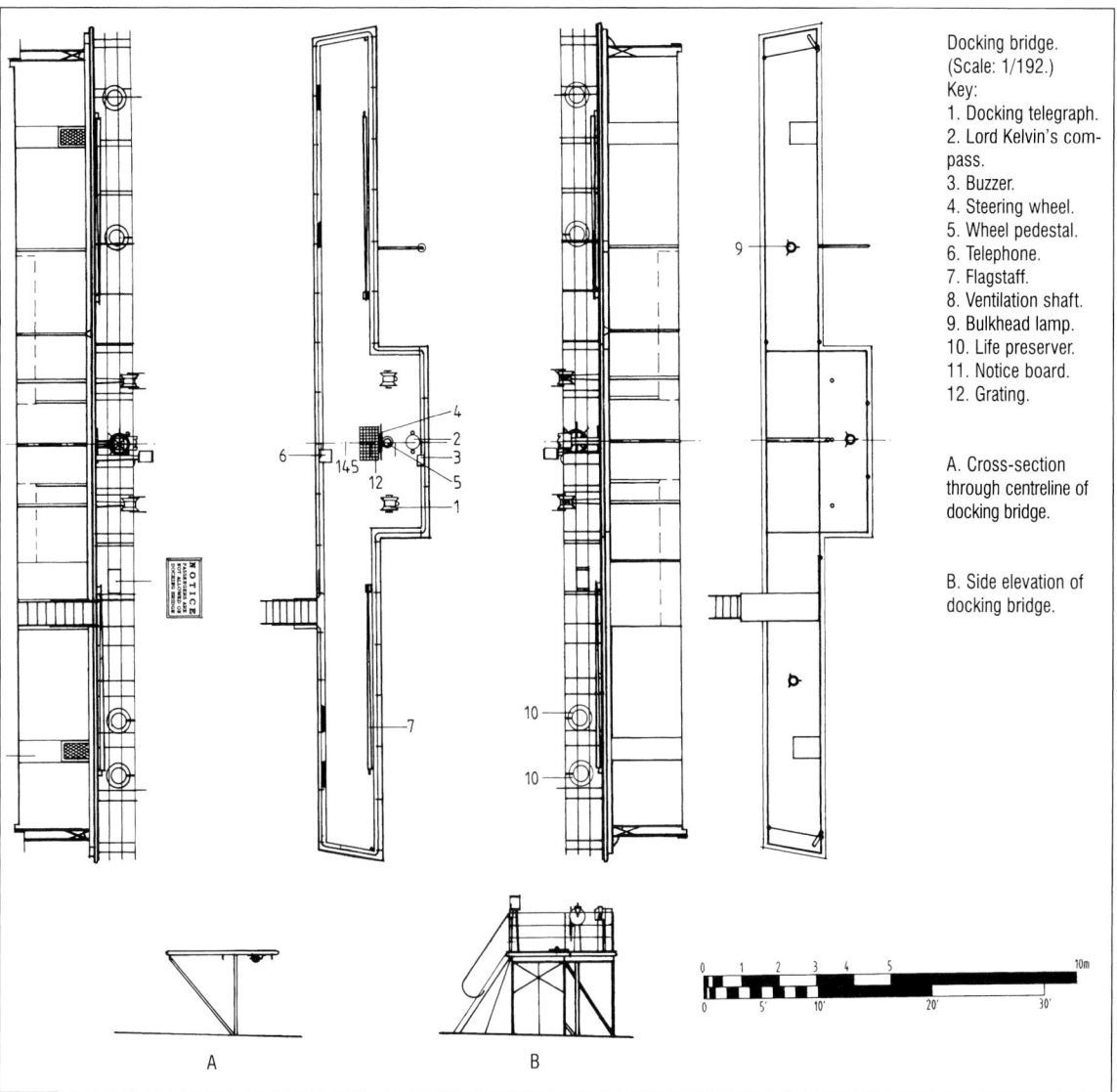

Docking bridge.
(Scale: 1/192.)
Key:
1. Docking telegraph.
2. Lord Kelvin's compass.
3. Buzzer.
4. Steering wheel.
5. Wheel pedestal.
6. Telephone.
7. Flagstaff.
8. Ventilation shaft.
9. Bulkhead lamp.
10. Life preserver.
11. Notice board.
12. Grating.

A. Cross-section through centreline of docking bridge.

B. Side elevation of docking bridge.

slope of the deck on this sheet of paper and transferring it to the sides of the supports. The docking bridge itself was horizontal. A vent duct was on the rear side of each support which was covered with wire mesh. The openings for these vents were cut out of very thin sheet-styrene and the mesh added with stretched sprue. First I made a template for this by drawing the mesh with the frame on paper and the styrene with the cut-out taped onto it. Using the drawn mesh as a guide, the pieces of stretched sprue were applied one by one. It was fairly easy with small openings such as these. However, it became tedious when I got to the large stokehold shafts in front of and behind the funnels, as they were much larger. I initially contacted the photo-etching company about this, hoping that the mesh could be photo-etched. Unfortunately, I was told it was not possible to etch the wires as thinly as I had hoped. In the meantime I have come across etched frets with pieces so thin that one can hardly see them, such as railings etc. Should I have to build more of these large models in the future then I will go for a different company that does photo-etching to save myself from having to complete the mesh by adding every single piece of wire by hand. Once the mesh was completed the vent cover was cut from the sheet-styrene and the mesh added to the supports.

POOP DECK

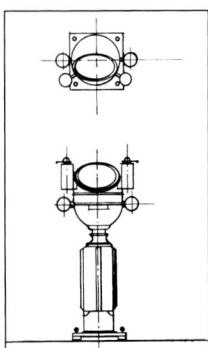

Lord Kelvin's compass binnacle. (Scale: 1/48.)

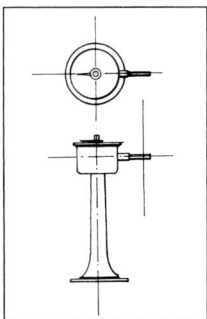

Buzzer. (Scale: 1/48.)

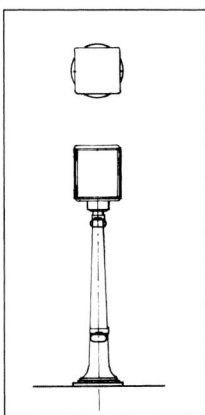

Wheel pedestal. (Scale: 1/48.)

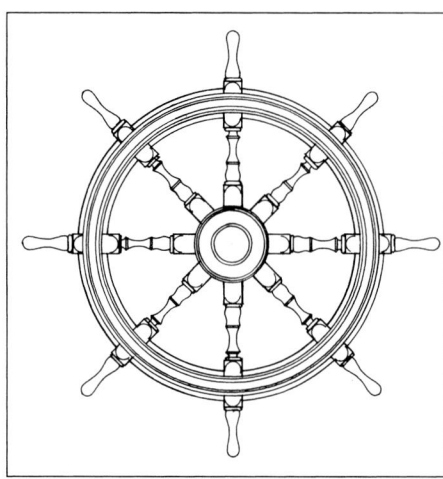

Docking- and navigating bridge wheel. (Scale: 1/18.)

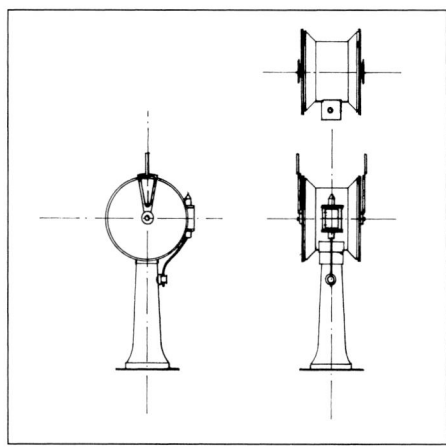

Docking- and navigating bridge telegraph. (Scale: 1/48.)

Underneath the stairway leading to the docking bridge was a small storage locker, possibly for deckchairs. The rear wall was angled closely to the angle of the stairs above it, while the front wall was lengthened to form a windshield for the door. The extreme end of this windshield was reinforced by a beading, for which I added a thin strip of half-round styrene. Three bulkhead lamps were attached to the bottom side of the docking bridge of the model. These were built the same way as described in Chapter 5.

Along the outline on the topside of the docking bridge we added thin strips of styrene as the margin strip. They were at the level of the decking of the docking bridge. They were 3mm (0.11in) wide and flush with the outer edges of the docking bridges. The stanchions for the railings were in the centreline of this strip. We took the locations of the stanchions from period photographs as best we could and marked them on the strip. We then drilled holes into the strip for the stanchions. The position of each stanchion was also applied to a long, straight piece of soft wood, but in a straight line, not in the outline of the docking bridge. On this board the railings were built, by first pushing in each stanchion and after that threading the brass wire through the openings in each stanchion. After they were painted we removed them from the board, folded them at the corners and the stanchions were pushed into their respective holes in the docking bridge margin strip.

We attached a bead of 2mm (0.07in) half-round styrene strip, painted dark brown, to the sides of the docking bridge. We did this after painting the docking bridge, as it would have been pretty awkward to get a straight line between the dark brown bead and the white.

Underneath the docking bridge was a vast array of struts. Some were vertical, others were angled. They were attached to the sides of the outer L-beams with a small flange. To create the flange, the tops of the rod struts were flattened slightly with a pair of pliers.

The deck of the docking bridge was cut out from a sheet of maple veneer and the planks drawn onto it. It was attached using contact cement, and then varnished.

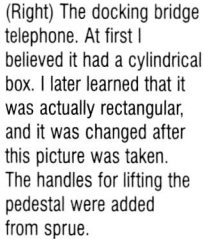

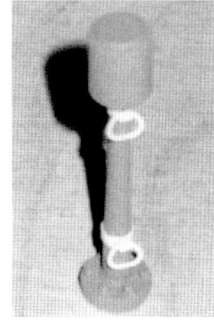

(Right) The docking bridge telephone. At first I believed it had a cylindrical box. I later learned that it was actually rectangular, and it was changed after this picture was taken. The handles for lifting the pedestal were added from sprue.

(Left) Telephone box. (Scale: 1/48.)

Navigational instruments

The navigational instruments on the docking bridge consisted of two docking telegraphs, one telephone, the wheel and its pedestal, one 'buzzer' and a 'Lord Kelvins' binnacle.

The docking bridge instruments were made from sheet styrene and wood. The sides of the telegraphs were wooden discs sanded to a conical shape in a hand drill. They were attached to the cylinder which was of styrene tube. A thin styrene ring was added to the outer side as a rim. The pillar was also made from a wooden rod which was also sanded to shape using a hand drill. The lamp box and cables were added from styrene and brass wire. The operating levers were cast in resin.

The *Titanic*'s wheels were 3.9ft in diameter on the navigating bridge and 3.6ft diameter in the wheelhouse. It is believed that the docking bridge wheel was also 3.9ft across. I was fortunate enough to find a superb wheel in a model shop in the correct size. Three of them were cast in resin and painted dark brown, and brass rings were painted onto them. The buzzer was carved from pear wood. The two flagstaffs on the docking bridge were made from brass wire. They were fastened to the deck when not in use.

Notice boards

Three large identical notice boards were attached to the outside of the poop deck railing, warning tug captains to keep well away from the rotating propellers. They read: 'NOTICE – THIS VESSEL HAS TRIPLE SCREWS – KEEP CLEAR OF BLADES'. It is believed that the letters were white on a red background. I made a replica of one of these boards in life-size a few years ago which I still have. I took a photograph of it in my garden from a distance. The photograph was colour-copied at the correct size and then cut out and glued to a small piece of styrene.

Another notice board indicated that 'PASSENGERS ARE NOT ALLOWED ON DOCKING BRIDGE'. This was typed on a computer and printed out on coloured cardboard. It was glued to a backing plate which was attached to the railing next to the stairs leading to the docking bridge.

Notice board

7 Forecastle Deck

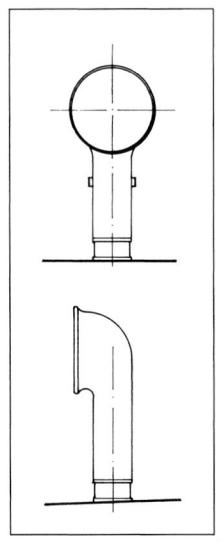

No 1 cowl-vent. (Scale: 1/48.)

Many visitors who come to my workshop are surprised when I tell them that passengers were not allowed on *Titanic*'s forecastle deck, because they have all seen Jack and Rose at the bow 'flying' or Jack and Fabrizio watching dolphins in James Cameron's 1997 movie 'Titanic'. In 1912 this area was strictly out of bounds for passengers. The regulations were relaxed a little in the 1920s, however, and photographs of *Olympic* entering New York harbour show the forecastle crammed with passengers.

The deck

On the forecastle deck, the waterways commenced underneath the foremost fairleads and ended at the forward well deck, forward bulkhead. As on the poop deck, the waterways were 5in wide on the real ship. There were two margin planks on the outer edges of the forecastle decks. The deck planks were 5in wide except in the area surrounding the anchor-handling gear, where they were 10in wide. This can be seen in the forecastle deck plan. These reinforced planks were also twice as thick as the deck planking, *ie* 6in. A second layer of veneer was attached to the decking to represent the reinforced area. The outer edges of the reinforced deck were chamfered. There was a single margin plank in front of and behind the breakwaters.

The complete forecastle deck was cut into a forward and aft section along the breakwaters. These sections were then mated to each other with a thin strip of styrene placed between them acting as a spacer with small wooden blocks glued underneath the deck to join the sections back together. After this had dried the spacers were removed.

Forecastle deck of *Olympic* after her first arrival in New York in June 1911. *Titanic* did not have the air shaft to the left on the forecastle, instead there was a large cowl-vent on the port side in front of the breakwater. (Library of Congress – LoC 908108 Z62 26817)

FORECASTLE DECK

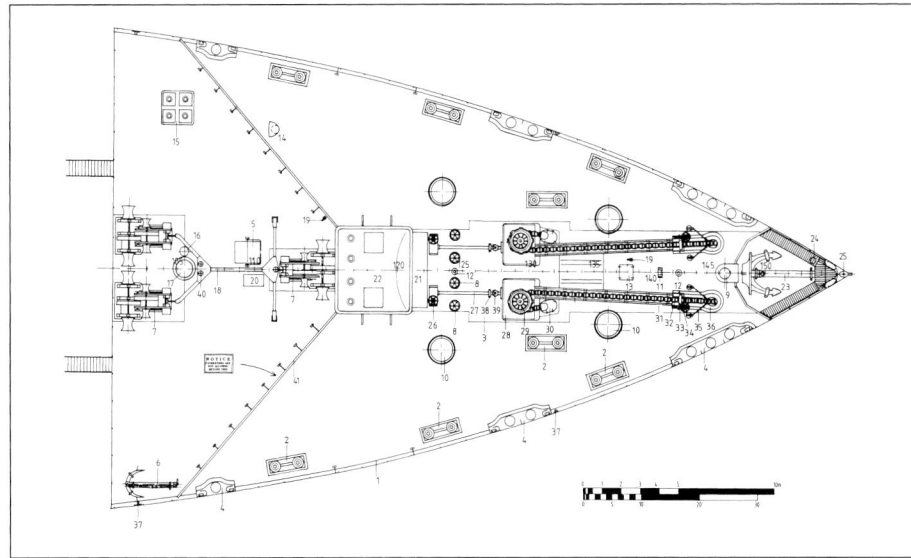

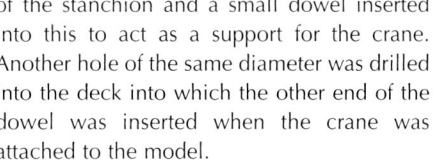

Forecastle deck plan. (Scale: 1/384.)
1. Waterway.
2. Bollard.
3. Reinforced deck planks.
4. Fairleads.
5. Rope reel.
6. Stream anchor.
7. Steam winch.
8. Capstan steam supply valve.
9. Reserve anchor crane.
10. Napier Brothers Ltd capstan.
11. Forestay bracket.
12. Telephone mount.
13. Hatchway.
14. No 1 cowl vent.
15. Crew galley skylight.
16. Crew galley flue.
17. Foremast.
18. Steam supply cover.
19. High-pressure water valve.
20. No 2 air vent.
21. Locker.
22. No 1 cargo hatch.
23. Reserve anchor.
24. Mushroom-head vent.
25. Flagstaff mount.
26. Windlass steam valve.
27. Motion shaft.
28. Windlass bedplate.
29. Windlass.
30. Chain pipe.
31. Chain races.
32. Compressor.
33. Bow stopper.
34. Bow stopper wheel.
35. Chain stopper.
36. Hawse pipe.
37. Rigging bracket.
38. Motion shaft bearing.
39. Universal joint.
40. Steam supply valves.
41. Breakwater.

Bollards, capstans, capstan valves, cable drums, cowl vents and fairleads

These were identical to those on the poop deck, so I will not repeat the construction method here.

Anchor crane

The crane stanchion was turned from a wooden rod and details added from brass, styrene rod and sheet. A hole was drilled into the bottom of the stanchion and a small dowel inserted into this to act as a support for the crane. Another hole of the same diameter was drilled into the deck into which the other end of the dowel was inserted when the crane was attached to the model.

The jib was made from thick brass wire with slots cut into both ends, one to accommodate the crane top, the other to accommodate the joint to the crane stanchion. Holes were drilled into the sides in both ends of the jib. A

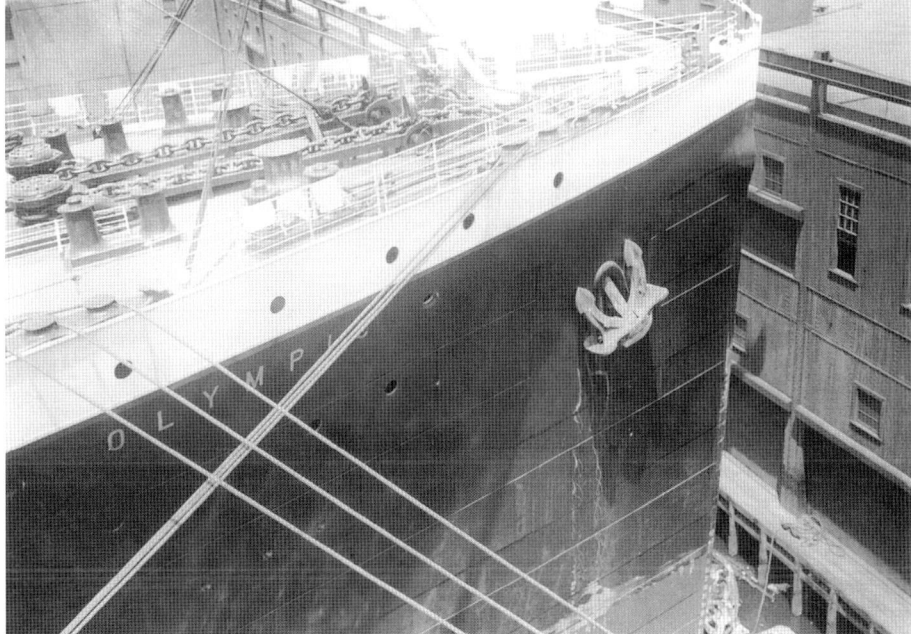

Taken on the same occasion as the previous picture, this too is *Olympic*. Apart from the name on the bows this view of *Titanic* would have been perfectly identical.
(Photograph: Brown Brothers)

FORECASTLE DECK

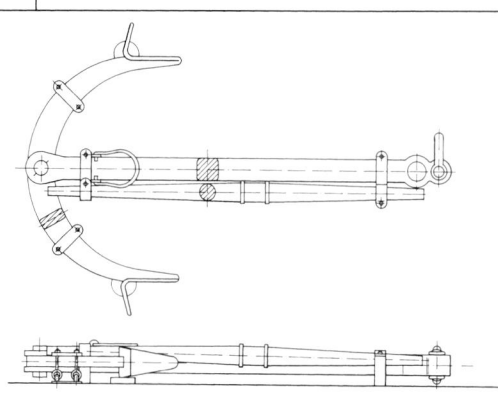

Stream anchor. (Scale: 1/48.)

(Above) Reserve anchor and crane (side elevation). (Scale: 1/192.)

(Top) Reserve anchor and crane (top elevation). (Scale: 1/192.)
Key:
1. Head.
2. Shank.
3. Fluke.
4. Bill.
5. Gravity bands.

(Far right) The reserve anchor and its crane.

(Right) The railings were completed as a whole straight unit on a wooden board. They were removed from the board after completion, bent to shape and then attached to the bulwarks. Here can be seen where segments of the wires were removed between portable rails and the railings.

small plate with a hole in the centre was attached vertically to the bottom end of the stanchion. This fitted snugly into the slot sawn into the jib's lower end, and a piece of brass rod was pushed into the holes to secure the jib. The top end of the jib was cut from thick styrene and pushed into the upper slot. The seams were filled and sanded smooth.

The drag wires connecting the jib to the top of the stanchion were also made from brass wire. Eyelets were formed at both ends of these wires, through which brass rods were also inserted when the wires were attached to the crane and the jib. Small slices of styrene tube were then push onto the rod ends acting as bolts. The crane was then rigged according to the plan.

No 1 cargo hatch

The walls of the hatch were built up the same way as those on the well decks. Two triangular supports were added to each side. At the forward edge of *Titanic*'s cargo hatch was a small locker with an angled front. The forward edge of the hatch cover continued this angle. There was a reason for this: on *Olympic* in 1911, the front of the cargo hatch was vertical. During a heavy gale the hatch cover, which weighed

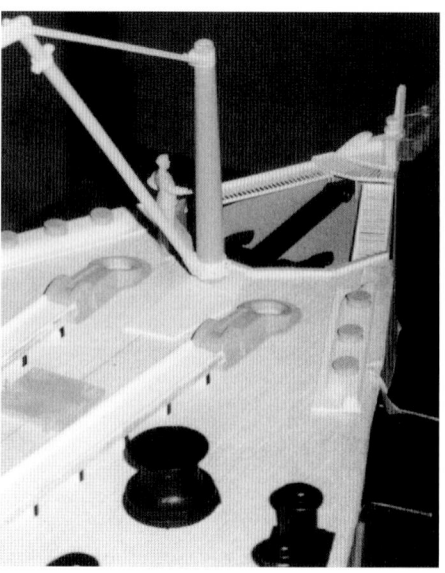

some 7 tons and was also bolted to the coaming, was torn off by an enormous wave and subsequently found in a corner of the forward well deck. This shows the force of the North Atlantic. As a result the forward edge of *Titanic*'s No 1 hatch was angled to reduce the impact of heavy waves on the front of the hatch. In addition, *Titanic*'s hatch cover was given twice as many bolts as *Olympic*'s.

The hatch cover was heat-moulded in an oven over a wooden former. Lids were added with styrene squares and hinges from strip and rod. Small slots were cut in to the hatch covers and the coaming rim to give access for the bolts. These were added from short pieces of rod. Four portholes were drilled into the hatch cover and their rims were cut out from styrene. The porthole glazing was added from clear styrene.

The breakwaters

These were made from four strips of 1mm (0.03in) styrene. Two of these were joined together to form the overlap near the centre of each breakwater. The beading on the top edge was made from 2mm (0.07in) styrene rod. The breakwaters were inserted into the slots in the deck after No 1 hatch was added. They extended right up to the hull side, with a cut-out in the corners above the waterways to allow water to pass through freely. The supports on the rear side of the breakwaters were also added from rod with small styrene plates forming the bedplates.

Small signs indicating that 'PASSENGERS ARE NOT ALLOWED BEYOND THIS' were printed on coloured cardboard, cemented to backing plates and added to the breakwaters.

The reserve anchor well

The well in the deck for the reserve anchor was built as a box-like construction with only the rear walls attached. The side walls would be part of the hull plating and would be added when the shell plating was being attached. The floor and the rear walls were left slightly oversize, as the joints to the shell plating would be determined while this work was being carried out. I found it was easier to remove excess material rather than to add material to the floor and walls. Part of the centre-frame of the hull had to be removed to give access to the well.

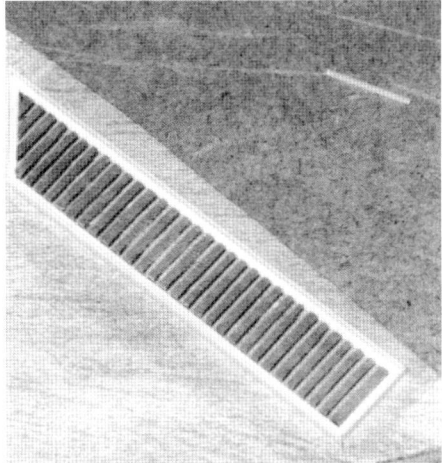

Anchor well gratings under construction.

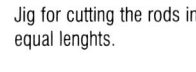

Jig for cutting the rods in equal lenghts.

Attaching the rods to the frame.

The gratings surrounding the well were made using a pre-built wooden jig. The jig was made in the shape of the outline of the gratings and adding thin strips of wood acting as spacers for the rods. To achieve an equal gap between

FORECASTLE DECK

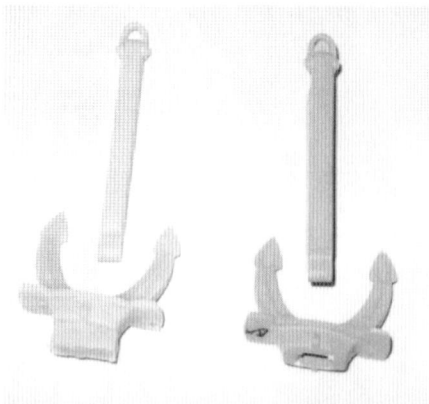

The master anchor and shank to the right with a resin-cast item to the left.

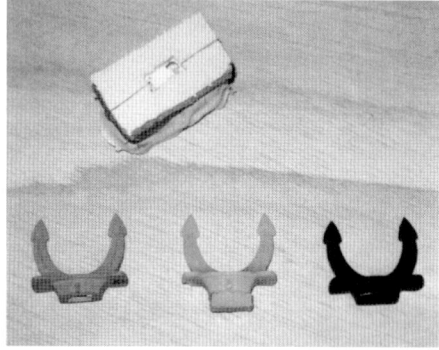

To the left is the master anchor, in the centre a resin item and to the right a cleaned painted item.

each wooden strip a small piece of 1mm (0.03in) styrene was placed between them and removed after the glue had dried. L-beams were cut and cemented to each other as the frame around the jig.

The rods were also cut to length using a jig to ensure that they were all of equal size. Two small pieces of wood, of the same length that the rod needed to be, were attached to a board so that the rod would fit snugly between them. One of the ends was closed with another piece of wood, then the rod was inserted and sliced off at the open end. These rods were then added to the frame between the wooden strips on the grating jig.

The anchors

These were amongst the first items to be built for the model. The shanks were built the same way as those of the stream anchors, so I will not repeat the method of construction here.

Again master items were built and resin cast items used for the model. A template for the flukes was cut out in styrene. The outline was then drawn onto 0.5mm (0.01in) styrene using the template to ensure that both flukes were the same size. After these were cut out they were cemented to each other but only at the 'Bill', ie the extreme top of the fluke. The bottom half was then slightly prized apart, giving the fluke the shape of an inverted 'V' when viewed from the side. This area was closed with long triangular pieces of styrene that were rounded over a dowel. These were cemented to the flukes and the seams filled and sanded. The tripping palm was cut out of 2mm (0.07in) styrene and scored lengthways so that it could be bent to shape. A square hole was cut into the palm for the stock. After the tripping palm was bent to shape (it was slightly curved when viewed from the side), the scores were given a coat of liquid poly and filler and left to dry for a few days, then sanded smooth. The head was added from several layers of styrene that were cemented to each other and filed to shape. The cut-out for the stock in the head was opened up by drilling holes alongside the edge of the opening. The remaining material was removed with a scalpel.

The reserve anchor was bolted to the floor of the anchor well with clamps. These clamps were made from thick styrene strips which had holes drilled into their outer edges. Rod was pushed into these holes and the clamp cemented to the well floor. The reserve anchor was placed into the well and another clamp, also with holes at the edges, pushed over the rods. The rods were then trimmed to the correct length after the whole assembly had dried.

Anchor-handling gear windlass bedplates

These were assembled from several layers of thick styrene sheet with the cut-out in the forward edge for the chain rails. The forward edge was rounded, viewed from the side. Very thin sheet styrene was added to the bedplates as the covers, which were slightly smaller in size than the bedplates proper. The chain sprocket was the lower part of the windlass which drove the chain around and into the chain pipes. These were made from two styrene discs which were chamfered at the edges and then cemented to each other.

I saw no other way of building the windlasses than to carve them from a single piece of thick styrene. First I drew the outlines on thick styrene and then opened up the holes, first by drilling two holes in the corners and then removing the rest of the material with a sharp scalpel. The windlasses were cut out with a belt saw and the sides then shaped with a file. The rounded caps were added with a thin styrene spacer between the windlass and the cap. The handwheels were assembled just like the capstan wheels.

The chain races or cable races were quite straightforward to build. They were made from long thick styrene strips with two small strips added to the edges as the guards and small styrene blocks as the supports.

The chain pipes were assembled from layers of styrene with a base plate of thin styrene. After this assembly had dried a hole large enough for the anchor chains to lead through was drilled into the forward half of the pipe. The cover was a thin sheet of styrene with a heat-moulded tunnel added. Hinges and fly-nuts were added from strip and rod. Before we added the covers, the chain pipes were placed onto the deck and the position of the pipes marked on, so they could be drilled out here too.

The windlass valves were made from thick discs which had six grooves filed into the sides. The wheel-rim was then added from rod formed over boiling water. The valve casings were built up from layers of styrene with a thin layer in the middle as the joint.

The motion shafts between the valve casings and the windlass bedplates were made from brass tube, the bearings carved from a small piece of styrene with bolts added from thin slices of rod. Small rings were cut from styrene tube and added to the front of the valve casings to accommodate the shafts. The universal joints were made by pushing a short piece of styrene tube over the forward end of the shafts which butted against the bearing and adding two triangular-shaped pieces of styrene to the sides to form the bracket, but before these were cemented to the tube, small holes were drilled into them to accommodate the swivels. Two pairs of brackets were made for each motion shaft. These were joined to each other by swivels which were made from two short rods of different diameters. A hole was drilled into the centre of the thicker rod in the same diameter as the thin rod which was then inserted into the first rod, forming an 'X'-shaped swivel, which connected the motion shafts to the extensions.

The anchor chain hawse pipes and their compressors were also built up from layers of thick styrene in one piece. This took some carving and shaping, but the finished items look just like the real thing. On top of these a small strip of thin, rounded styrene was attached as the bow stoppers. Two small slots were cut out in their sides before attaching to accommodate the stopper bar. This was also made from styrene strip and attached after the chains were in place. The bow stoppers were to secure the chains while the ship lay at anchor.

The compressor rotating worm gear was cut from a small brass screw which had the

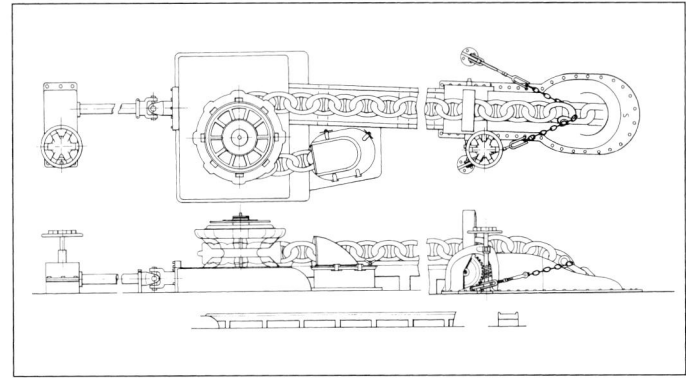

Anchor-handling gear. (Scale: 1/96.)

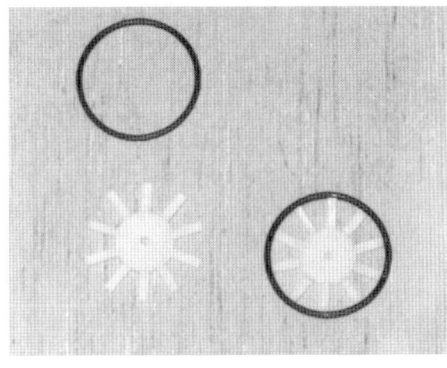

The windlass wheels under construction.

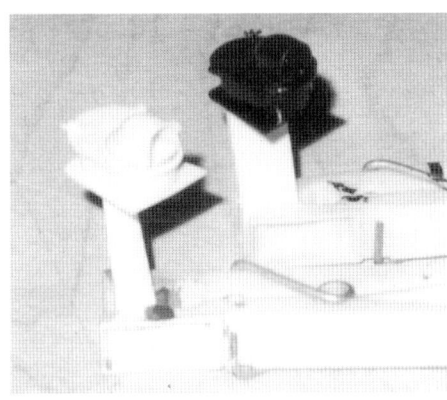

Chain pipes before and after painting.

FORECASTLE DECK

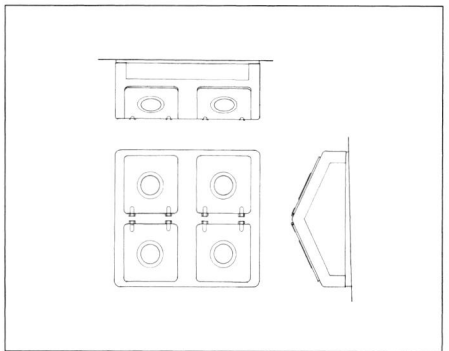

Crew galley skylight. (Scale: 1/96.)

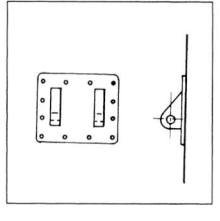

Forestay bedplate. (Scale: 1/48.)

Hatch cover between chain races. (Scale: 1/48.)

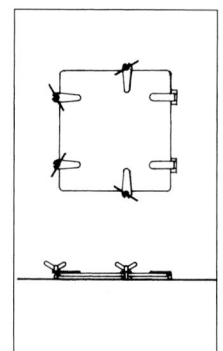

same wheel on top as the windlass valves. It was attached to the side of the rubber with strips and a bedplate was made from a square of thin styrene.

For the chain stoppers we used brass chain and small turnbuckles, intended for radio-controlled model aircraft. Luckily I found a suitable stud-link anchor chain in a mail order catalogue. The ends of the chains were tied to each other with wire underneath the deck before the deck was attached to the hull. Between the chain races were further hatches which were also assembled from different layers of styrene just as the forestay bedplate.

Crew galley skylight

This item was also heat-moulded using a wooden former. After the skylight cover had been removed from the backing sheet, the sides were opened up to give access to the inner plating. The lids were attached with styrene squares after adding the portholes as on the No 1 cargo hatch cover.

Steam winches

It took me 11 full working days to build these very complex items. I found suitable spur wheels, intended for radio-control model drive gears, in a model shop. The interiors of these wheels had to be altered to represent those of *Titanic*, so they were completely removed which left me with spur wheel rings. The interior was remodelled with the cogs cut out from thin styrene. Thin styrene strips were added to the cut out cogs to act as spacers between both sides. After the wheel ring was

The forward well deck and forecastle deck under construction.

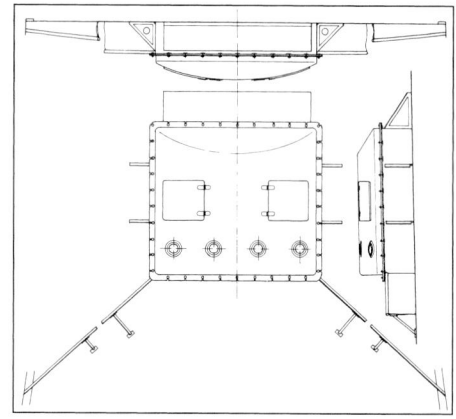

No 1 cargo hatch. (Scale: 1/192.)

FORECASTLE DECK

attached the joints were filled and sanded.

The steam winch bedplates were cut from sheet styrene and the walls added. The cylinders were made from tube. The triangular frames were made and motion bars added from brass tube. The warping drums were made like those described in Chapter 5, so I shall not repeat the method here. The piston rods were added, and the exhaust valve from rod. The finished assembly was airbrushed satin black. The deck area surrounding the winches (and also the Sirocco vents) was filled with Portland cement on many Harland & Wolff ships, and this also applied to the *Olympic* class liners, possibly to reduce vibration and the resulting noise. To replicate this we painted the thinnest sheet light grey and attached it to the deck underneath the winches before they were fitted.

Steam supply cover

This was an 'Y'-shaped pipe-cover which can be seen on footage and photographs of the wreck of *Titanic*. At first I tried to heat-mould the cover but the result was unsatisfactory. I then made it from styrene strip and added the blocks underneath it. The steam pipes were formed from brass wire and fed into the steam supply casing at the front of the winches. The supply valves were added and the assembly airbrushed satin black.

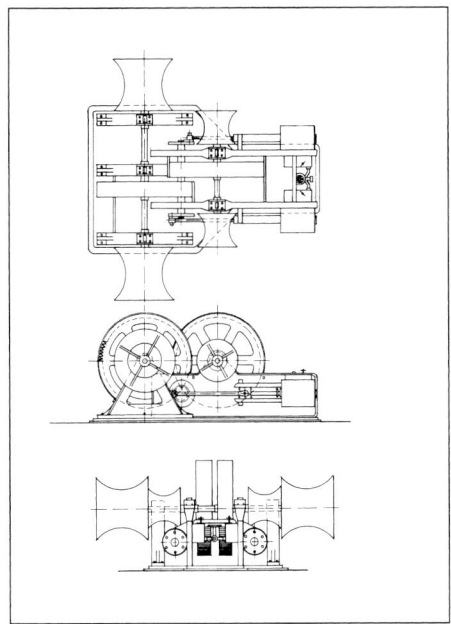

Steam winch. (Scale: 1/96.)

No 2 vent

This was assembled from sheet-styrene. I found the easiest method was to cut out the front and then add the rounded side before it had been trimmed to the correct length. The length was determined by the sides after they had been attached.

(Above) The spur wheels under construction. At top left the items as they were bought, top centre shows the wheel after the interior had been cut out, to the right is a completed wheel. The cogs are drawn on sheet styrene and are being cut out.

Steam winches under construction. The master warp-drum can be seen before it was filled and sanded to shape. One of the cylinders is lying on the deck next to the winch.

FORECASTLE DECK

(Right and far right) The steam supply cover with supply valves.

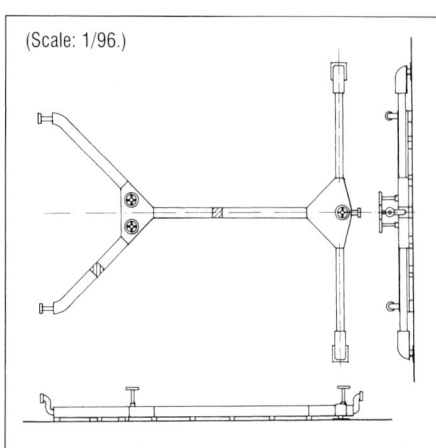

(Scale: 1/96.)

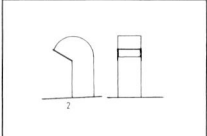

No 2 vent. (Scale: 1/192.)

(Right) No 2 vent with a rope reel in the background.

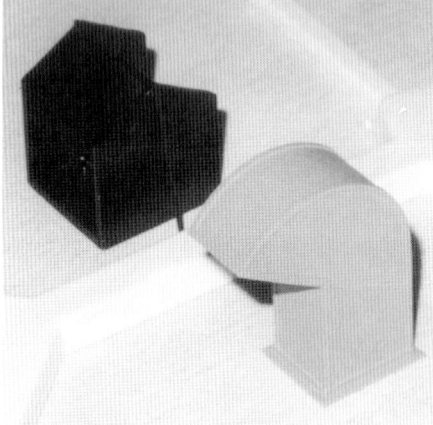

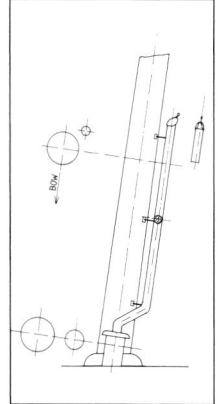

Galley flue. (Scale: 1/192.)

Crew galley flue

The galley flue was made from a wooden dowl as the base and styrene rod for the funnel. Two bends were required in the funnel and to achieve this slots were cut into the rod were the bends were to take place. After the funnel was shaped the mating edges in the slot were secured with superglue and later filled and sanded. On the top of the funnel was a rotating 'fishtail' cap, which ensured that rain did not run into the funnel and consequently into the crew galley. This cap was heat-moulded and attached to the funnel with the director made from brass wire. The galley flue was secured to the mast with brass wire.

Telephone

This was the same as on the docking bridge, but an additional telephone mount was located in front of No 1 hatch. The telephone could be removed from the bow and reinstalled on this mount in heavy weather giving the lookout a little more protection from the elements. This small mount was simply a small styrene ring attached to a disc of equal diameter. We painted it satin black.

Railings

These were built the same way as described in Chapter 6, *ie* small holes were drilled into a long wooden board at the same distance as the rail stanchions. The stanchions were pushed into the holes and brass wire fed through the openings in the stanchions. The wire was straightened by attaching one end in a vice and carefully stretching the other end with a pair of pliers before they were fed into the stanchions. This was done with care as overstretching the wire could easily cause it to snap, and this left us with some nasty gashes on our hands. The wires were left slightly too long which gave us some additional material to work with should some stanchions have to be relocated whilst the railings were being attached to the hull. After the railings were painted and the paint had dried, they were removed from the board and pre-folded at the bow over a wooden dowel. The stanchion brackets had been attached to the inside forecastle bulwarks in the meantime, so the stanchions could be inserted into these brackets. The railings were then folded at the aft corners of the forecastle deck and inserted into the stanchions attached to the inside of the forward well deck forward bulkhead. The wires were then trimmed to the required length. The surplus wire between the portable rails and the railings were removed. A little patching-up with white paint completed the railings.

8 B Deck

As on *Olympic*, *Titanic*'s B deck was originally planned to have promenades along the sides. However, Bruce Ismay, the chairman of the White Star Line, noticed during early trips in *Olympic*'s career that only a few passengers took advantage of this promenade space. The decision was therefore taken to add extra staterooms in this area on *Titanic*. This resulted in a window arrangement completely different to that on *Olympic*.

RMS *Olympic* on 24 April 1912, the first scheduled trip after the loss of *Titanic*. Many crew members were very concerned about the extra collapsible boats that had been installed after the original number of boats was found inadequate. Several collapsibles were lowered and tested and at least one leaked, which caused the first members of the crew to leave the ship. *Olympic* finally left Southampton after a delay of several hours, but further endless bickering between striking crew members and White Star Line officials led to the crossing being cancelled, adding insult to injury to the White Star Line after the loss of *Titanic* some 10 days previously. Apart from some minor details, the same view of *Titanic* would have been absolutely identical. A window shutter is in place above No 4 cargo hatch to prevent the window from being damaged by swinging cargo.
(Photograph: *The Sphere* – Günter Bäbler collection)

B DECK

B Deck fore and aft
(Scale: 1/384)
Key:
1. Waterway.
2. Deck beams on the promenade deck.
3. No 4 cargo hatch.
4. Promenade deck crane support.
5. Bulkhead lamp.
6. Entrance light box.
7. Harland & Wolff builders' plaque.
8. Storm shields.
9. Drainage pipe.
10. Jackstay.
11. Aft well deck rain tent bracket.
12. High-pressure water valve.
13. 9/3in teak rail (between frames 76 and 88 aft; between frames 75 and 80 fore).
14. 7/3in teak rail (aft of frame 88 aft).
15. 8/3in teak rail (forward of frame 80 fore).
16. 6/6in T-bar.
17. 6/6in angle.
18. Stiffeners 3/2.6in L-beam.
19. Limber board. (1/48)
45. 20in cowl vent.

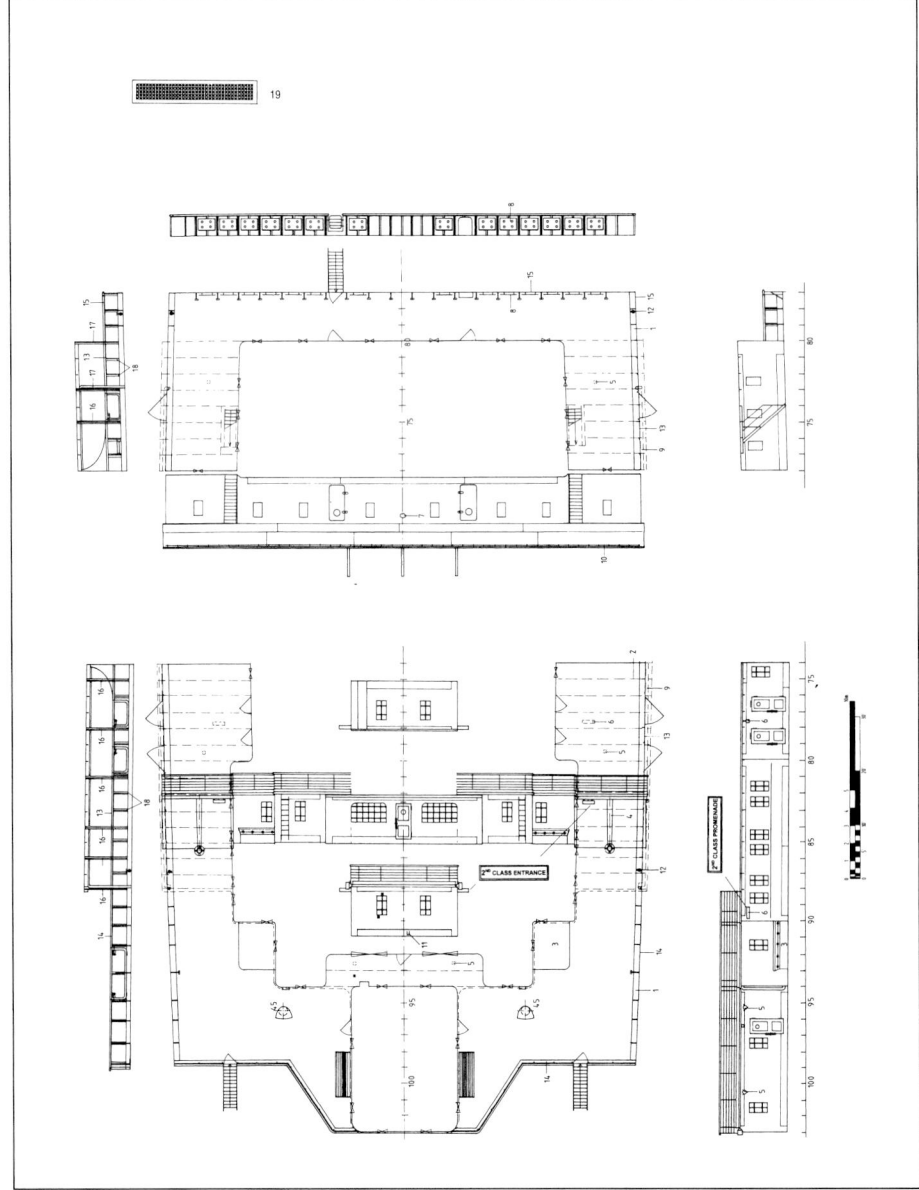

There is a rumour (the basis of a highly successful book) that *Titanic* was swapped with *Olympic* while *Olympic* was undergoing repairs at Harland & Wolff for some gigantic insurance swindle which was too fantastic even for the authors themselves to explain. However, wreck footage of the ship on the ocean floor clearly shows the window configuration of *Titanic* and not *Olympic*. The story goes that the major differences between these two ships were changed within a week or so, so nobody would notice the switch. I can hardly imagine that, should this story be true, a workforce of several thousand men involved in the switch would have kept this fraud to themselves, especially after the sinking of *Titanic*.

Besides all this, a number of staterooms and public rooms from the surviving ship have been discovered in the past decades, some bought by private individuals for their homes, others by factories and hotels at an auction while *Olympic* was being scrapped. They all have one thing in common: the yard number 400 for *Olympic* written on the inside of the wood panelling

(*Titanic* had the yard number 401). I wonder if the two individuals who set up the switch theory possibly believe that the interior of several hundred staterooms and public rooms of liners this size could have been transferred from one ship to another within a week? I hardly believe so. Now back to the model!

Deckhouses

The angles of the deckhouse walls on B deck were designed as described in Chapter 5. The position of the hull frames was drawn on the deckhouse walls as this enabled us to locate the position of windows and doors accurately. These walls were basically a complete outer plating with, in most cases, two thin strips of inner plating at the bottom and top edges respectively which had to be cut out of the walls as well as the windows and doors. The top inner plating applied only to deckhouses that had another deck on top of them, *ie* boat-deck deckhouses did not have them. In addition, some of the walls facing the bow or the stern consisted only of outer plating. This can be seen in the plans.

Each deckhouse was cut out of sheet styrene in one piece, which was folded at the corners and joined at the centre of a wall, not at a corner. This made filling and sanding the seam much easier for us. Thin strips of styrene were added to the inside of the walls as the inner plating.

The corners were carefully bent to shape over a wooden dowel. Before the ends were mated, wooden strips were attached to the inside of the walls to ensure that they remained flat. The bottom strips were attached at the bottom line of the deckhouses, as these would be glued to the deck when the deckhouses were being mounted.

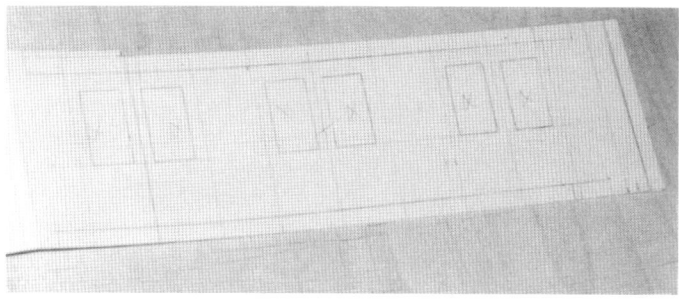

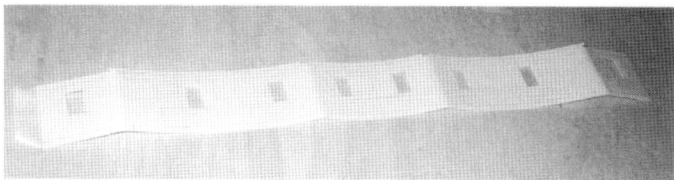

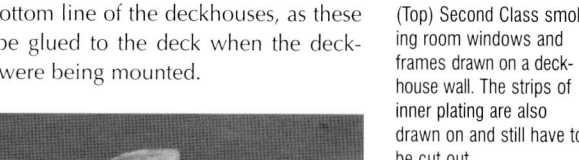

(Top) Second Class smoking room windows and frames drawn on a deckhouse wall. The strips of inner plating are also drawn on and still have to be cut out.

(Centre) Second Class entrance cut out and folded.

(Above) The Second Class entrance assembled. Note the stiffeners on the inside.

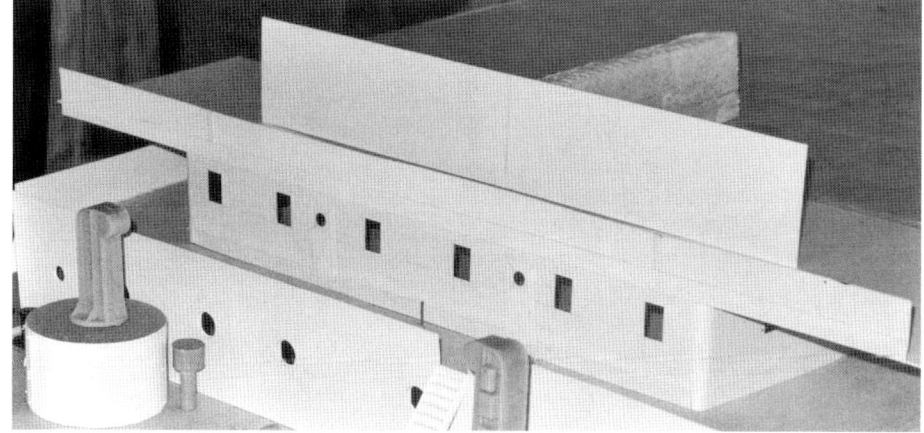

(Left) The forward end of B deck under construction.

B DECK

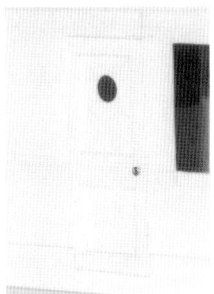

(Below) The doorknobs were made from small polished brass nails.

(Below) The Second Class promenade deck roof was actually the aft end of the First Class promenade deck. The roof was cut from thick styrene.

(Right) Second Class smoking room and entrance. The roof has been attached to the deckhouses and the assembly painted. Deck beams were added from brass L- and H-beams. Handrails and entrance light boxes have also been fitted. The wooden jig inside the deckhouse can be seen. This ensured that the assembly could be lifted and moved around without distorting or damaging it. The wooden strips at the bottom edge of the deckhouse were used to mount the construction to the deck.

The deckhouse ends were then joined to each other and a thick strip of styrene attached to the inside of the joint for added strength. Large triangular gussets made from wood were glued to the inside of the corners to ensure that the corners were at a 90° angle and remained so. On complex houses, such as the Second Class smoking room, a wooden jig was built inside the deckhouse which held it in shape and also enabled us to lift and work with the construction without distorting or damaging it.

Doors

The doors were assembled from two layers of thin styrene on top of each other. The inside layer forming the panels with the porthole cut out, the top layer with the panels cut out. The door openings in the deckhouses were covered from the inside with styrene strips to which the door was glued. Of course the porthole had to be opened up in these strips too. The porthole glazing was added from 3mm (0.11in) Perspex. Door hinges were added from rod, and small doorknobs made from small polished brass nails.

Second Class promenade deck roof

This is actually the aft end of the First Class promenade deck. It was cut from thick styrene and the deckhouses attached to it. Deck beams were then added from brass L- and H-beams. However, the flanges on one side of every third beam had to be removed at the outer end as the deck supports on the hull side would be mated here. The area that needed to be removed was only about 3mm (0.11in), the width of the support, and this was done with a belt saw. The mating surface between the beams and the roof was roughened with a sanding disc as if this had not been done, the glue would not secure the brass beams to the styrene roof. These were fixed to the roof with superglue. The binding was very strong, as we later found when some had to be removed again with great difficulty. After this assembly was complete it was spray-painted satin white.

Windows

At first I was thinking of photo-etching all window frames, but gave this up after giving it

considerable thought. The snag was that the frames had raised rims, and in some cases the cross bars stood slightly behind the frame. I wanted to replicate this as accurately as possible, so I decided to build a master for each window and cast the items for the model in resin. First I cut out the window in a piece of styrene. The outer raised rim, made of thin strip, was inserted in this cut-out in one piece, folding it at the corners and without gluing it to the sheet as the completed window would have to removed again later. Inside this rim the actual frame was added from strip, which was slightly flatter than the outer rim. The window frame was then removed from the styrene sheet and glued to a styrene backing plate. The location of the cross bars was then drawn on the backing plate as a guide for applying them. These were then added from styrene strip. This gave us a complete window glued to a styrene sheet. A box was built around it and silicon rubber poured into it to produce the mould. A second mould of the same size was made, but without window frames. This flat mould was pressed onto the first mould after resin had been applied to squeeze out any excess; basically a two-piece mould, but one mould with a perfectly flat side which could be used for other windows too. I realised that it was of paramount importance to remove the cast frames from the mould after the resin had fully hardened, ideally after 24 hours, or the windows would break while removing them. Of course a little flash needed to be removed and the odd frame was unusable because of air bubbles, but after they had fully set they turned out to be very flexible and strong items that could take a great deal of stress.

The window frames were all painted chocolate-brown. The glazing was attached to the inside of the deckhouse from oversized 3mm (0.11in) Perspex. The frames were then placed into the opening and secured with a tiny amount of superglue applied to the mating edges. After this had dried, the glue was overpainted with clear varnish. In some cases the inside of the glazing was painted black to prevent viewers from looking through the model.

Handrails

The mounting rings for the handrails on the deckhouses were located at the frames. Small holes were drilled into the deckhouse walls to give access to the rings. We used Display Models' one-wire railing stanchions for the rings which had been chemically blackened and were fed into the holes. A wooden strip was applied to the inside of the walls, through which the holes were drilled, to give these stanchions additional support. The wire was also blackened and then straightened in a vice and finally fed into the rings. They were secured with small blobs of black paint.

Light boxes

These indicated where the entrances were and also the passenger class of the particular area. The boxes were made from a thick oblong

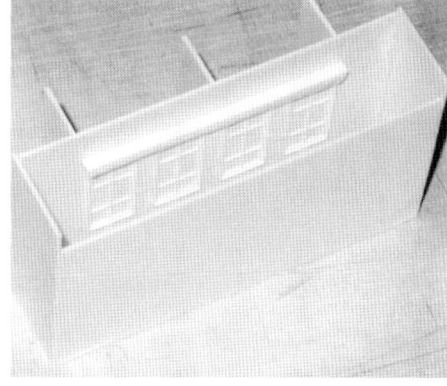

(Below) One of the master Second Class windows. Note the raised outer rim.

(Top left) The box for the silicon rubber mould. The silicon was poured into the box; when it had hardened the box was broken up and the rubber mould was ready for use.

(Left) The mould for the window frames. After liberal amounts of resin had been poured into the mould, a second flat mould was pressed onto it and any excess removed.

Resin-cast Second Class window frames, cleaned and painted.

B DECK

Private promenade deck on the starboard side.

Deck beam supports attached to the inside bulwarks.

piece of styrene with thin strip added to the outer edges as the frames. The notices themselves were written on a computer and printed out on paper and attached to the boxes with double-sided tape.

Private promenade decks

Even though the model contract said that none of the ship's interior would be featured, we felt that it would be a shame to ignore it completely as we learned that some of the windows were large enough for some of the interior to be easily seen. We then decided to add the private promenades, the Café Parisienne and the veranda cafes on A deck, albeit all *sans* furniture as this would have delayed completion considerably. Steve Rigby of the British *Titanic* Society did a masterful job of painting the floors and walls of these rooms onto cardboard; they were colour-copied and attached to thick styrene walls with double-sided tape. The private promenades were built up as box-like assemblies which were attached to the inside of B deck. They were located between frames 13 and 29 (bow) and were 13ft wide.

Deck support beams

These were also made of brass L- and H-beams. They were cut to the required lengths with a belt saw and the bottom end chamfered with a sanding disc. Here too the flanges needed to be removed to give access to the deck beams to which they would be joined. All surfaces that were to be glued were also roughened with a sanding disc to ensure that the glue would attach them firmly.

The support beams were attached to the inside of the bulwarks before the B-deck assemblies were attached. The deckhouses were placed onto the model and held down with weights to prevent any movement while the supports were being added. Spacers were placed between the deck and the roof to gain the correct height. With this all secured, the supports were attached to the inside of the bulwarks with superglue using the roof as a guide for the height. After this had been completed the deckhouses were removed again. This left us with B deck entirely open but with the support beams all attached to the bulwarks inside.

Small L-beams were made as in the well decks and also attached to the bulwarks. The complete Second Class entrance and smoke room could then be attached to the model. The wooden strip attached to the inside of the deckhouses was also the base of the deckhouses that was glued to the deck surface. The joints between the deck supports and the deck beams were glued with superglue.

B DECK

(Above) Side view of the forward end of B deck. Deck beams and bulkhead lamps can be seen.

(Above) The Second Class entrance nearing completion.

Storm shields

On the film of the wreck, plates were seen mounted to the inside of the forward well deck aft bulkhead. Their purpose has been the cause of much debate among historians, but the feeling is that they were storm shields or shutters which were attached to the B deck forward stateroom windows as a protective measure in heavy seas. We painted them dark brown on the model, but I now believe they should have been white. They were also fitted to the windows above No 4 cargo hatch while cargo was being loaded, to prevent swinging cargo from damaging the windows, but their location when not in use is unknown.

Builders' plaque

This was attached to the B deck forward bulkhead. It was a small oval brass plaque, approximately 5in wide stating that the ship was built by Harland & Wolff, Queens Island, Belfast. We do not know for sure what the plaque really looked like. It was mounted on a wooden backing plate, which apparently has been found and salvaged.

Limber boards

These were gratings which covered the waterways for the passengers to stand on at deck level. We did not know of their existence when we were building the model, and so they were not included. I would photo-etch them if I were to build another model of the same scale.

Storm shields being attached to the inside of the forward well deck aft bulkhead. They were painted dark brown. I now believe they should have been white.

9 Promenade Deck

This deck was a completely First Class area which included many of the First Class public rooms such as the reading and writing room, the lounge, the smoking room and the veranda cafes. One of the major differences between *Olympic* and *Titanic* was the enclosure of the promenade deck forward. *Olympic*'s promenade was entirely open. However, while the ship was underway, the deck had a tendency to wetting, even in relatively light seas. As a result the forward half of the open promenade on *Titanic* was enclosed with panels with sliding windows. This feature was also adopted for the third ship of this class, *Britannic*. It might have seemed obvious that the White Star Line would have wanted the promenade on *Olympic* enclosed too but after the loss of *Titanic* her boat deck was crammed with lifeboats, to meet the new Board of Trade requirements which left this deck with hardly any view to the open sea. To give the passengers a complete open promenade deck with an unobstructed view to the sea it was decided not to enclose *Olympic*'s promenade deck.

Port-side promenade deck on *Olympic* looking aft. The large windows are of the First Class smoking room.
(Photograph: Harland & Wolff – Claes Göran Wetterholm collection)

Starboard-side promenade deck on *Olympic* looking forward in June 1911. The large veranda cafe windows are prominent. The same view on *Titanic* would have been identical.
(Photograph: Harland & Wolff – Claes Göran Wetterholm collection)

PROMENADE DECK

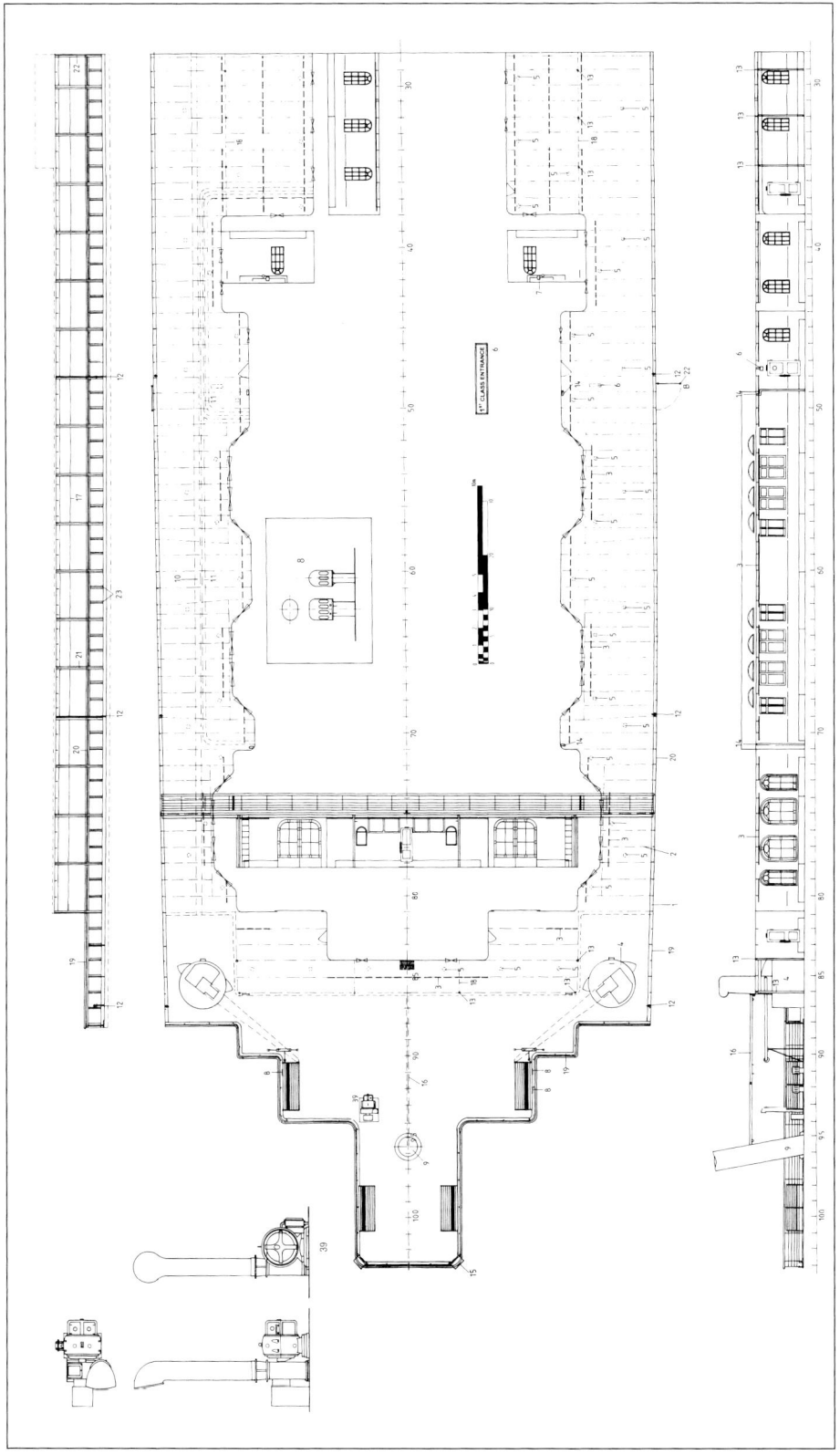

Promenade Deck aft.
(Scale: 1/384.)
Key:
1. Waterway.
2. Boat deck beams.
3. Deckchair number boards.
4. 1½-ton Stothart and Pitt electric crane.
5. Bulkhead lamp.
6. Entrance lightbox.
7. Electrical outlet.
8. Fyfe vent.
9. Rear mast.
10. Cable channel.
11. Water pipe.
12. High-pressure water valve.
13. Deck support stanchion.
14. Drainage pipe.
15. Aft well deck crane jib clamp.
16. Raintent beam.
17. Jackstay.
18. Girder beneath deck beams.
19. 6/3in teak rail (aft of frame 81).
20. 8/3in teak rail (between frames 28 and 81).
21. 5/5in T-bar (all).
22. 5/2.6in angle.
23. 2.6/2.6in angle (all).
39. 10in cowl vent.
    (Scale: 1/96.)

PROMENADE DECK

Promenade deck amidships. (Scale: 1/384.)
Key:
1. Waterway.
2. Boat deck beams.
3. Deckchair number boards.
4. 8/3in teak rail.
5. Bulkhead lamp.
6. Entrance light box.
7. Electrical outlet.
10. Cable channel.
11. Water pipe.
12. High-pressure water valve.
13. Deck support stanchion.
14. Drainage pipe.
15. 5/5in T-bar (all).
16. 5/2.6in angle.
17. Jackstay.
18. Girder beneath deck beams.
19. Scupper.
20. Sliding windows.
21. Sliding window case.
22. Outrigger.
23. Outrigger mounting rod.
24. 2.6/2.6in angle (all)

C. Coaling outrigger.

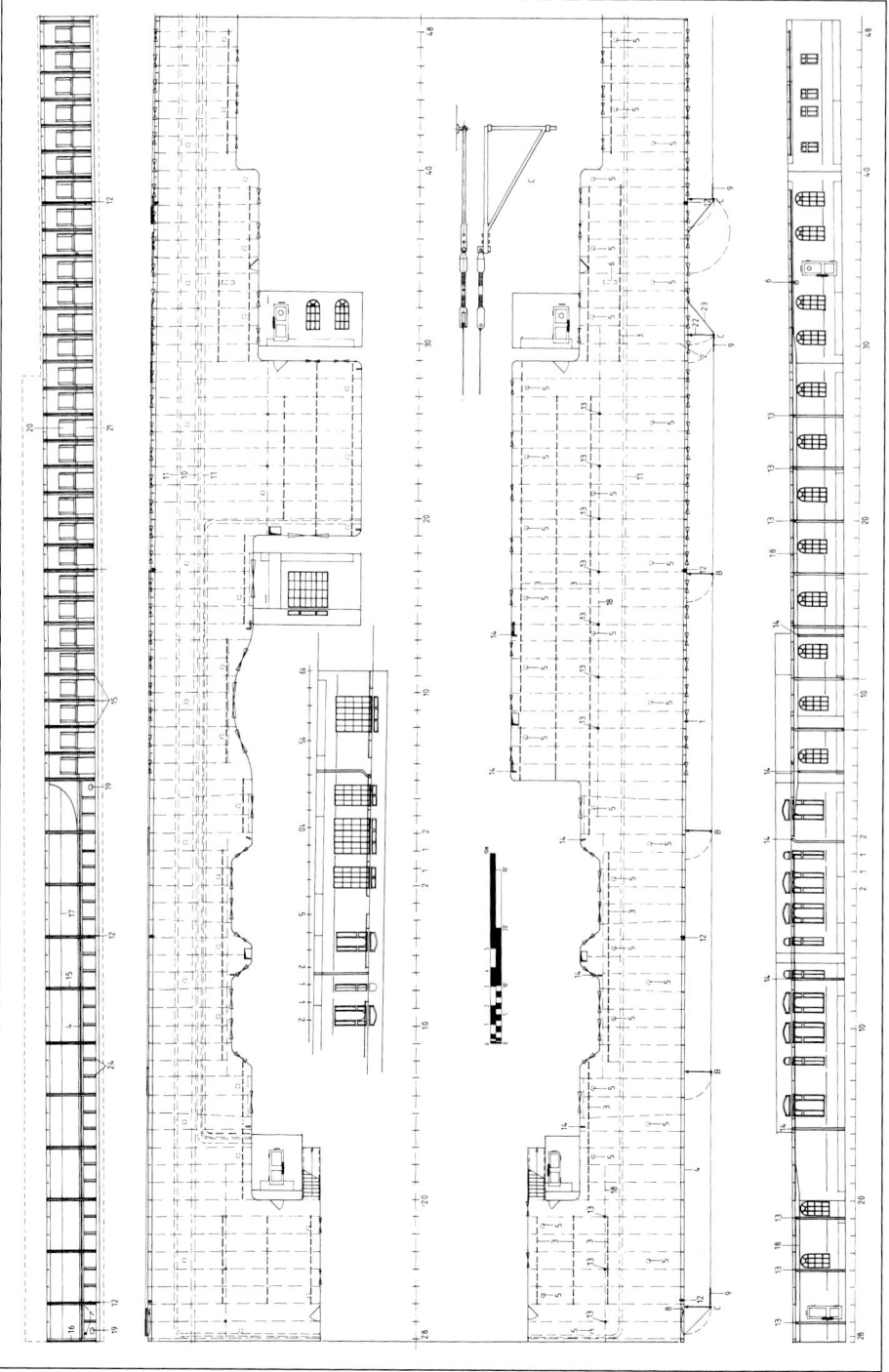

The deck

According to the Harland & Wolff plans we had, the extreme width of *Titanic*'s promenade and boat deck was 94.5ft, so there was an overhang of approximately 19in on top of B deck on both sides. The top of the hull was covered with 5mm (0.19in) plywood for the under-deck apart from the areas above the Second Class entrance, the smoking room and

PROMENADE DECK

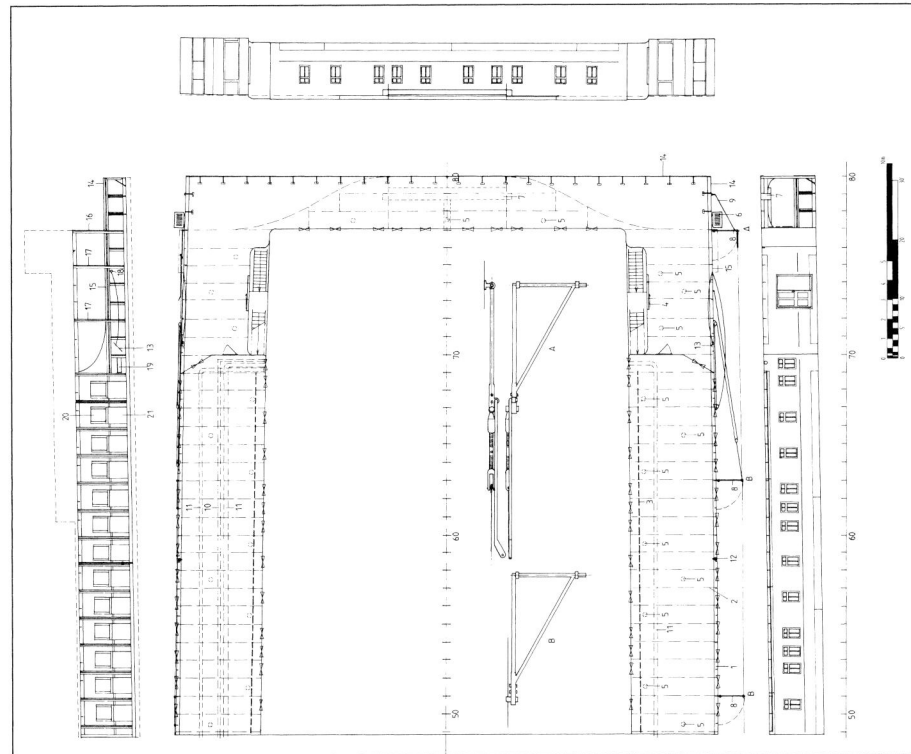

Promenade deck foreward. (Scale: 1/384.)
Key:
1. Waterway.
2. Boat deck beams.
3. Deckchair number boards.
4. Sliding door.
5. Bulkhead lamp.
6. Leadsman's platform.
7. Bridge telegraph gearbox.
8. Coaling outrigger.
9. Outrigger mounting rod.
10. Cable channel.
11. Water pipe.
12. High-pressure water valve.
13. Outrigger tackle cleat.
14. 7/3in teak rail.
15. 8/3in teak rail.
16. 6/6in angle.
17. 5/5in T-bar.
18. Outrigger tackle scuttle.
19. Scupper.
20. Sliding windows.
21. Sliding window case.
A & B. Coaling outriggers.

the small promenade at the bow, as these were already dealt with while these parts of the ship were being built (see Chapter 8).

The deck was divided into three sections, separated at the expansion joints and cut out of maple veneer. These sections were coated with contact cement, applied with a spatula, and carefully attached to the hull using the centreline which had been drawn onto the under-deck and the veneer as guides and pressed onto the hull with weights.

The underside of the overhang was then covered with thin styrene strips, adding the width of the waterways to it. Another 2mm (0.07in) wide styrene strip was then attached vertically to the lower side of the outer edge of the promenade deck. The bottom strake of the promenade deck walls would be attached to this strip at a later stage.

Looking from underneath, the promenade deck beams would be visible under the overhang and these were also added from styrene strip. The drainage pipes on both sides were then added from plastic tube. A very thin styrene strip was added to the outer edge of the veneer forming the waterway channel. The waterways were then painted black. It seems there were no limber boards in the promenade deck waterways. The deck seams were then drawn on the veneer, starting at the waterways margin planks as described in Chapter 5. The promenade deck planks were 5in wide.

The deckhouses

These were also divided into three sections, split at the expansion joints. The deckhouse walls were cut out of styrene in one piece and

Port-side promenade deck on *Titanic* looking forward. Taken in Southampton in April 1912, a lot of detail can be seen such as water pipes, cable channels and deckchair number boards. To avoid arguments between passengers over the best deck space, deckchairs could be hired out for the whole trip. Once a deckchair had been hired passengers were not permitted to move deckchairs around the ship.
(Photograph: *The Illustrated London News* – Günter Bäbler collection)

PROMENADE DECK

(Above) Reading and writing room windows on the portside promenade deck on *Olympic* looking aft. The same view on *Titanic* would have been identical.
(Photograph: Harland & Wolff, Claes Göran Wetterholm collection)

(Top right) Port-side First Class lounge windows on *Olympic* looking forward. The photographer tried to add the missing handrails in the picture by scratching them onto the glass negative.
(Photograph: Harland & Wolff, Claes Göran Wetterholm collection)

(Middle right) Starboard-side promenade deck on *Olympic* looking aft.
(Photograph: Library of Congress LC-USZ62-116096)

(Right) Starboard-side promenade deck on *Olympic* looking aft. The stateroom windows are of the 'Utleys' heavy brass style.
(Photograph: Author's collection)

then carefully folded at the corners. A copy of the Harland & Wolff promenade deck plan served as a template. Wooden frames were built up inside the deckhouses for support. Drainage pipes were added from bent brass rod and vents shafts from thick styrene strip.

Deckhouse roofs (boat deck)

This was dealt with in the same manner as described in Chapter 8 only in much larger proportions. The boat deck was cut out of styrene and attached to the promenade deckhouses, deckbeams, cable channels and water pipes added to the beams. In large open areas the deckbeams were additionally supported by stanchions which were attached to girders attached underneath the deckbeams. After these girders had been glued to the deckbeams a small slot was cut into the brass rod stanchions and these were inserted into the girders and secured with superglue.

There are, of course, no plans showing the exact location of the water pipes. There are two known photographs of *Titanic*'s promenade deck, but these are both of the port side. As there are no known photographs of the starboard side promenade deck, all we could do was duplicate the arrangements of pipes that can be seen in pictures of *Olympic*'s promenade deck. We

PROMENADE DECK

(Right) There was an overhang of approximately 19in above B deck. The deck beams are visible when viewing from underneath. These were added from styrene strips. A 2mm (0.07in) wide strip was attached to the outer edge of the promenade deck to which the shell plating would later be applied.

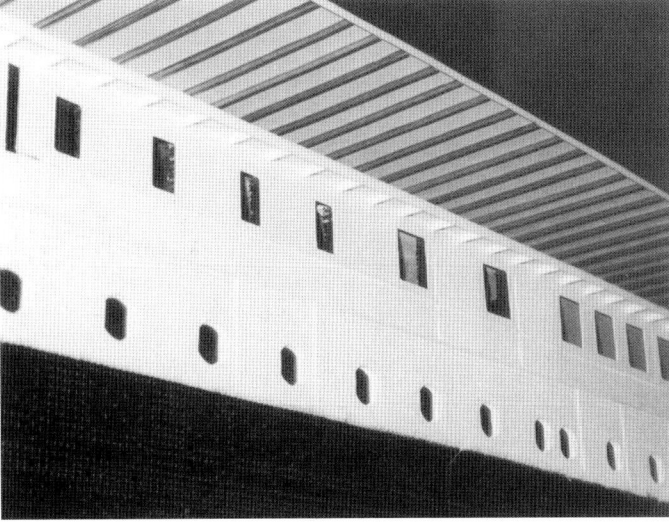

are not sure if this is correct, as we could see that there were differences in the water pipe and cable channel arrangements between *Olympic* and *Titanic* on the port side, so there were most probably differences on the starboard side too. The arrangement of these pipes on the starboard side of *Titanic*'s promenade deck is a mystery, but the most sensible approach, to us, was to replicate *Olympic* here.

The deckhouse between the expansion joints before painting.

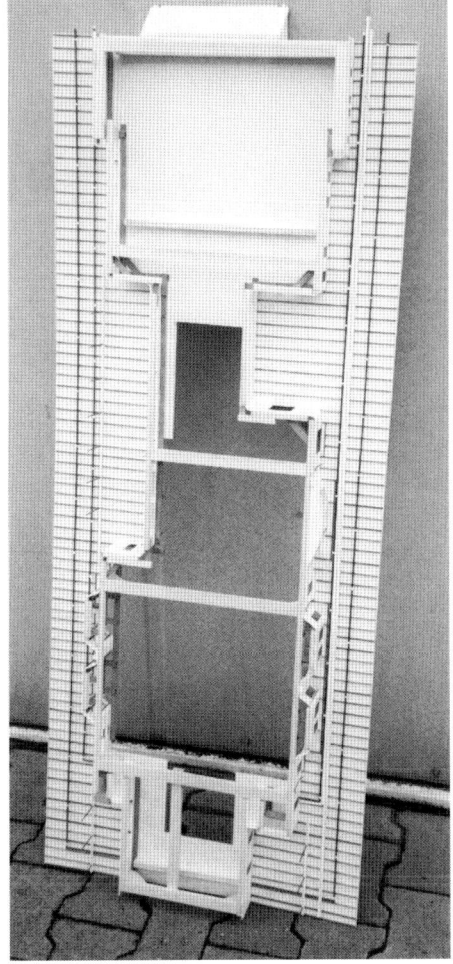

Windows

The promenade deck staterooms were located towards the bow. These had very heavy brass-framed 'Utley's' windows. Forty-four of these windows were needed, and every one of them consisted of eleven pieces. Each backing plate was cut out individually. Master window frames were made from styrene strip and the required items cast in resin. For the glass we

(Below) The promenade deck walls were cut out of sheet styrene and folded at the corners. A copy of a Harland & Wolff deck plan acted as a template.

(Bottom) Wooden jigs were attached to the inside of the deckhouses to keep them in shape.

PROMENADE DECK

(Right) An 'Utleys' heavy brass window showing the eleven pieces needed for each window at left and an assembled window to the right.

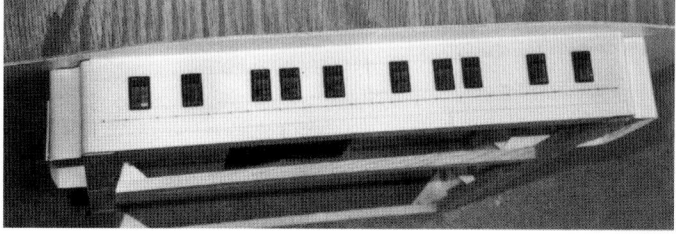

(Below) Painted and attached windows at the promenade deck forward bulkhead.

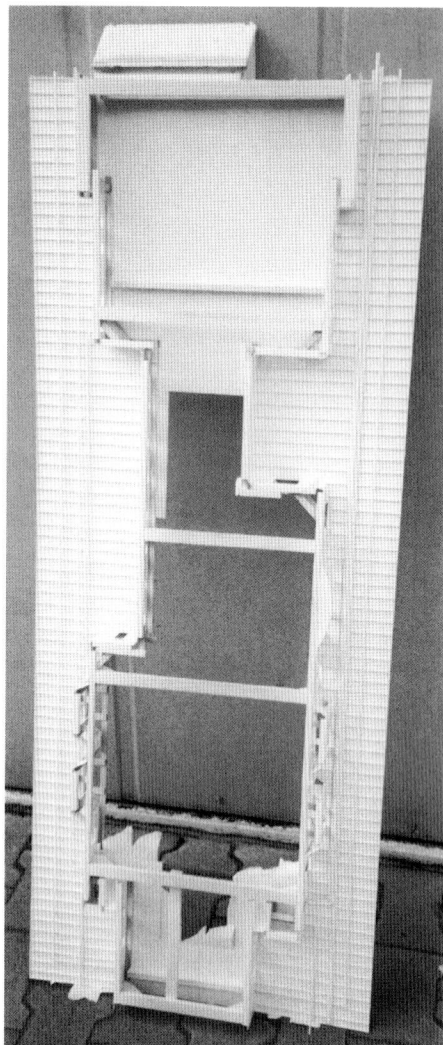

The deckhouse after painting. Note the deck beams and water pipes.

used 1mm (0.03in) Perspex, which had the same dimensions as the window frames, which was attached between the backing plate and the frame.

Three hinges made from rod were added to the sides. The window frames were all painted in chocolate brown. Some of the glass had to be painted black on the inside to prevent viewers from looking in one side of the ship and out of the other.

The First Class lounge had leaded glass windows. This leaded glass was drawn on draughting paper at 1:24 scale and photocopied, reduced in size by half also on draughting paper in the amount we needed. The copies were attached to 3mm (0.11in) Perspex with clear double-sided tape and the resin-cast frame added.

The same applies to the First Class smoking room windows as these were also leaded glass. The basic colour scheme of this room was blue and red (buff and grey on *Olympic*). We do not know the colours of the window glass, but I opted for blue and red. The copies were coloured with a felt pen and also attached to 3mm (0.11in) Perspex with clear double-sided tape

Promenade deck walls

The promenade deck walls were made of 0.3mm styrene using the Harland & Wolff shell plating plan. The whole assembly was very much like that of the real ship, starting at

First Class lounge windows with leaded glass. This was drawn on draughting paper and photocopied, reduced in size by half and attached to 3mm (0.11in) Perspex with clear double-sided tape.

PROMENADE DECK

Four of these windows mounted to the deckhouse walls. The leaded glass windows also obscured the wooden jig inside the deckhouse.

the stern and attaching the plates moving towards the bow. The bottom strake was glued to the thin styrene strip which had been attached to the overhang previously. Small styrene L-beam stiffeners were attached to the inside of the walls in accordance to the Harland & Wolff plans.

One of the last alterations whilst building the *Titanic* was the enclosure of the forward half of the promenade deck as *Olympic*'s promenade deck was prone to wetting through spray in heavy weather. Before we added this enclosure on our model, we took photographs to illustrate what *Titanic* would have looked like if this final alteration had not been made.

The deck supports were attached to the walls as described in Chapter 8. Some supports, however, were made from styrene to ensure that the enclosure would be glued to them securely with polystyrene glue. The enclosure is not shown in the Harland & Wolff shell plating plan so we did not know the actual size of the shell plates in this area, or where the overlaps were. We figured this out as best we could from photographs of *Titanic* and *Britannic*. The windows in this area were added from 3mm

(0.11in) Perspex which also gave these walls added strength and helped to flatten them.

A jackstay was added to the top of the upper strake in the open area. This was to tie down a canvas cover to protect the promenade deck in heavy weather.

Coaling outriggers

The coaling outriggers were made of brass wire and were silver soldered. They were fastened to the promenade deck walls with brackets and linked to each other by wire attached to the ends. The aftmost outrigger apparently was not rigged. This one served the galley a few decks beneath it. The outriggers were rigged in

(Left) First Class lounge windows of *Olympic* today at the White Swan Hotel in Alnwick, Northumberland. Every *Titanic* enthusiast should visit this hotel as it has the almost complete First Class lounge from *Olympic* along with parts of the First Class grand staircase. The size of the First Class lounge is incredible.

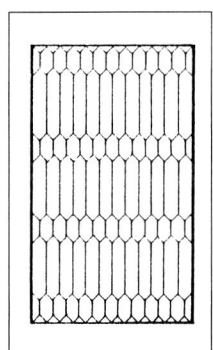

First Class lounge leaded glass.

(Far left) Resin-cast First Class smoking room windows during a test fit.

(Left) The First Class smoking room windows complete. The dominant colours in this room on *Titanic* were blue and red.

89

PROMENADE DECK

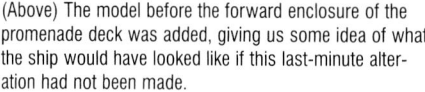

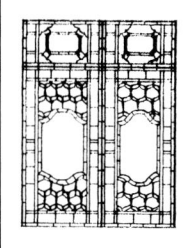

First Class smoking room leaded glass. The left half is for the large windows (flat walls), the right half for the small windows (angled walls).

(Above) The model before the forward enclosure of the promenade deck was added, giving us some idea of what the ship would have looked like if this last-minute alteration had not been made.

two groups on each side. The forward group consisted of four outriggers, the aft group of five. The foremost and aftmost outriggers in each group had rigging screws or turnbuckles attached to the ends to tighten the wire. Mounting rods held these outriggers in position when they were in use. The rods were attached to the two foremost outriggers. The other four rods were attached to the hull side between outriggers 4 and 5, counted from the bow.

The promenade deck plans show the outriggers on the port side in the stored position, and in use on the starboard side.

(Above) A jackstay was mounted to the top edge of the promenade deck walls. A jackstay wire can also be seen attached to the deck supports. This was to fasten a canvas cover which was installed in heavy weather. It is known that part of this canvas cover was actually installed on *Titanic* by the time she reached Queenstown. If it was still like this, or even completely installed when she sank is not known.

(Right) Coaling outriggers in use.

(Far Right) The same coaling outriggers in their stored 'at sea' configuration. The turnbuckles are hanging down as the wire has yet to be added to them.

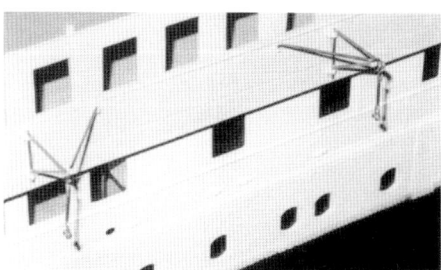

PROMENADE DECK

Olympic in the 1920s showing two Fyfe vents to advantage.
(Photograph: Andreas Pfeffer collection)

Handrails

On the model, the wooden handrails were all made from pear wood. On the deck supports on the promenade deck walls they were 8in/3in on the real ship, aft of the supports they were 6in/3in. We cut wooden strips with a rotary saw, and cut a slot into the bottom to give access to the promenade deck walls. The edges were then rounded with a sanding block. Slots were also cut into the bottom side to give access to the supports.

Expansion joints

There were two expansion joints on *Titanic* which commenced above C deck to allow the hull to move and flex while at sea. To picture them, imagine someone has cut down into the hull with a massive chainsaw and stopped at C deck. The gaps between the decks were covered with brass strips which were attached to one side of the strip. On the other side one would have been able to see the deck movement underneath this brass strip.

The gaps in the superstructure were covered with leather that was battened down on each side with iron strips, as were those on the deck roofs. The brass and leather strips on the model were made from styrene strip painted in the appropriate colour.

Fyfe vents

Three Fyfe vents have been located at the aft end of the promenade deck on period photographs (a further two on the boat deck). They were also made and filed from thick sheet styrene.

10 Boat Deck

The boat deck was divided into First and Second Class areas, engineers' promenade, officers' promenade and navigating bridge. No part of the boat deck was allotted to Third Class passengers, and consequently none of the lifeboats were meant for them. It is report-

Boat deck aft.
(Scale: 1/384.)
Key:
1. Channel waterway.
2. 30ft lifeboat
   (in Southampton).
2A. 30ft lifeboat (at sea).
3. Funnel guywire bracket.
4. Boat fall bitt.
5. Boat fall roller.
6. Davit mount.
7. Sunderland Forge and Engineering Company 15cwt boat winch.
8. 7/3in teak rail.
9. High-pressure water valve.
29. Hot air fan
48. Thermotank

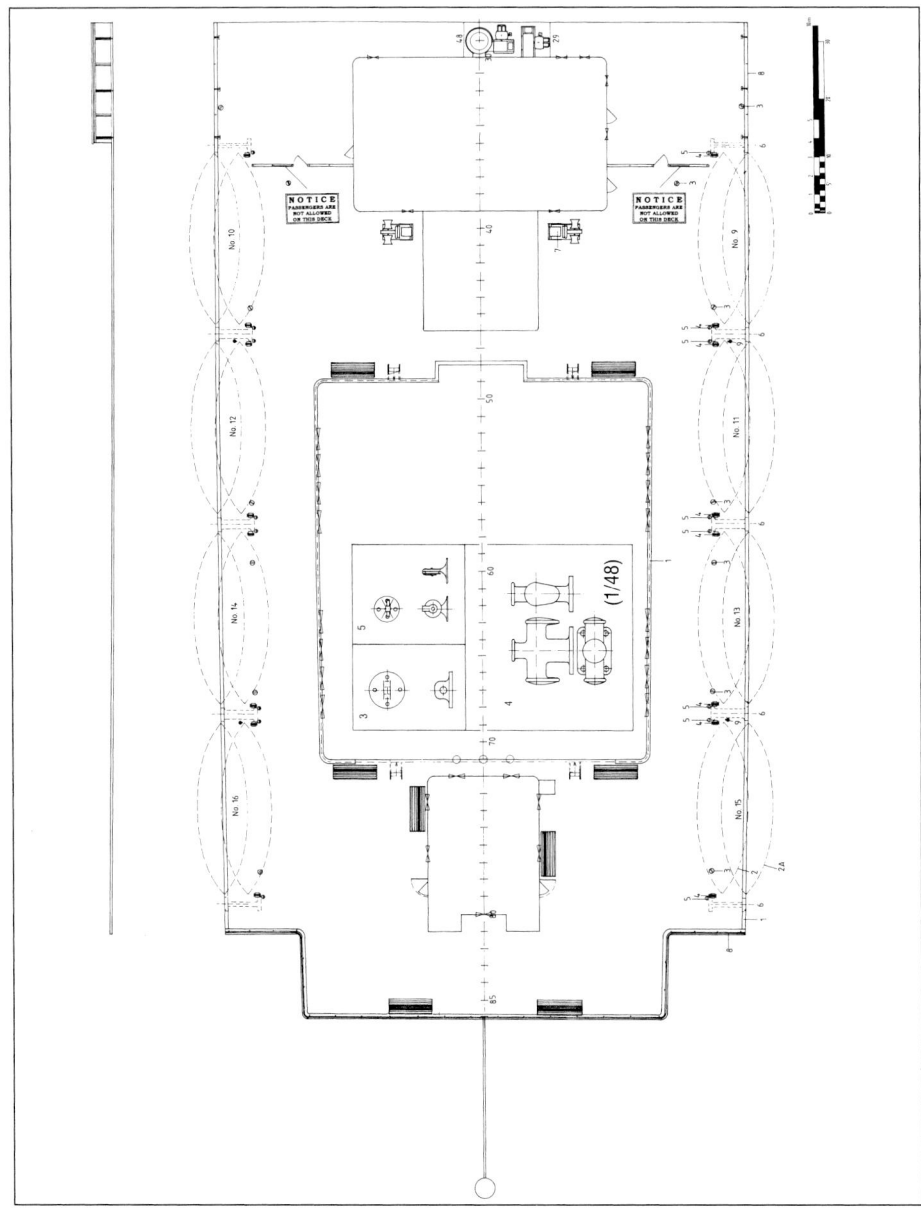

BOAT DECK

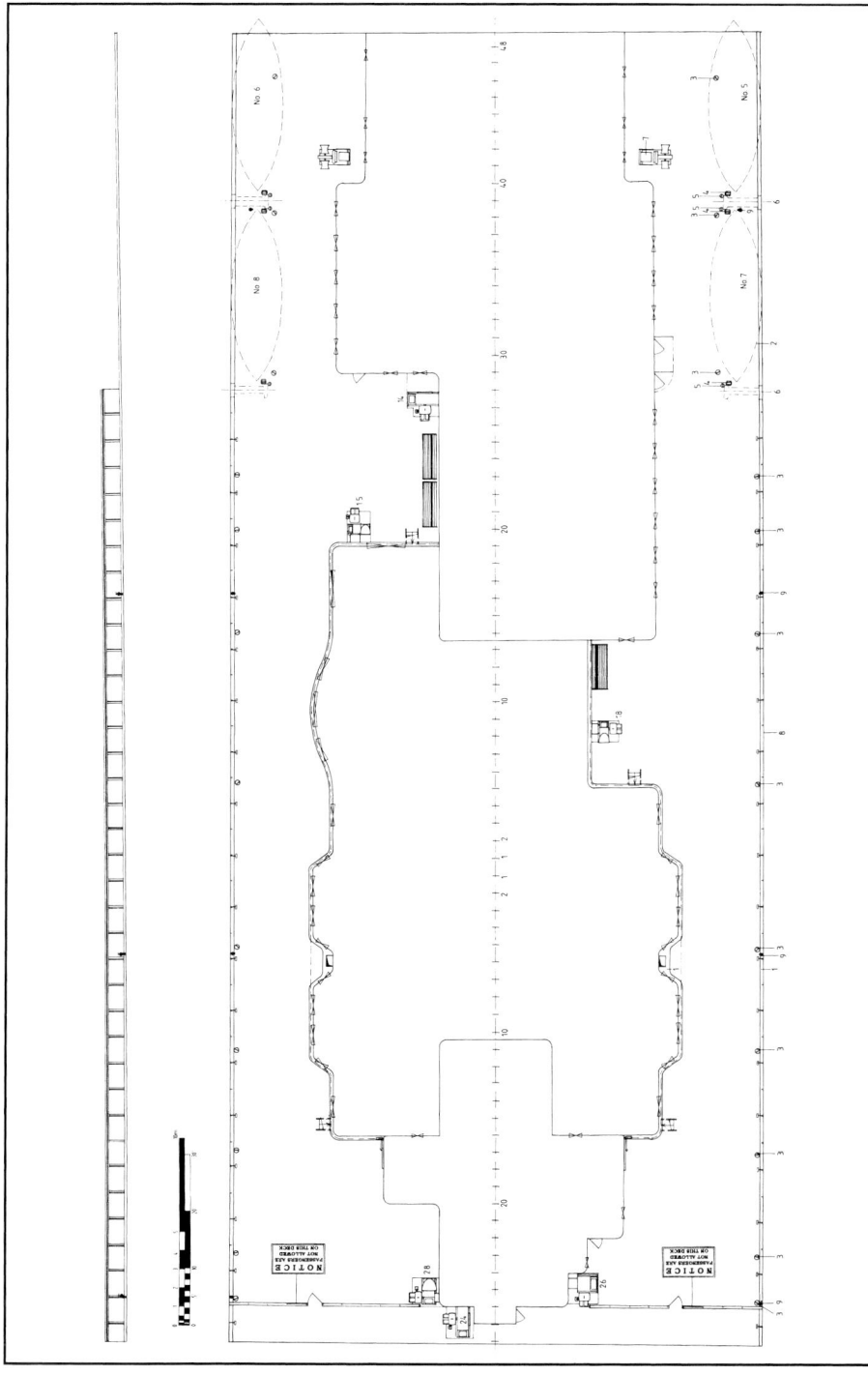

Boat deck amidships.
(Scale: 1/384.)
Key:
1. Channel waterway.
2. 30ft lifeboat.
3. Funnel guywire bracket.
4. Boat fall bitt.
5. Boat fall roller.
6. Davit mount.
7. Sunderland Forge and Engineering Company 15cwt boat winch.
8. 7/3in teak rail.
9. High-pressure water valve.
14. Hot air fan.
15. 20in cowl vent.
18. 20in cowl vent.
24. Hot air fan.
26. Hot air fan.
28. 30in cowl vent.

ed that during the sinking, stewards went below decks to guide Third Class passengers up to the boat deck. After they had been placed in a boat the stewards went back down again to fetch more. They did not survive.

The deck

The deck planks here were also 5in wide. The veneer was applied to the boat decks (promenade deck roofs) before these were attached to

BOAT DECK

Boat deck forward.
(Scale: 1/384.)
Key:
1. Channel waterway.
2. 30ft lifeboat.
3. Funnel guywire bracket.
4. Boat fall bitt.
5. Boat fall roller.
6. Davit mount.
7. 25ft emergency cutter (at sea).
7A. 25ft emergency cutter (in Southampton).
8. 27ft Engelhardt collapsible lifeboat.
9. Lord Kelvin's Sounding Device receiver locker.
10. Sounding spar.
11. Bridge bulwark ledge.
12. Pelorus.
13. Life preserver.
14. Rigging cleat.
15. Navigation lamp.
16. Bulkhead lamp.
17. Telegraph.
18. Wheel pedestal.
19. Grating.
20. Bridge roof support.
21. Steam whistle operating lever.
22. 9in bell.
23. Sliding window case.
24. Sliding window.
25. Electrical outlets.
26. Morse lamp.
27. Helm indicator.
28. Portable wall mounting sockets.
29. 8/3in teak rail.
30. Lord Kelvin's compass.

Titanic at Queenstown, 11 April 1912, taken by the *Cork Examiner* photographer Thomas Barker. To the left can be seen boats No 10, 12, 14 and 16 (boat No 16 in the foreground). Little did the passengers know that they would be loaded into these boats three days later during one of the worst maritime disasters in history.
(Photograph: *Cork Examiner* – Claes Göran Wetterholm collection)

BOAT DECK

(Above) Taken on the same occasion as the previous photograph and by the same photographer. The 'mystery box' next to the Second Class entrance can be seen in the far left of the picture.
(Photograph: *Cork Examiner* – Claes Göran Wetterholm collection)

(Left) *Olympic*'s boat deck seen around April 1912 in New York. This is the port side looking forward. The funnel guy wire brackets and the gammonning lashing
fastening the guy wires to the brackets can be seen as well as a Fyfe vent in front of the sliding door to the right.
(Photograph: Brown Brothers)

BOAT DECK

The Lord Kelvin's Sounding Device locker.

The sounding spar in its stored position.

the promenade deckhouses as described in Chapter 9. A 2mm (0.07in) styrene strip was also attached to the bottom of the outer edge of the boat deck to which the promenade deck walls would be glued at a later stage. Slots were cut into this strip to give access to the deck support beams.

After completion of the promenade deckhouses they were glued to the promenade deck as described in Chapter 8. The outer edges of the boat deck were weighed down with weights on a stiff wooden board, so that the deck rested flat on the support beams, and the shell plating added to the outer edge of the boat deck, along the waterway. In the open area the support beams were pushed slightly inwards, a small blob of superglue was applied to the top of the beam and the beam was then pulled back into position thus gluing the top of the beam to the inside of the shell plating. The beams in the enclosed area of the promenade deck did not need to be glued as the shell plating would secure the whole assembly. By this time the promenade deck forward enclosure had been added, but the strakes above it still had to be completed. The strake with the windows was an outer strake so the bottom edge of the inner strake above this needed to be pushed behind it, glued to the boat deck edge and secured to the lower strake with liquid poly. Here too the decks rested on the supports with weights placed on a board on the boat deck to ensure that the deck was perfectly flat when the final strakes were attached.

The final shell plating added to the model was the boat deck bulwarks and the bridge front. Small L-beam stiffeners were attached to the inside of the bulwarks and the bridge.

There were no limber boards in the boat deck waterways, which were painted black. High-pressure water valves were cast in resin, painted red and fitted to the waterways.

Funnel stay brackets

For these, 5mm (0.19in) diameter styrene discs were punched out of sheet styrene as the bed plate. For the brackets a row of holes was drilled into 2mm (0.07in) styrene and the brackets cut out, producing a small square with the opening in the middle. Two corners were rounded with a file and the brackets were cemented to the bedplate. The brackets were painted white and attached to the decks with superglue.

Boat fall bitts and rollers

The boat fall bitts were cast in resin. The master was made from styrene tube and the base from two layers of styrene. The boat fall rollers were made from three small discs cemented to each other with a styrene bracket connecting the disc to the bedplate, to guide the boat falls while the boats were being lowered. A small styrene disc served as the roller and the bedplate was also punched out of sheet styrene. The bracket was cut out and folded around the disc and cemented to it. The rollers for the model were cast in resin.

Lord Kelvin's sounding device

The lockers for the Lord Kelvin's sounding device were made from sheet styrene and painted dark brown. The sounding spar was

BOAT DECK

cut from a thick piece of brass rod and tapered at one end by attaching it to a hand-drill chuck and holding it against a sanding disc with a block of wood. The hinge at the end of the spar was bent from brass wire and silver soldered to the spar. At the other end of the spar a small slice of plastic rod was attached and to this four small eyelets were glued for the spar-rigging. The sounding spar was attached to the outside of the hull with the same type of bracket that was used to attach the railing stanchions to the bulwarks.

The bridge

As viewers of the model can see inside the bridge, the whole interior was added right up to the bulkhead lamps on the bridge roof. The bridge instruments and telegraphs were built the same way as described in Chapter 6 so I shall not repeat the methods here. The compass was slightly larger than on the docking bridge but it was built in the same way.

The bridge front was built up of several layers of sheet styrene. The outermost layer was the bridge front with the windows cut out. Another layer with slightly smaller windows was added to the inside of this as the window frames. These were painted dark brown. A very thin sheet of clear styrene was added to this as the glazing. A further sheet was attached to the inside of this, also with the windows cut out (the same size as the window frames). This also had the openings in the centre of the storm shutters drilled out, and this complete sheet was painted dark brown. Attached to this was another sheet with the windows cut out (in the same size as on the bridge front) as well as the storm shutter frames all painted white. Styrene strip strengtheners were then added. The bridge side walls were made up of thick styrene, also with a thin sheet of styrene for the window frames and clear styrene as the glazing. Folding tables for navigational charts were attached to the inside walls.

Along the inside of the bridge bulwarks

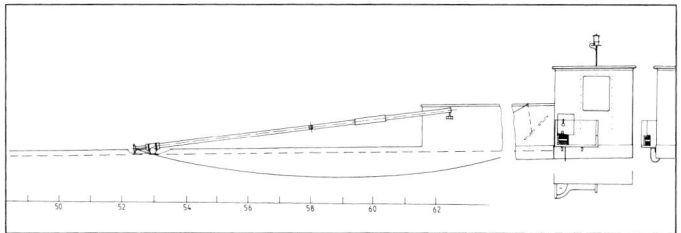
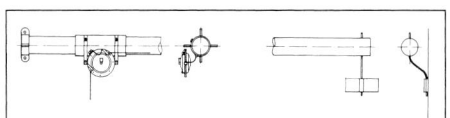

Sounding spar. (Scale: 1/192.)
(Left) Sounding Device carrier and block and sounding spar mount. (Scale: 1/48.)

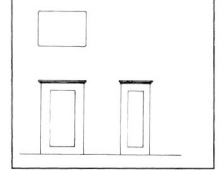

Sounding Device locker. (Scale: 1/96.)

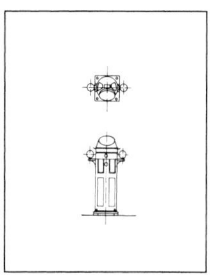

Lord Kelvin's bridge compass. (Scale: 1/48.)

(Above) The bridge bulwarks under construction.

(Far left) The bridge of the model under construction. The storm shutters can be seen underneath the windows and also the helm indicator beneath the top edge of the bridge front. The telegraph levers still need to be added.

(Left) The bridge bulwarks and wing cab in an advanced stage of construction. The forward bulwark ledge has been added as well as the pearwood handrails.

BOAT DECK

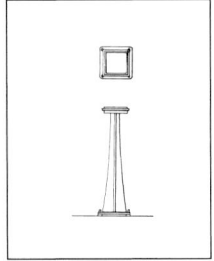

(Above) Pelorus (blind compass). (Scale: 1/96.)

(Right) *Olympic*'s starboard bridge wing cab in December 1912. The wing cabs were identical on *Titanic*. Note the forward bulwark supports, the ledge and the morse lamp on the cab roof.
(Photograph: Harland & Wolff - Claes-Göran Wetterholm collection)

The finished stairway bulwarks. Note the handrail and the stiffeners on the inside of the walls.

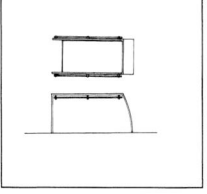 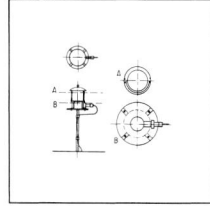

Stairway walls. (Scale: 1/192.)

Morse lamp. (Scale: 1/96.)

was a wide ledge for the officers to stand on. This ledge was possibly made of teak on the real ship; it is still visible in wreck footage of the sunken ship. It was attached to wooden chocks which were located behind the bulwark stiffeners. The ledge was cut out from the same maple veneer that was used for the decks, which had an additional layer of birch veneer glued to one side to give it the required thickness and strength.

The inside of the bridge bulwark was additionally supported by rods which were fed through openings in the ledge. These holes were drilled into the ledge and the support rods fed into them after they had been painted and the bedplates added. Spacers were attached to the bottom side of the ledge and the assembly cemented to the boat deck. After that the top of the support rods were cemented to the stiffeners of the inside of the bridge bulwark.

Bridge wing cabs

As these were also large enough to allow viewers to see inside them, the interiors were completely detailed. Window cases were cut out of thick styrene and the sliding rails added from styrene L-beams. The glazing was then inserted from the top before the wing cab roofs were attached. Further details such as stiffeners and handles for the navigation lamp doors added.

The cab roofs were built up from layers of styrene. The Morse lamps were made from clear Perspex rod, styrene rod and brass wire. The navigation lamps were purchased items.

Stairs

Behind the aft bridge bulwarks, two stairways led down to the promenade deck. These were surrounded by walls which had a round beading along the top edge.

BOAT DECK

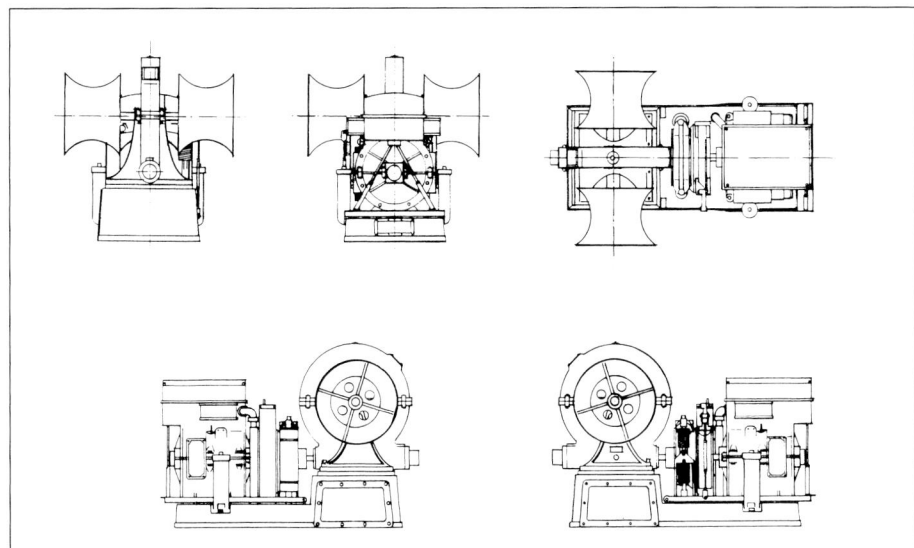

Sunderland Forge and Engineering Company 15cwt boat winch. (Scale: 1/48.)

Deck tennis court

On *Olympic* there was a deck tennis court on the port side next to No 2 funnel. *Titanic* had a large cowl vent in this space which made the tennis court redundant. However, two bench seats were installed next to the court alongside No 2 funnel casing for spectators. We do not know whether these two bench seats were also installed on *Titanic*, but I was advised by several *Titanic* historians to install them.

Officers' quarters on *Olympic* under construction.
(Photograph: Harland & Wolff-Claes Göran-Wetterholm collection)

11 Deckhouses

The deckhouses on the first two ships of the *Olympic* class, *Olympic* and *Titanic*, were at the time of building virtually identical. As Harland & Wolff did not draw plans for both ships, the plans of the prototype, *Olympic*, were used for building *Titanic*.

Officers' quarters.
(Scale: 1/535)
Key:
1. Chartroom prismatic skylight.
2. Rigging bracket.
3. Fidley grating.
4. Awning cover strut.
5. Mushroom vent.
6. Fresh water tank.
7. Sirocco vent.
8. Cowl vent.
8a. Hot air fan.
9. Sirocco vent.
10. Sirocco vent.
11. Cowl vent.
12. Cowl vent.
13. Cowl vent.
14. Hot air fan.
15. Grand staircase dome skylight.
16. Sirocco vent.
17. Sirocco vent.
18. Stokehold vent.
19. Cowl vent.
20. Marconi room skylight.
21. Officers' lavatory skylight.
22. Marconi aerial padeye.
23. Marconi aerial trunk.
24. Expansion joint.
25. Thermotank.
26. Tent spar.
27. Lightbox.
28. Funnel guywire bracket.
29. Portable wall socket.
30. Margin strip.
31. Breakwater.
32. Skylight vent duct.
38. Gibbs extractor.

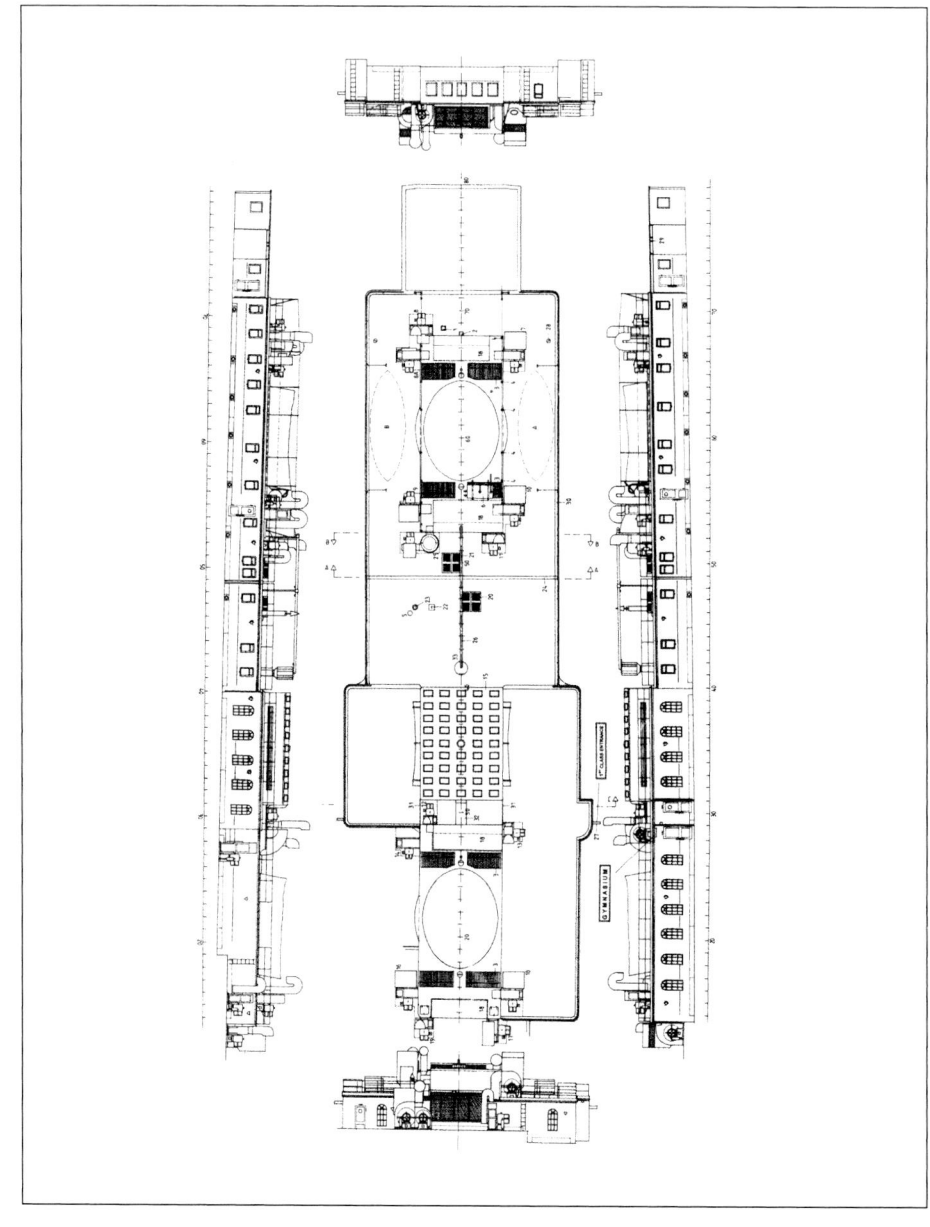

DECKHOUSES

However, during *Olympic*'s first year in service it became clear that some alterations in the design were needed to further improve the ship.

As most of the alterations were not added to the plans, for the many areas of *Titanic* that were not photographed one can safely use photographs of the early *Olympic* (before the First World War) as a guide. The major difference between the two, with regard to the deckhouses, was the bridge, which was longer on *Olympic*, and her wheelhouse also had a rounded front which was flat on *Titanic*. In addition to this the side walls of the bridge wing cabs were flush with the promenade deck walls on *Olympic* while they were moved further outboard on *Titanic*. During *Olympic*'s December 1912 refit the bridge was altered to the same configuration as *Titanic*. Also the portholes at the foot of the officers quarters' walls were elliptical on *Olympic* but round on *Titanic*. A further alteration was the addition of a stairway at the aft bulkhead of No 3 funnel deckhouse on *Titanic*; this too was added on *Olympic* in December 1912. There were substantial differences in the arrangement of vents and siroccos between the first two sisters but there is no need to describe these in detail here.

Officers' Quarters

Building the officers' quarters was, apart from the shell plating, the most complex part of the whole work. The enormous array of vents, siroccos, thermo tanks and skylights housed on the roof were tedious to redesign and reconstruct accurately.

Apart from a few First Class staterooms at the aft end of this deckhouse, and the gymnasium, of course, the officers' quarters were inhabited by the captain and his officers. Beyond that were the wireless operators' cabin and the adjoining silent room.

The complete deckhouse was built in two sections which were separated at the expansion joints. The deckhouse was built in the usual sheet-styrene on a wooden frame, taking the inner plating at the foot of the

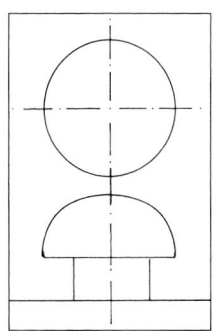

Mushroom vent.
(Scale: 1/12.)

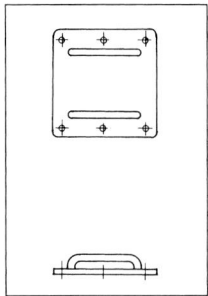

Rigging bracket.
(Scale: 1/24.)

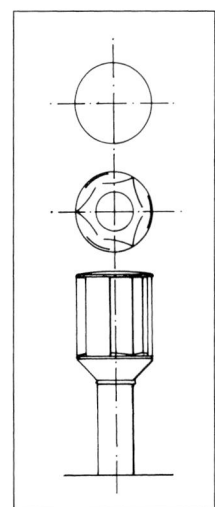

Gibbs extractor vent.
(Scale: 1/48.)

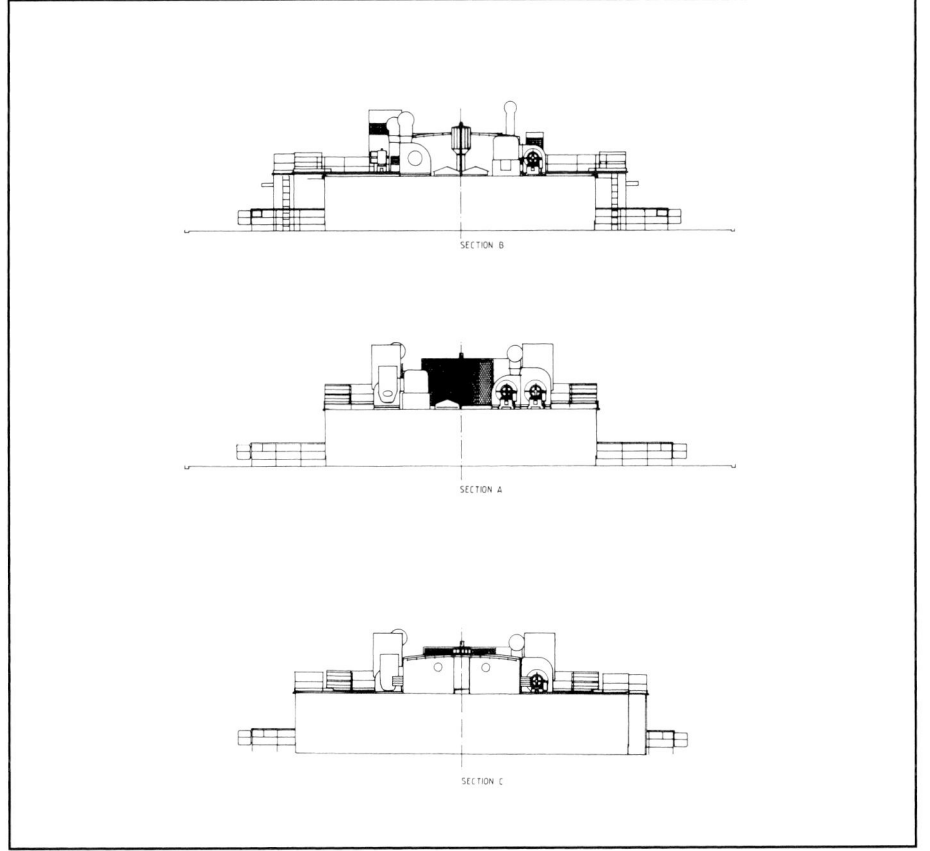

Sections through officers' quarters.

Section A (looking forward)
Section B (looking aft)
Section C (looking forward)
(Scale 1/384)

DECKHOUSES

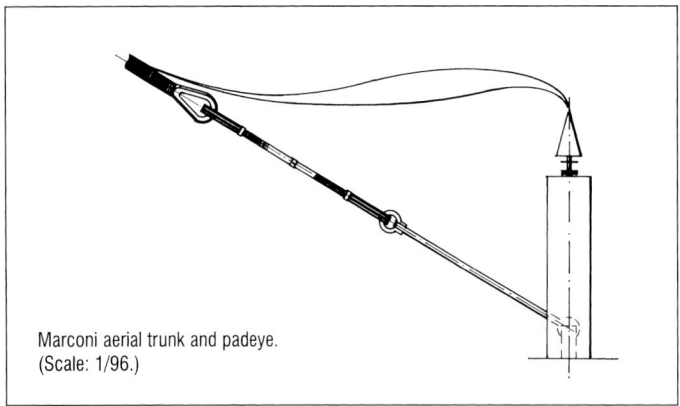

Marconi aerial trunk and padeye. (Scale: 1/96.)

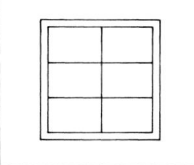

Chartroom prismatic skylight. (Scale: 1/24.)

walls into account. All windows were cast in resin as described previously. For the frosted glass for the gymnasium windows we sanded a 3mm (0.11in) sheet of Perspex with fine wet-and-dry sandpaper and gave it a slight polish afterwards to remove any remaining scratches. This Perspex was then given a few coats of gloss varnish, applied with an airbrush to replicate the structure of the glass. The result is very satisfying.

Large portholes were located at the foot of the walls on the inner plating. They were to give light to companionways one deck below. The resulting 'tunnel' in the officers' quarters was covered with cabinets or beds. We made one master for these and cast the items needed in resin. For the master a small thin disc served as the backing plate. The top and bottom edge of this plate was straightened for it to fit underneath the outer plating. A small ring cut from a tube was attached to the plate as the porthole rim. The locking bolt and the hinge were added from short rod. After the portholes were cemented to the deckhouse and painted white, a small disc of clear styrene with the inside painted black was attached to the porthole as the glazing.

The officers' quarters window frames were cast completely in resin. All resin pieces were painted before the glass was attached. The glass was 1mm (0.03in) pieces of Perspex and after the glass was glued to the frames an outer frame was cemented onto it. Hinges were added from sprue and the unpainted areas like the glass edges were painted with a fine brush.

The decks were strengthened underneath with MDF boards and wooden strips. Margin strips at the top edge of the deckhouse were made as described in the section on the lounge roof below, but here a half-round strip was attached to the outer face of the strip and painted dark brown.

Above the chartroom a glass skylight was mounted into the deck at deck level. This consisted of six small panels in a large frame. It has apparently been salvaged from the wreck site, located near the stern. A small square the size of the light was cut out of the deck and a piece of 1mm (0.03in) Perspex placed into it after the inside had been painted black. The six panels were scribed into the Perspex and a brass frame painted to it.

This rare snapshot was taken on the officers' quarters roof, above the gymnasium looking forward. It is the only photograph I know that was taken on the officers' quarters roof on any of the *Olympic* class liners. Handwriting on the back says it was taken by a group of sightseers taking part in a guided tour around *Olympic* in Southampton. Surprisingly passengers were not normally allowed on this deck.
(Photograph: Author's collection)

DECKHOUSES

Bridge roof

Though most of the pictures in this book show the bridge roof on the model in natural wood, it appears that it was actually covered with canvas and enamelled grey. So as not to disturb the navigational instruments on the bridge on the real ship, the complete structure was built from wood. Thus there was no steel deck as the bridge roof. The planks were laid in tongue and groove, and this was apparently covered with canvas and enamelled to seal the roof. A photograph of *Titanic*, taken from the roof of the officers' quarters looking down onto the forecastle, shows part of the bridge roof. One might believe that deck seams can be seen on the bridge roof and this was misleading me as the deck seams show through the canvas cover. At the time of writing I am thinking about changing the bridge roof on the model.

The first funnel casing top was built around an 8mm (0.31in) wooden plank, the sides and top covered with styrene. The stokehold shafts were also made from styrene and the mesh from stretched sprue. As mentioned in Chapter 6, this was not the most exciting job. I first drew the mesh on a sheet of cardboard and used the drawing as guide for attaching the threads accurately. Every thread was attached by hand. Where threads crossed each other I applied a slight touch of liquid poly.

Four 'fidley gratings', two at each end of the first three funnels covered the fidleys leading down to the stoke room. These gratings were built in a wooden frame similar to the reserve anchor grating described in Chapter 7.

Awning lines

Alongside the first funnel on each side were long struts supporting a single wire leading from the aft stokehold vent to the aft end of the bridge. These were to attach a canvas cover over this area, possibly to protect it against the sun.

We made these struts from thick brass wire which was tapered at the end using a disc sander with the brass rods in a hand drill. The eyes at the top of the struts were bent to shape using thin pliers.

Small bedplates were cut out from styrene which had holes drilled into them in the same diameter as the struts. The foot of the struts were then inserted into these holes.

Further holes were also drilled into the

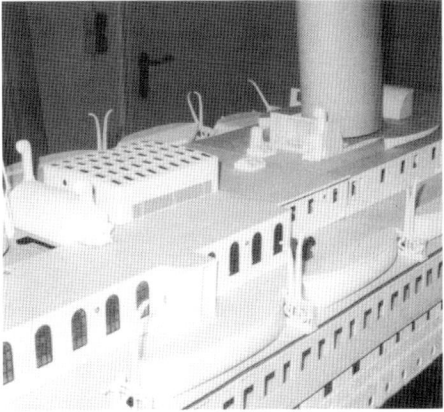

The officers' quarters on the model under construction.

The gymnasium windows are completed. The perspex windows were sanded slightly with fine wet-and-dry sandpaper and then given several layers of gloss varnish applied with an airbrush. This gave the perspex a slightly rough texture just like the real windows. The result is very convincing.

Captain Edward J Smith, commodore of the White Star Line, on board *Titanic*, possibly on 10 April 1912, shortly before her departure. Many photographs supposedly showing Smith and the officers on board *Titanic* were actually taken onboard *Olympic*. This, however, is *Titanic* as the porthole at the bottom of the image is round, those on *Olympic* being elliptical.
(Photograph: *Illustrated London News* – Günter Bäbler collection)

DECKHOUSES

No 1 funnel casing top. The base was an 8mm (0.31in) thick board covered with sheet styrene.

The officers' quarters fresh water tank. To the left is the funnel pipe.

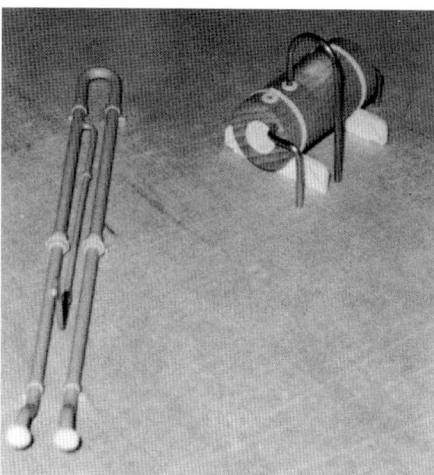

Fresh water tank. (Scale: 1/48.)

funnel casing top edge, the same size as the struts and the struts inserted into these after painting. Very thin steel thread was used for the awning lines.

Fresh water tank

Behind the first funnel was the fresh water tank which contained water for the officers' quarters. *Olympic* had two next to each other; *Titanic* had only one tank on the starboard side. The tank was made from a thick wooden dowel; the supports and bands were added from styrene and strip. The pipes were added from brass wire and small hand-wheels made as described in Chapter 6.

Sirocco vents

There was no possibility of casting these items in resin as the walls were too thin. Each had to be made individually if they were to be reproduced accurately. The same applied here as to many other items of the model: do it as it was done on the real ship. The only difference was I used styrene and glue, not steel and rivets. The method described here applies to all vents and thermo tanks as the method was the same; only the shape and size varied a little.

First I cut out the side shells which contained the fan case and the duct in one piece. These were joined together with styrene strip between them in the required width. The width differed on some vents (this can be seen in the plans).

The bed plate was made from two small rectangular pieces of styrene cemented on top of each other. These were attached to the fan casing and small L-beams cemented to the joint. Pieces of thin strip were attached to the bottom as the feet.

The motor axle plate was riveted, cut out and attached to the side plate at which the motor would be mounted. The motors and their pedestals were the only items that were cast in resin. The master motor was made from small discs of thick styrene cemented to each other and filed to shape. The 'cross' at the motor's forward side was carved from one piece of styrene, cemented to the front

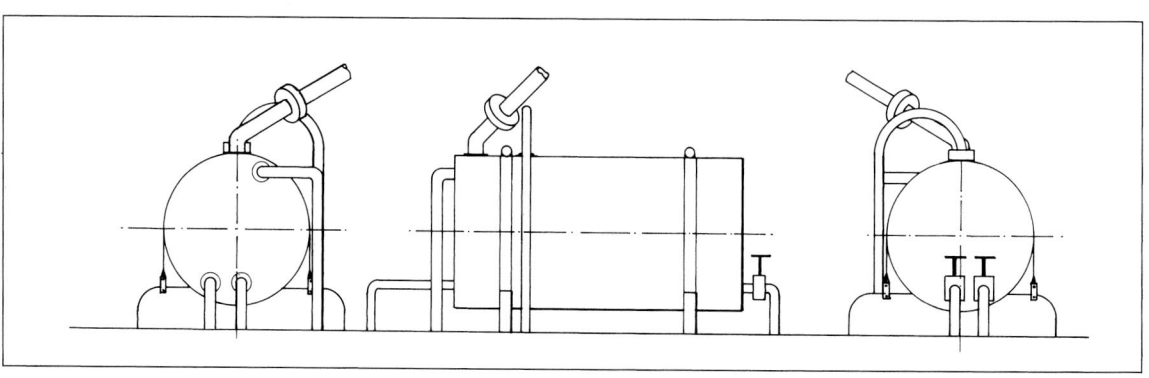

DECKHOUSES

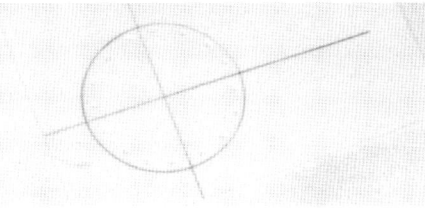

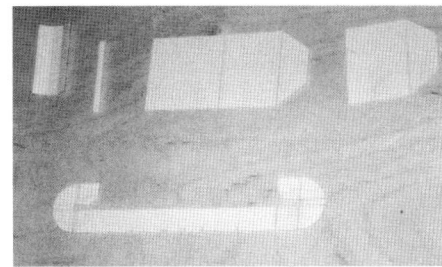

(Far left) Assembly of a sirocco vent fan casing. The side plates were cut out including the duct. These were then joined together with a thin strip of styrene between them. The plate on the left has the strip already attached. (Middle) The bed plates were made from two rectangular pieces of styrene in different sizes. The styrene strips in the foreground are the mounts for attaching the vent to the decks. (Bottom) L-beams were attached at the joint between the base plates and the fan casing.

(Top left) The motor axle backing plate riveted and ready for cutting out. (Middle left) The vent casing under construction, showing all items needed. I initially planned to attach the side parts in one piece but this was difficult and not really satisfying. (Bottom left) The cut-out axle plate ready for attaching and the resin-cast motor casing and its pedestal.

and the arms carefully folded backwards so as not to break them and cemented to the sides. The motor pedestal was also made from laminates of styrene and the sides added from sheet styrene with their cut-outs. Of course the pedestals on the real ship were hollow inside so the openings on the sidewalls on the model pedestals were painted matt black to give the impression that it was the dark interior the viewer is looking at.

The sirocco vents were also constructed as a box-like item. At first I planned to cut out the side pieces in one piece and fold them accordingly around the bottom, but this did not always work out. In the end I cut them out in one piece but sliced them in half at the bottom. Should a resulting gap needed to be filled after assembly, it could easily be done with styrene strips and filler.

The mesh for the siroccos was also made from stretched sprue but it was thankfully not as large as that covering the stokehold vents. The siroccos were then joined to the vent casing with a small slice of thick rod.

DECKHOUSES

(Right) Assembling the vent casing. The sides were cut into two pieces and attached separately. The joint at the bottom was then filled and sanded

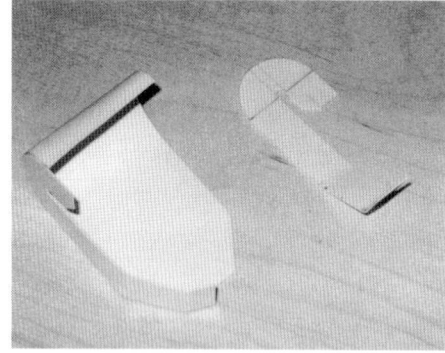

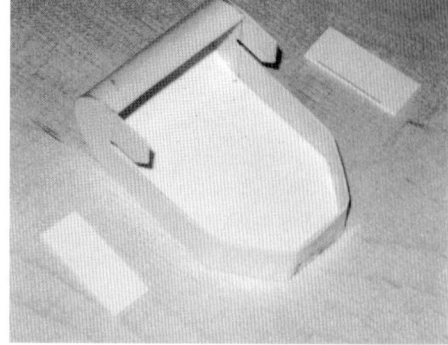

(Far right) The two spacers that were attached to the inside of the walls to ensure that the front plate would not slip too far inwards when being attached.

(Right) The vent nearing completion.

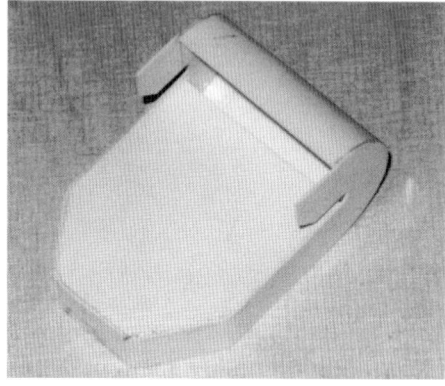

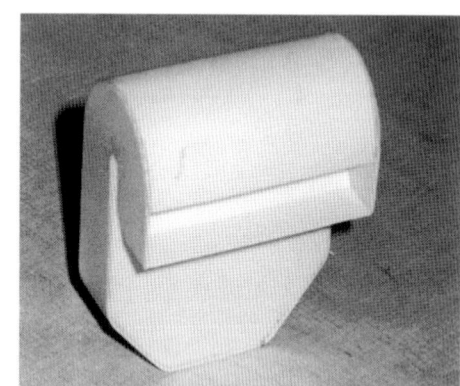

(Far right) The complete vent ready for the mesh to be attached.

(Right) The mesh under construction. The positions of the wires were drawn on with a pencil. These lines served as guides to attach the wires from stretched sprue in equal spaces.

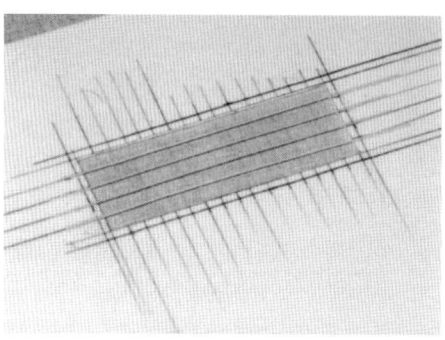

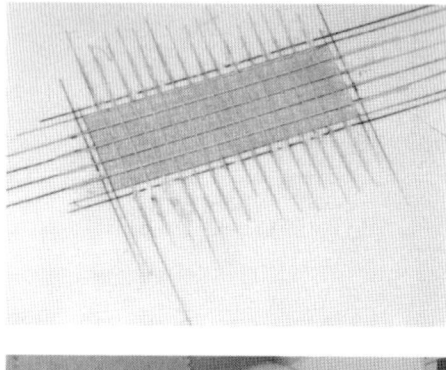

(Far right) The completed mesh ready to be cut from the sheet.

(Right) The cut-out mesh ready for cementing to the vent.

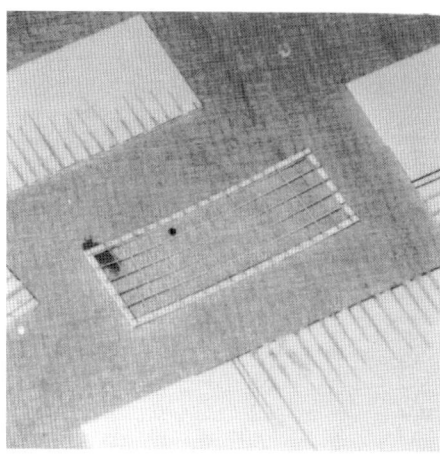

(Far right) A finished vent ready for painting.

DECKHOUSES

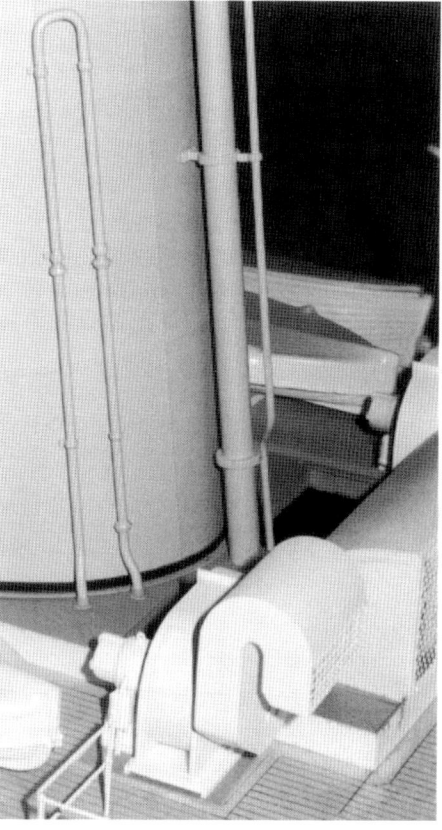

(Far left) A completed and painted sirocco vent to the starboard side forward of the first funnel.

(Left) A cowl vent, thermotank and sirocco vents behind the first funnel. Note the water tank and the tent spar.

Officers' quarters skylights

There were two skylights on the roof of the officers' quarters, one for the Marconi operator's cabin, the other above the officers' lavatory. These were simple to construct, with the side walls made from thick styrene and the covers from thinner material. The rods were added as well as jackstays on the sides and the skylights airbrushed dark brown. The glazing was attached to the inside of the covers from 3mm (0.11in) Perspex which had the inside painted black.

A tent spar was attached to the aft stokehold vent behind No1 funnel and the Gibbs extractor in front of the grand staircase skylight. Here too a canvas tent could be erected, possibly to prevent the officers' quarters from an excessive build-up of heat in very hot weather. Several aerial views of *Olympic* have emerged in the past years showing this canvas tent in place.

The tent spar was made from a strip of pear wood with small eyes attached to the bottom bent from thin steel wire.

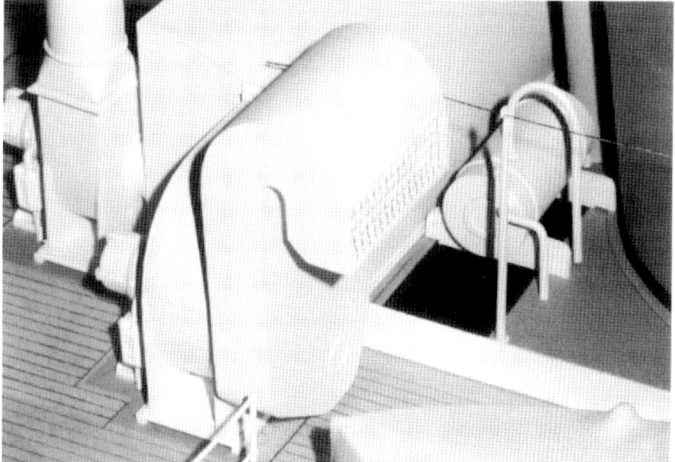

(Below) A completed and painted sirocco vent from the starboard side slightly aft of the funnel. Note the water tank and the fidley grating.

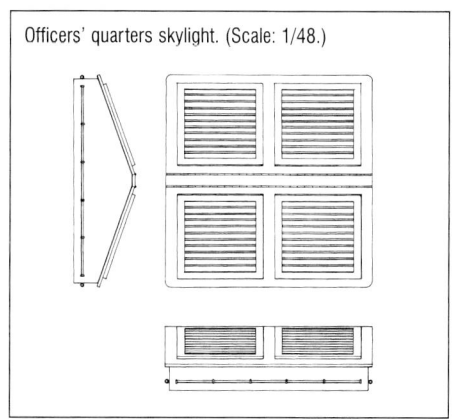

Officers' quarters skylight. (Scale: 1/48.)

Officers' quarters skylight before painting. Note the jackstays at the bottom edge. After painting the skylights dark brown the glazing was attached to the inside.

107

DECKHOUSES

Shielded bulkhead lamp. (Scale: 1/12.)

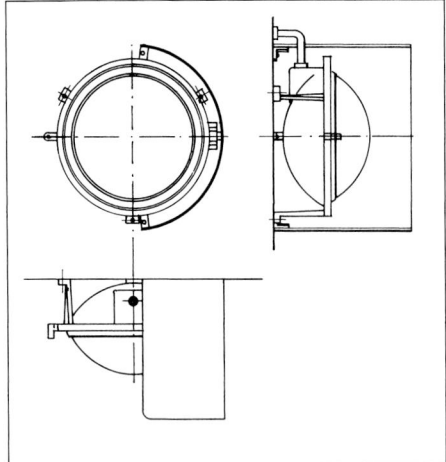

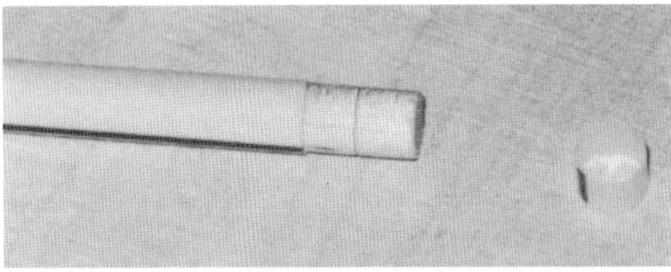

The lamp shields or screens were produced from drinking straws. A straw was cut in slices and each slice was cut in half. This resulted in two lamp shields.

Grand staircase dome skylight

This was also a large box-like construction, and here the side walls were cut out in one piece and folded at the corners. The inside of the walls was strengthened with strips of wood. The skylight top was slightly rounded. The top was cut out of styrene and frames added to the inside to reach the rounded shape. The top then was attached to the walls and a thin strip added to the top edge of the walls sealing the joint. Jackstays were attached slightly beneath the top edge. *Olympic*'s skylight had openings in all sides with portholes that could be covered by louvres. On *Titanic*, however, there were only two portholes in the aft side.

It is here where we meet yet another mystery amongst the many mysteries of *Titanic*. On each side of *Titanic*'s grand staircase skylight were two long dark 'boxes'. Their purpose remains a mystery, and has been the cause of many endless (and heated) debates amongst historians. Some say these boxes might have been the casing for steam pipes to heat the skylight interior to avoid condensation. The skylight was, however, ventilated at the rear with a duct leading to the stokehold vent behind it. Contrary to the heating theory, in wreck footage and photographs no openings have yet been found in the skylight walls through which the steam pipes could be fed into the skylight interior. Besides, why place the heater outside when it was the inside that needed to be heated?

For what it is worth, my opinion is that these dark boxes were merely wooden boards stacked on top of each other used to cover the skylight as a protective measure. *Olympic* also had these dark objects initially but they were removed before the First World War.

We have a similar situation near the aft staircase skylight. On the tank room roof we also see wooden boards of an apparently similar nature stored on top of each other (this is described more thoroughly in the tank room section below). As we have two stacks of wood (well, actually three: one on each side of the forward staircase skylight), both within easy reach of the skylights, the assumption I have is that they related to the skylights. My theory is that these boards were used to cover the skylights, placed on top, with a canvas cover mounted on top of these boards, possibly to protect the glass from getting damaged or the skylight interior from heating excessively in sunlight.

Now back to the model. I made these boxes from thick strips of pear wood, which were slightly rounded at one side for them to fit snugly on the rounded skylight top.

The glass skylight panes on the model were constructed in one sheet of thin clear styrene. We first scored the outline of each panel onto the styrene and then covered the whole sheet with masking tape. The glazing outlines were drawn onto the tape and the frames cut out and removed, leaving only the glazed windows masked. The whole sheet was then airbrushed white and after the paint had dried the individual panels were snapped off by bending them at

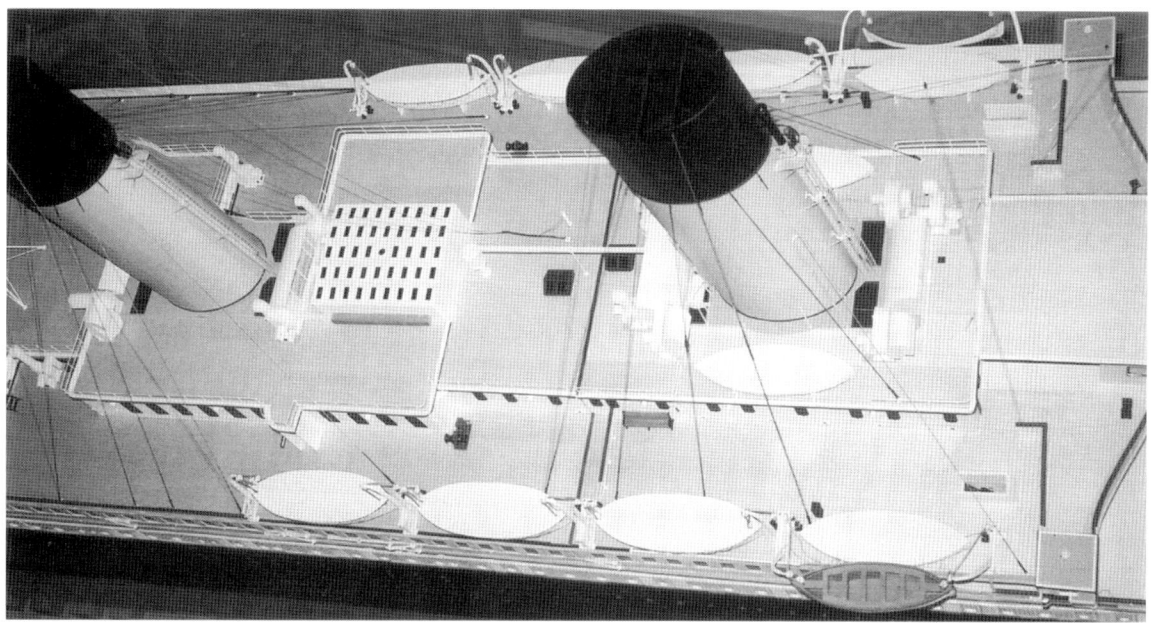

the scored lines. The corners of the panels were slightly rounded with sandpaper and they were attached to the skylight top. The duct leading to the stokehold shaft was made from thick strip and the two breakwaters, one on each side, leading from the aft edge of the skylight to the stokehold vent behind it were added from thin sheet with beadings at the top outer edges added from half-round strip.

Final details for the officers' quarters were light boxes at the First Class entrances and the gymnasium. The bulkhead lamps were fitted with metal screens to prevent the glare of light reflecting on the bridge while the ship was underway at night and disturbing the crew. The bridge of an ocean liner was pitch-black at night when the ship was at sea.

The bulkhead lamp screens were made from drinking straws cut into slices and then in

The completed officers' quarters viewed from above. The natural wood bridge roof was later changed to grey.

(Below) A cowl vent and hot air fan forward of No 1 funnel.

(Left) The same vent and fan as before, viewed from the rear. Note the bulkhead lamps with shields.

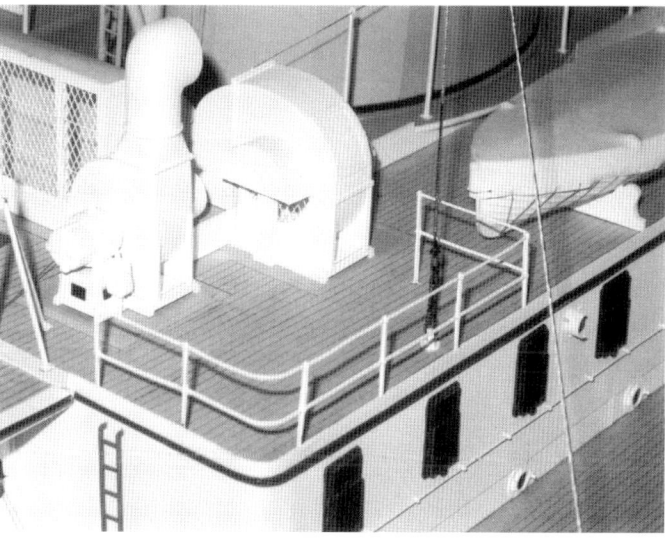

DECKHOUSES

half, producing two screens from each slice. They were attached to the bulkheads with superglue and then painted white.

Lounge Roof

The lounge roof was a large open deck space on which passengers could play shuffleboard and other deck games. Like the First Class smoking room roof, the lounge roof was raised approximately 3.6ft higher than the boat deck.

In the centre of the lounge roof was a compass platform which housed the main compass to which the bearings of all other compasses were adjusted. To prevent the steel and other metals from manipulating the bearings, the compass was located as far away from the funnels as possible and high above deck level. The platform walls were made of wood. A notice board to the right of the entrance indicated that 'Passengers are not allowed on Compass Platform'.

The deck

The lounge roof was made from 3mm (0.11in) plywood which had reinforcing ribs attached underneath. In addition to this small chocks were attached inside the edges to allow the roof to be placed onto the lounge walls and locked into position with the chocks meeting the wooden deckhouse frame.

The plywood was covered with maple veneer and planks seams drawn on. These planks were also 5in wide. The underside was painted white.

Shuffleboards

The shuffleboard fields' were chalked, not painted, onto the deck surface by seamen. We drew them on the model deck with a draughtsman's ruling pen dipped in white paint. A template was used to draw the fields but the numbers were drawn by hand, as on

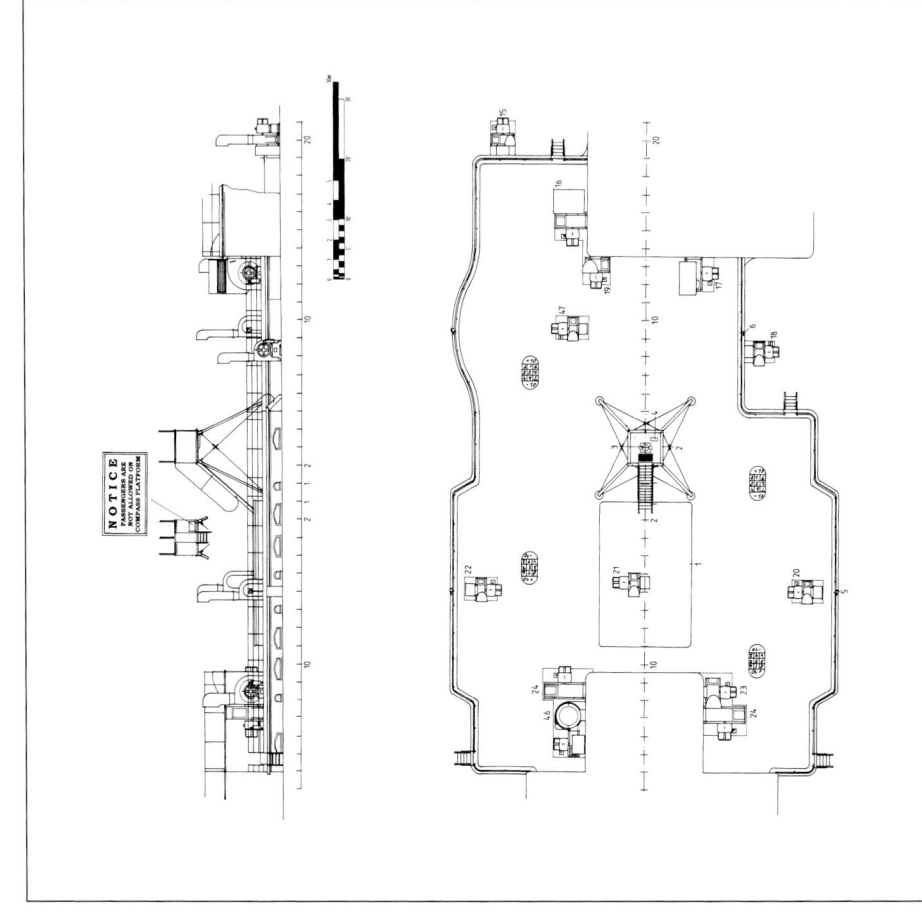

Lounge roof.
(Scale: 1/384.)
1. Raised roof above lounge chandelier.
2. Compass platform.
3. Lord Kelvin's compass.
4. Buzzer.
5. Shielded bulkhead lamp.
6. Unshielded bulkhead lamp.
15. 20in dia. Cowl vent.
16. Sirocco vent.
17. Sirocco vent.
18. 20in dia. cowl vent.
19. 30in dia. cowl vent.
20. 20in dia. cowl vent.
21. 20in dia. cowl vent.
22. 20in dia. cowl vent.
23. 30in dia. cowl vent.
24. Hot air fan.
46. Thermo-tank.
47. 20in dia. cowl vent.

the real ship. As it was crucial for these to be convincing and tidy, I tried about seven or eight test runs before I reached a satisfactory result and could apply them to the lounge roof. Many visitors to my workshop are surprised to see that even such 'minor' details have been included.

Deck margin strip

The plywood deck was used as a template to draw the outer edge of the margin top on thin sheet. Then the inner edge was drawn approximately 5mm (0.19in) inside of the outer edge following the shape drawn using the wooden deck. After this I cut out another strip, in the same height as the plywood deck and this was attached to the bottom outer edge of the margin strip. The railing kicking strips were then glued to the top of the margin strip approximately 2mm (0.07in) inside the outer edge. Gaps for stairs were cut out of the kicking strip and the resulting marks cleaned. The complete assembly was then painted white and glued to the deck and the deck was then attached to the lounge deckhouse.

We calculated the location of the railing stanchions as best we could from period photographs, and marked the position of each stanchion with a pencil. Small holes were then drilled through the margin strip into the deck and after the railings had been completed they were folded to shape and the stanchions inserted into the holes. Where the railings met

Olympic's lounge roof in June 1911. Shuffleboard fields can be seen chalked onto the deck surface.
(Photo: Brown Brothers)

DECKHOUSES

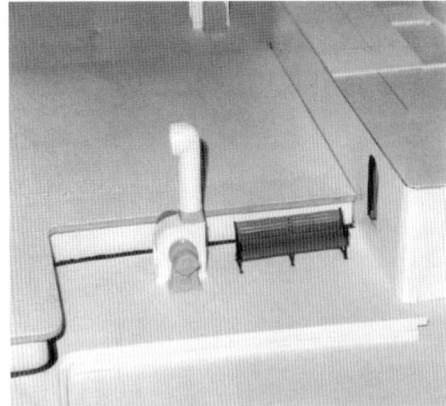

The lounge roof behind the gymnasium. The margin strip can be seen in the foreground.

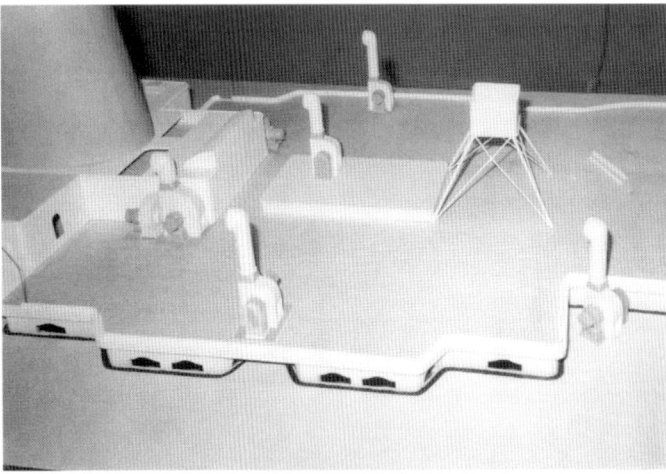

(Above) The lounge roof under construction. The margin strip is now attached and the kicking strips have received the cut-outs for where the stairs will be attached.

All vents are painted and attached to the lounge roof.

a deckhouse, holes for the rods were drilled into the deckhouse walls, the rods bent to a 90° angle and inserted into these holes. Finally the rods were cut out where stairs were to be added.

Bulkhead lamps were mounted to small styrene backing plates and attached to the railings with a second plate from the inside. The second plate had a smaller plate glued to it, acting as a spacer to reach the first backing plating between the railings. The electrical cables were added from brass wire inserted into holes drilled into the rear backing plate and the margin strip. Lamp shields were added as described for the officers' quarters above.

The centre of the lounge roof was a raised steel casing which housed the large chandelier inside the First Class lounge. This was a simple box-like construction made from thick styrene. The vast number of vents, fans and thermo tanks were constructed as described in the section on the officers' quarters above.

Compass platform

As mentioned above, this housed the main compass, the bearings of which were used to adjust all other compasses. The platform legs were made from rod and tube. At first I drew the legs and drag wires on a white board and used this as a template. The two sides were

DECKHOUSES

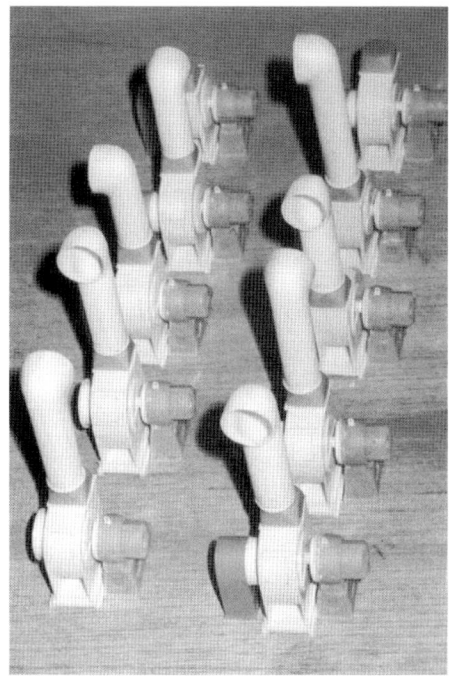

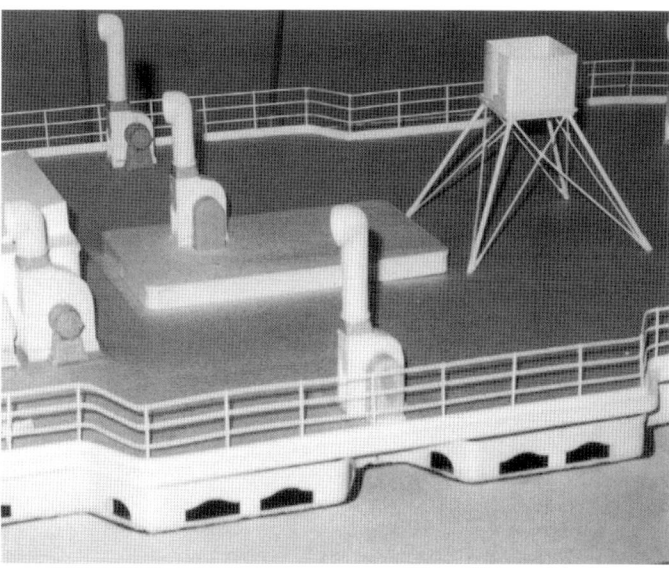

built with the legs and the drag-wires while the forward and aft ends were built as drag-wires only. After this had dried the four sides were assembled. The platform floor and the drainage pipe leading down the starboard side forward leg were added. A small rim was then fitted to the top of the floor into which the walls were later placed. The outer edges of this rim were sanded round. Stiffening strips were attached to the bottom of the floor using thin strips.

Like the superstructure, the compass platform walls were also made in one piece and folded to shape. The planks were scored into this sheet with a scriber before cutting them out. Jackstays were added to the top edge of the walls from sprue-eyelets and rod. After the walls were attached the compass platform was airbrushed white. Then handrails were added from thin strips of pear wood which had slots cut into the underside so the handrails could be inserted onto the wall tops. All wooden handrails were stained in dark oak.

The compass platform deck was cut out of maple veneer, the planks drawn on and the deck varnished and attached to the platform floor. The buzzer, compass and grating were identical to those on the docking and navigating bridges and their construction will not be repeated here.

The stairs leading to the compass platform were built in a wooden jig and the handrails formed from brass wire. Two holes were drilled into the platform walls into which the handrails were inserted.

Lounge windows

The lounge windows that are at boat deck level were made from thin clear styrene that was sanded with very fine sandpaper to give them the appearance of frosted glass. The glazed area was then masked with masking tape cut out in the shape of the glazing. After the whole sheet had been painted white, the windows were cut out including the frames and attached to the deckhouse walls.

(Above) Lounge roof railings partly completed.

(Far left) An assembly of cowl vents ready for painting.

The completed lounge roof looking forward.

113

DECKHOUSES

No 3 Funnel Deckhouse

No 3 funnel deckhouse contained the officers' mess, storage rooms for deck chairs and the No 3 funnel casing. One fundamental difference between *Titanic* and *Olympic* was the stairway behind the aft bulkhead leading down to the lounge pantry on the promenade deck. *Olympic* did not initially have this stairway, though it was also installed on her during the December 1912 refit.

Shortly before *Titanic* went down, chief baker Charles Joughin was in the lounge pantry:

'I went to the deck pantry, and while I was there I thought I would take a drink of water, and while I was getting the drink of water I heard a kind of crash as if something had buckled, as if part of the ship had buckled, and then I heard a rush overhead.'

Q: 'Is that the pantry on A-deck?'
A. 'Yes'
Q: 'So that the deck above would be the boat deck?'
A: 'Yes, I could hear it.'
Q: 'You could hear it?'
A: 'Yes.'
Q: 'People running?'
A: 'Yes. When I got up on deck top I could see them clambering down from those decks. Of course I was in the tail end of the rush.'
Q: 'Clambering down, climbing down from where?'
A: 'These rails here and steps. They came down this way' (showing on model).
Q: 'They had run along as far aft as they could on the boat deck, yes?'
A: 'Yes.'
Q: 'Did you see them clambering down to get onto the A-deck so as to get further aft?'
A: 'Their idea was to get onto the poop.'

It is interesting that Charles Joughin was in the lounge pantry when apparently the ship started to break in two. It is also interesting that he could actually hear the passengers running on the boat deck above him. Reading his narrative, one might come to the conclusion that he went up to the boat deck and then went outside. If this was the case, then he might have left A deck by the stairs behind the deckhouse.

The complete deckhouse was built up like the other deckhouses, *ie* sheet styrene walls built up on a wooden frame. The difficulty with this deckhouse was that the forward half mated onto the lounge roof which was approximately 3.6ft higher that the boat deck. The margins of the lounge roof had already been attached so the area of the deckhouse joining the lounge roof had to be cut out to fit accordingly. This enabled us to push the deckhouse into position after it was complete.

The beading at the top edge of the deckhouse was added from half-round styrene

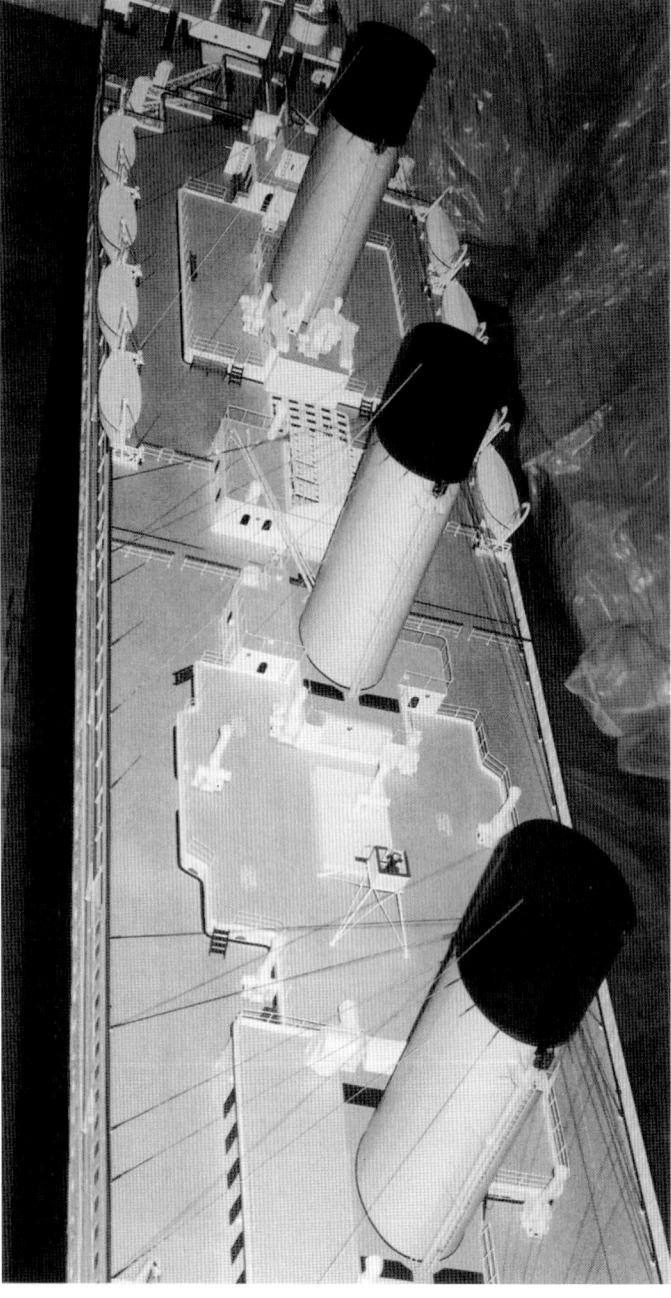

The lounge roof on the completed model. Note the shuffleboard fields.

114

DECKHOUSES

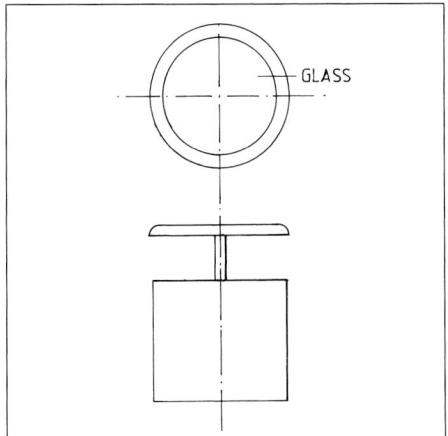

Mushroom vent. (Scale: 1/12.)

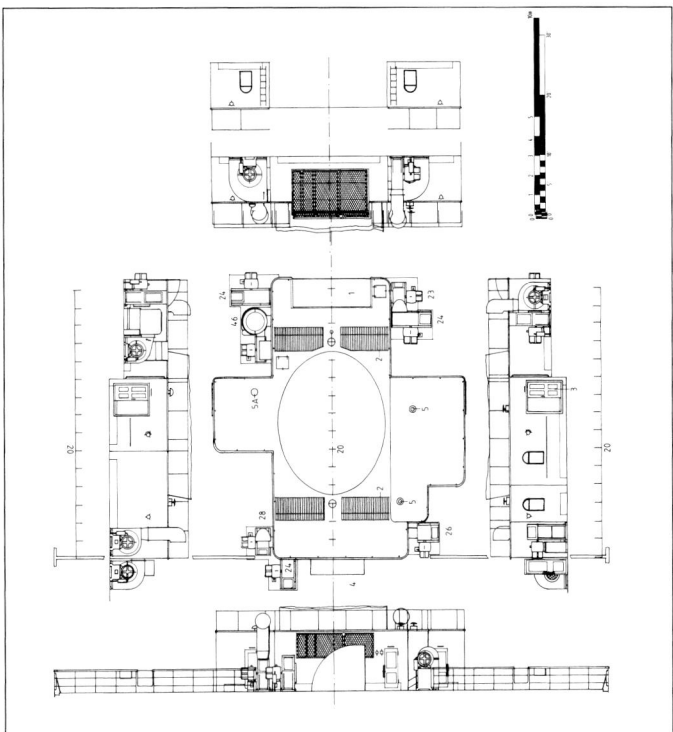

No 3 funnel deckhouse. (Scale: 1/384.)
Key:
1. Stokehold vent.
2. Fidley grating.
3. Sliding door.
4. Stairway leading to lounge pantry.
5. Mushroom vent.
5a. Mushroom vent.
23. 30in cowl vent.
24. Hot air fan.
26. Hot air fan.
28. 30in cowl vent.
46. Thermotank.

strip. Only a few weeks before the model was completed, Ken Marschall sent me a large batch of snapshots taken by passengers on board *Olympic*, possibly before the First World War. In one of these photographs ladders could be seen attached to the deckhouse walls. I was completely unaware of these before, as they could not be seen in the pictures I have and they were one of the final items to be added to the model. If it had not been for the photographs that Ken sent me, I would have missed them.

The sliding doors were made from styrene after the frame was built from thick strip. The door panels were scored into the surface with a scriber. A small handle was made from sprue formed to shape over boiling water.

The roof was painted dark grey. The roof above the officers' mess was insulated with deck planks which seem to have been covered with canvas and enamelled in grey.

There were two types of mushroom vent on the deckhouse roof. Those on the starboard side were made from styrene tube with the cap attached to a short piece of rod and glued to the roof so that the cap was in the open position, *ie* the cap slightly higher than the top rim of the tubes. These caps had glass centres, as they also served as skylights when closed. The single mushroom vent on the portside was heat-moulded.

Tank Room

As the name says, the tank room housed the fresh water tanks. It also housed the reciprocating engine room casing and the engineers' smoking room.

The deckhouse walls were built in one piece with the adjoining edges located at the centreline of the forward bulkhead. The inner plating at the foot of the walls was added as on all other deckhouses. Wooden reinforcements were attached to the inside of the walls to give the whole assembly added strength.

We decided to add the complete engine room casing in its full height as one can see most of it when looking down into the casing through the open skylight covers. I have a

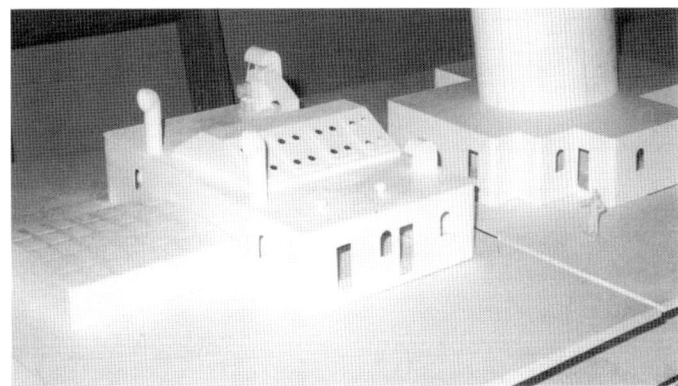

The tank room, aft staircase skylight and the No 3 funnel deckhouse under construction.

115

DECKHOUSES

No 3 funnel deckhouse at an advanced stage of construction. The fidley gratings still need to be added and the first water pipes have been test-fitted. At this stage of construction the roof of the officers' mess was also finished with maple veneer.

(Right) Sliding doors made from sheet styrene and strip. The panels were scored into the doors with a scriber.

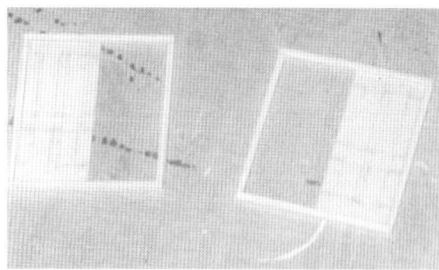

(Below) The port side of the completed deckhouse.

photograph of the inside of *Oceanic*'s casing, and the walls are a maze of walkway gratings and pipes. As it is unknown what these walls looked like on *Olympic* and *Titanic*, no detail was added to the model's casing.

The skylight openings had small rods attached to the inside which were added from styrene rod. The covers were small pieces of sheet with four portholes drilled into each corner. A styrene ring was attached to each porthole as the rim.

A thin strip was added to the edge of each cover and the covers were mounted to the skylight at the top edge with small strips of rod acting as hinges. After the covers had been painted, a small clear disc was attached to the inside of the porthole as the glazing. The roof was painted dark grey and heat-moulded mushroom vents attached to the roof.

Aft of the skylight a number of wooden boards were mounted to the skylight roof. Their purpose is also unknown and they too have been the cause for much debate amongst historians. At first I was told that these boards were to cover the engine room skylight openings. However, when I tried this out on the model I realised that they were far too short. As mentioned above, I believe that these boards were part of some protective measure for the staircase skylight windows behind the tank room. In one picture I can make out eight boards if the bottom board is obscured by the top edge of the deckhouse walls, which it undoubtedly is. There are seven rows of skylight windows parallel to the keel. So one of these boards could have been placed between each window and at each end of the skylight, as they fit perfectly across the skylight. Perhaps canvas was spread over these boards when needed to protect the

DECKHOUSES

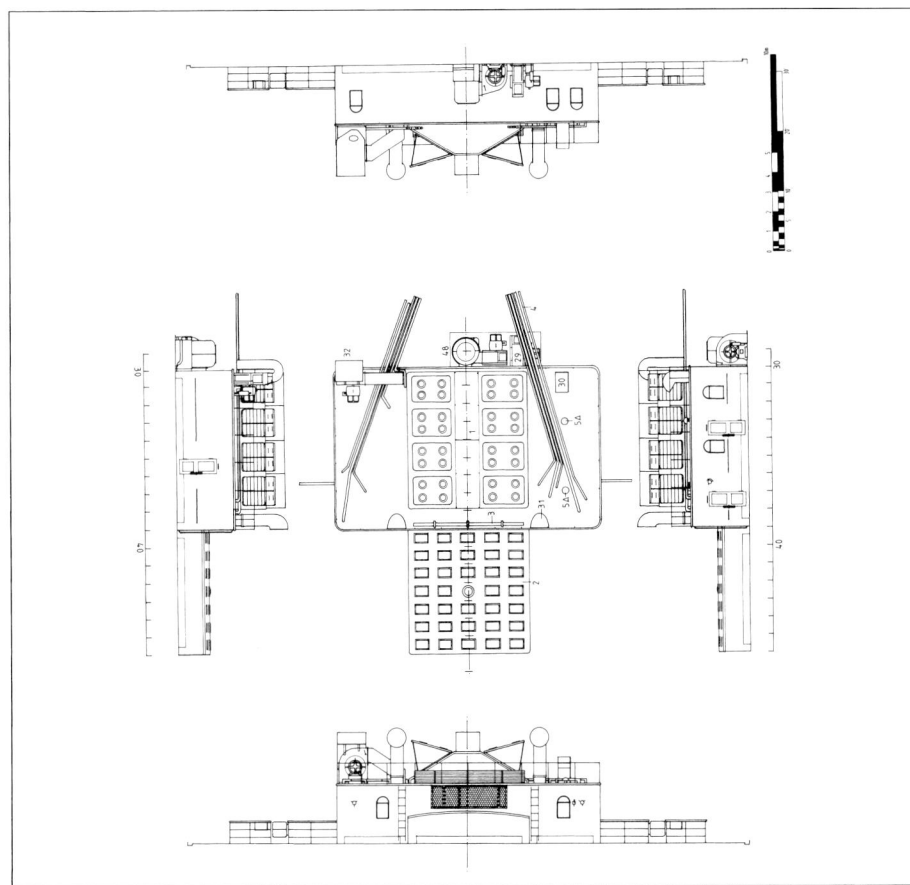

Tank room.
(Scale: 1/384.)
Key:
1. Reciprocating engine room skylight.
2. Aft staircase dome skylight.
3. Wooden boards.
4. Water overflow pipes.
5a. Mushroom vent.
29. Hot air fan.
30. Air duct.
31. 20in cowl vent.
32. Sirocco vent.
48. Thermotank.

The tank room before painting. The reciprocating engine room casing was added in its entire height. No detail was added to the inside of the casing as there are no plans or photographs available to show us what it looked like in reality. Note the wooden frame inside the deckhouse.

glass from ice splinters in winter gales. The funnel guy wires could ice up severely and ice breaking loose from the wires could hit and damage these windows. On the other hand, maybe this canvas cover was rigged up in summer to prevent excessive heat from building up inside the skylight from the sun. This is only my assumption. Their true purpose remains yet another mystery until definite proof arises as to what their purpose really was. For the model, these boards were made from a thick piece of pear wood into which the seams were scored with a scriber. The mounting brackets were made from styrene rod and strip.

DECKHOUSES

Rods were added to the inside of the reciprocating engine room skylight openings. The skylight covers have yet to be attached.

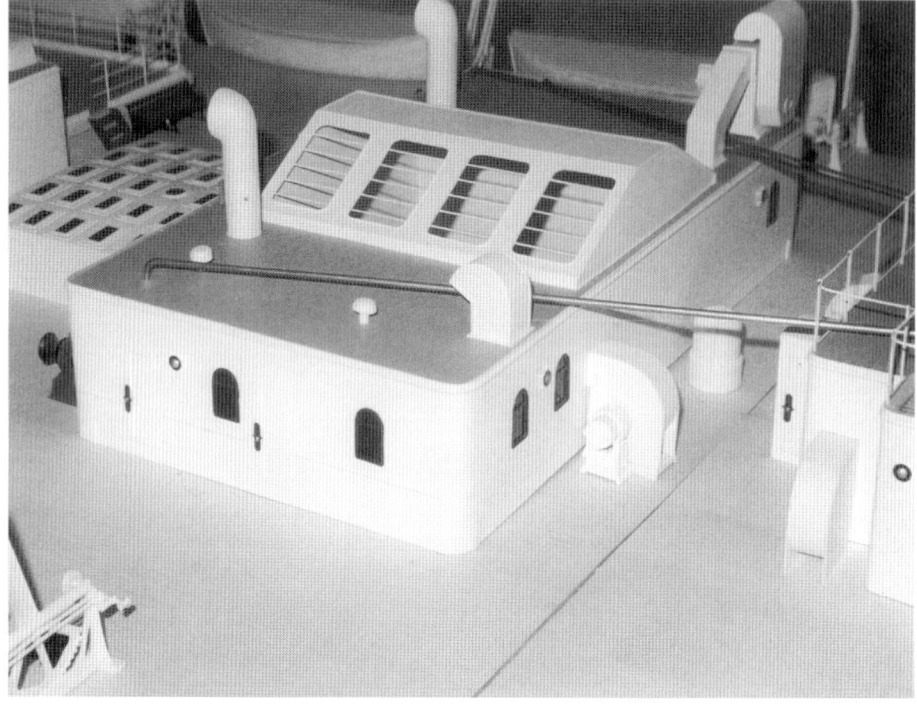

(Below) Detail of the tank room. In the upper left corner wooden boards can be seen attached to the tank room roof with brackets. Their purpose remains a mystery.

The aft staircase skylight was similar to the forward staircase skylight, but smaller. The model skylight construction was identical to that of the forward skylight described above.

No 4 Funnel Deckhouse & First Class Smoking Room Roof

The smoking room roof was built in the same manner as the lounge roof described earlier. As this roof was rectangular, it was easier to construct the margin strips. On the starboard side boat deck picture one sees a rather misplaced bench seat mounted at the right edge of the roof. Thinking about this, it might not be that

(Right and far right) The first Sirocco vent that was made for the model. The motor and its pedestal were cast in resin. The rest was built from sheet styrene as described for the officers' quarters.

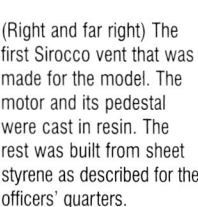

118

Port side view of the tank room looking aft.

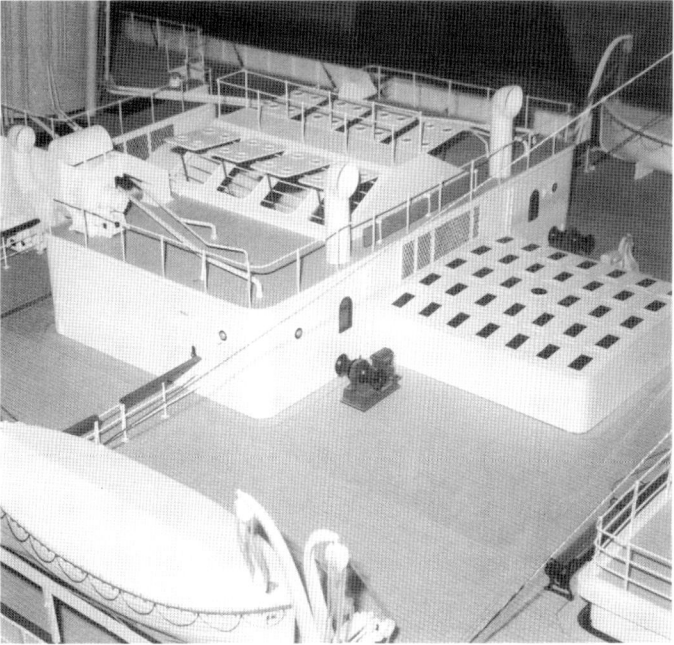

Port side view of the tank room looking forward.

misplaced after all: it is now believed that shuffleboards were also chalked onto the smoking room roof which gave the Second Class passengers their shuffleboards, and this bench was for the passengers who were playing or watching the game. Looking more closely at this picture, it appears that the bench is the second known 'short' bench. The average bench seat with a centre support was 7.6ft feet long. The two short benches appear to have been some 6ft long. They did not have the centre support. The first known short bench was placed at the aft end of the deckhouse. The story goes that one bench seat was removed from between the shafts aft of the Second Class entrance while the ship was in Southampton. Some sources say that this bench was given to the White Star Line agent in Southampton. I can hardly imagine that the White Star Line would have been happy with people dismantling parts of their ships and giving them away as souvenirs. Perhaps the bench seat on the starboard side of the smoking room roof is the one that was removed from between the shafts.

The railings were added as described for the lounge roof above. These were the first railings that were installed on the model. They only needed to be bent to shape in two places on each side so they were quite straightforward and gave us a little practice before we tackled more complicated railings such as those on the aft end of the promenade deck and the lounge roof.

DECKHOUSES

No 4 funnel deckhouse and First Class smoking room roof. (Scale: 1/384.)
1. Vent ducts.
2. First Class smoking room fireplace flue.
3. Porthole.
5a. Mushroom vent.
33. (port) 20in cowl vent.
33. (stb). 20in cowl vent.
34. Sirocco vent.
36. 20in dia. cowl vent.
48. Thermotank.
49. Thermotank.

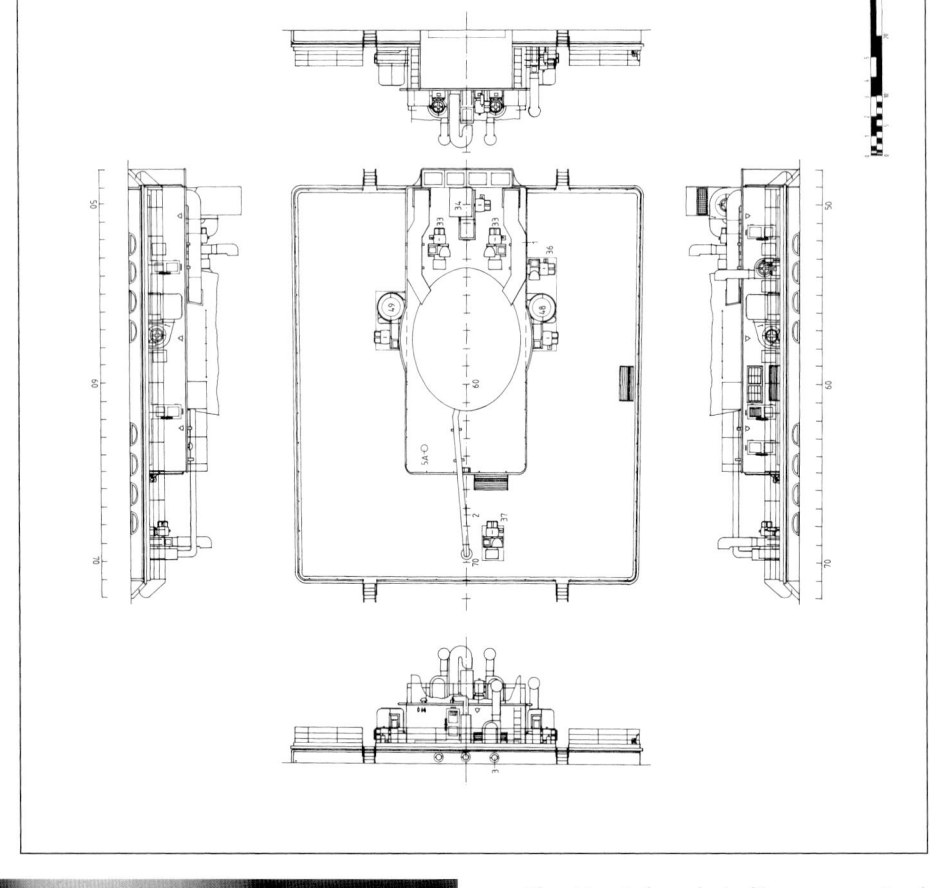

The deckhouse under construction. The bench seats had not yet been attached to the model when this picture was taken. The bench seat to the right was later replaced with a short bench. Another short bench can be seen at the aft end of the deckhouse.

The No 4 funnel deckhouse contained storage rooms and the turbine engine room casing leading into the dummy fourth funnel. After completing the deckhouse, several vent grilles and a few doors needed to be added to the deckhouse walls. These were all made from strip and rod. On the deckhouse roof two large ducts emerge from the forward end and lead into the funnel. They were made as boxes from styrene. The flanges which attached them to the funnel were made from L-beams.

Behind the deckhouse a flue lead from the open fireplace in the smoke room into the fourth funnel. The flue was made from a length of tube into which V-shaped slivers were cut where the tube needed to be bent to a 90° angle. This area was given a generous treatment with superglue at the bend while we had the tube secured to a board between nails keeping it in place and in the right shape. The foot of the flue was covered with an asbestos mantle. This

DECKHOUSES

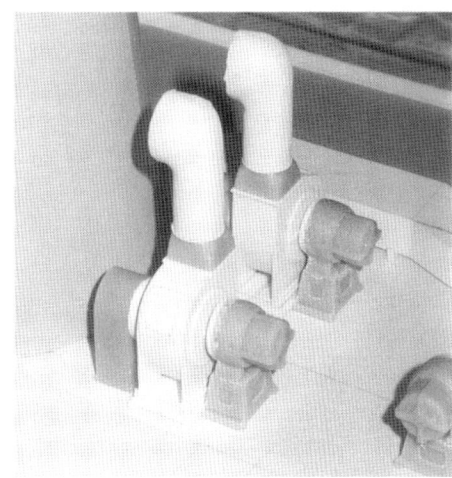

was added from thick rod into which the tube was inserted. The two brackets securing the flue to the deckhouse roof were cut out of thick styrene and attached to the tube. A large hole with the same diameter as the tube was drilled into the funnel and forward end of the tube inserted into the funnel and the aft end attached to the smoking room roof.

The windows in the deckhouse were frosted. We used 3mm (0.11in) Perspex which had been sanded with fine wet-and-dry sandpaper.

After polishing them with a soft cloth they were attached to the inside of the deckhouse with superglue.

Second Class Entrance Boat Deck

Surprisingly, it is still possible to make out this little deckhouse in footage of the wreck and pictures of the mangled stern, even though it

(Top left) The deckhouse nearing completion. These were the first railings that were attached to the model. As there were only two bends required on each side, they were fairly straightforward to construct. This gave us a little practice before having to fold the lounge roof railings or the railings at the aft end of the promenade deck.

(Above) Cowl vents and vent ducts ready for painting.

Port side view of No 4 funnel deckhouse.

121

DECKHOUSES

Second Class entrance.
(Scale: 1/192)
Key:
1. Stay bracket
   (as on forecastle deck).
2. Gibbs extractor vent.
3. Lightbox.
4. 'Mystery box'.

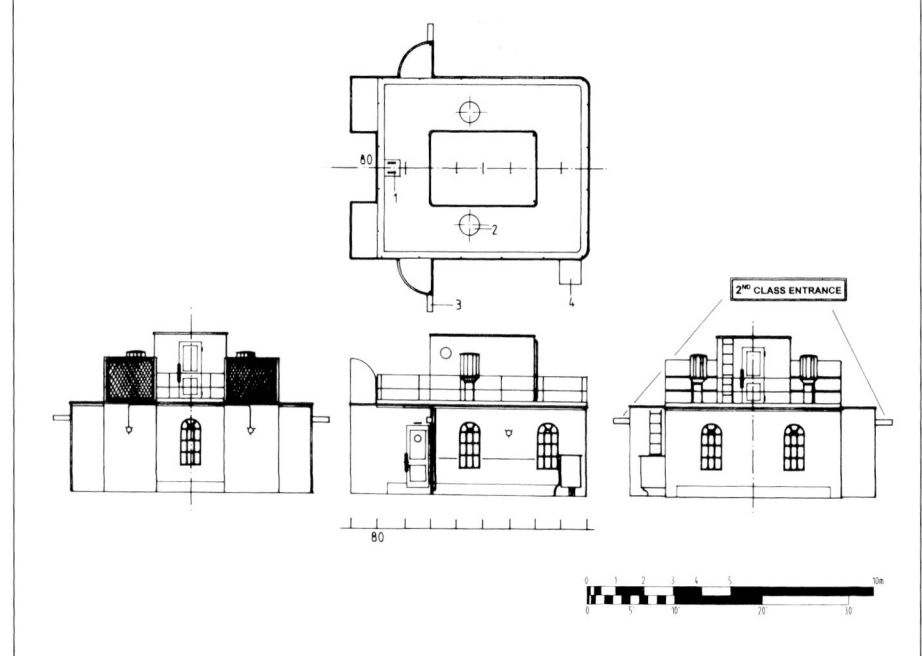

The Second Class entrance at a very early stage of construction.

Windows still have to be added. The bench between the shafts was removed later and placed on the starboard side of the smoking room roof. The openings of the shafts still have to be cut out. Later the mesh would be added to these.

was crushed by the fourth funnel when it toppled backwards and crashed onto it during the sinking.

This is also where we encounter the last unknown object to be discussed in this book, something *Olympic* did not have and about which there has also been much speculation: the little box mounted on the starboard side of the deckhouse. Nothing like this has been found anywhere else on any of the *Olympic* class. On the starboard side boat deck photograph, you can see an electrical wire leading into it, but that is the only indication we have with regard to its use. Thus its function was possibly electrical, but other than this its purpose is another complete mystery, and I have yet to hear a feasible suggestion regarding the use of this box.

The final deckhouse to be assembled was also built with styrene inner and outer plating, in one piece save for the two vents aft which were built as separate units and attached to the deckhouse later when they were completed. The windshields for the doors were added from styrene with a thin strip added to the outer edges.

The elevator shaft was also made in one piece and also with the inner plating at the bottom edge. Ladders were added as described in Chapter 5. It seems that there was no ladder attached to the port side windshield.

DECKHOUSES

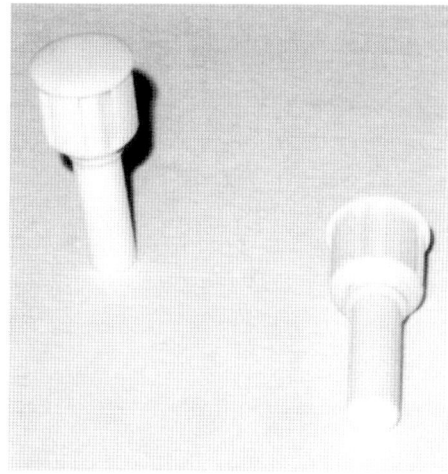

Two Gibbs extractor vents.

Second Class entrance looking aft. The 'mystery box' can be seen on the starboard side.

The nearly completed Second Class entrance.

The electrical wires leading to the bulkhead lamps and sign boxes were added from thin brass wire.

The Gibbs extractor vents were built on a plastic rod column to which a conically sanded disc was attached. In the centre of this disc a large square piece of strip was attached, large enough for the corners to mate evenly with the edge of the disc. Four small side pieces were cut out and attached to the disc edge, so that the corners of the square were central between each side piece. The cap was made from a disc of thick styrene and a slight camber sanded to the edges.

123

12 Funnels

The first four-funnelled liner was North German Lloyd's *Kaiser Wilhelm der Grosse* of 1897. This was followed by four other German liners and the Cunarders *Lusitania* and *Mauretania* (1907). The *Olympic* class liners did not actually need their fourth funnel; it was a dummy, added for the sake of appearance but as the flue of the First Class smoking room and the galley were led up through it, it did perform some function. There was also a ladder leading up to the top of it and it is reported that the coal-stained face of a stoker was seen at the top of the funnel while the ship was in Queenstown. Some considered this a bad omen.

Funnels

The funnels were all of different heights, the first being the lowest, the height then rising to the third, which was the highest, the fourth being slightly lower than the third. This was to improve the flow of smoke from them.

The funnels for the model were built by plank-on-frame construction. The frame was covered with a 5mm (0.19in) plywood skin which had grooves cut every 5mm (0.19in) to make the plywood flexible so it could be wrapped around the frame. The height of the plywood skin was left lower than the funnel so it would not be visible when looking into the completed funnel. This was then glued to the funnel with white glue and held in place with strong tape while the glue dried.

The shell plating of each funnel was made as a complete unit from a very large piece of styrene which would be wrapped around the funnel after riveting, forming a kind of 'sleeve'. This sheet too was left slightly higher than needed as the bottom edge was trimmed off after the 'sleeve' had been pushed over the funnel.

Rivets were punched into the sleeve as described in Chapter 4. We later calculated that some 8000 rivets were punched into each funnel. After riveting, a thin styrene strip was attached to one side on the inside of the outer

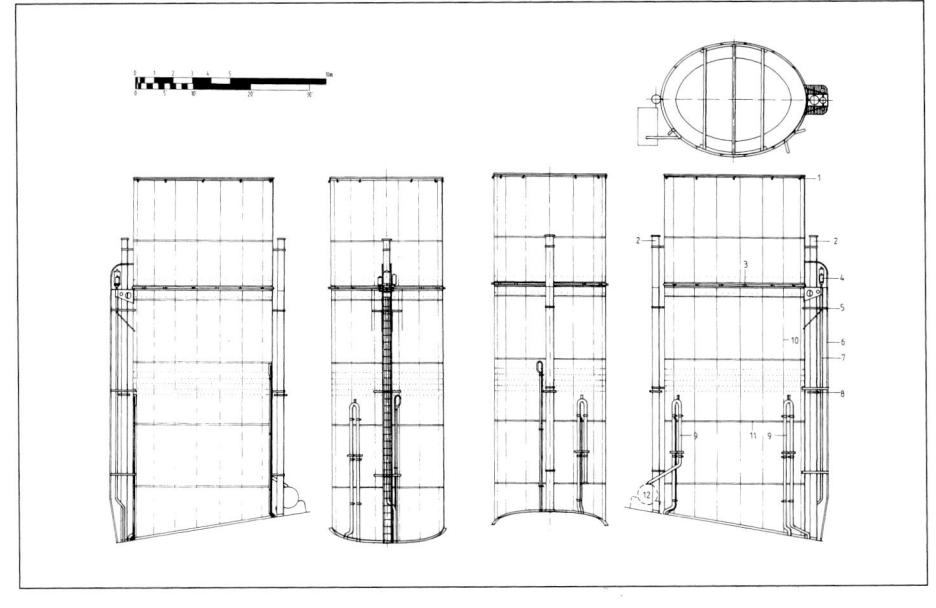

No 1 funnel.
(Scale: 1/384.)
Key (All funnels):
1. Painters' line block.
2. Steam exhaust pipe.
3. Guy wire bracket.
4. Whistle.
5. Whistle platform.
6. Ladder.
7. Whistle steam pipe.
8. Flange.
9. Water overflow pipe.
10. Vertical rivet line.
11. Horizontal rivet lines.
12. Water tank.
13. Air duct mount.
14. Smoking room fireplace flue mount.
15. Handrail.

FUNNELS

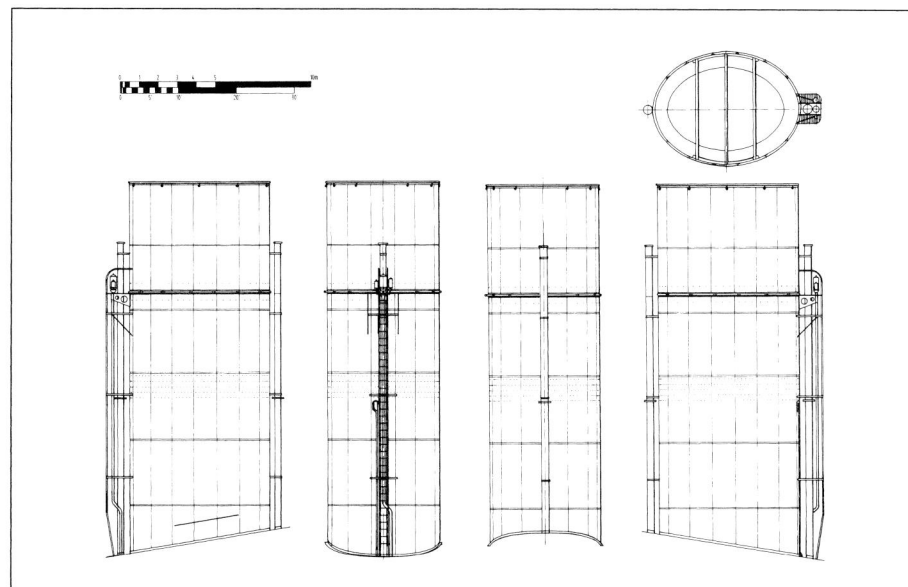

No 2 funnel.
(Scale: 1/384.)

skin. The other side was also cemented to this, which resulted in a sleeve which could be pushed over the funnel and remain in place without gluing. Bands of half-round styrene strip were added to the top rim and to the bottom edge of the black funnel tops.

On the real ship the funnels were attached to the superstructure with large L-beams at the foot. We simplified this a little on the model by cutting out a large oval which was approximately 4mm (0.15in) larger in diameter than the funnel itself. A thin strip was added upright to this to form the L-beam, when viewed from the outside. However, the angle of the funnel had to be taken into account. The simple solution was to roll the funnel over a large sheet, following the roll with a pencil along the bottom edge of the funnel. This gave a wavy line and a second line was drawn 2mm (0.07in) above the first line. The strip was then cut out

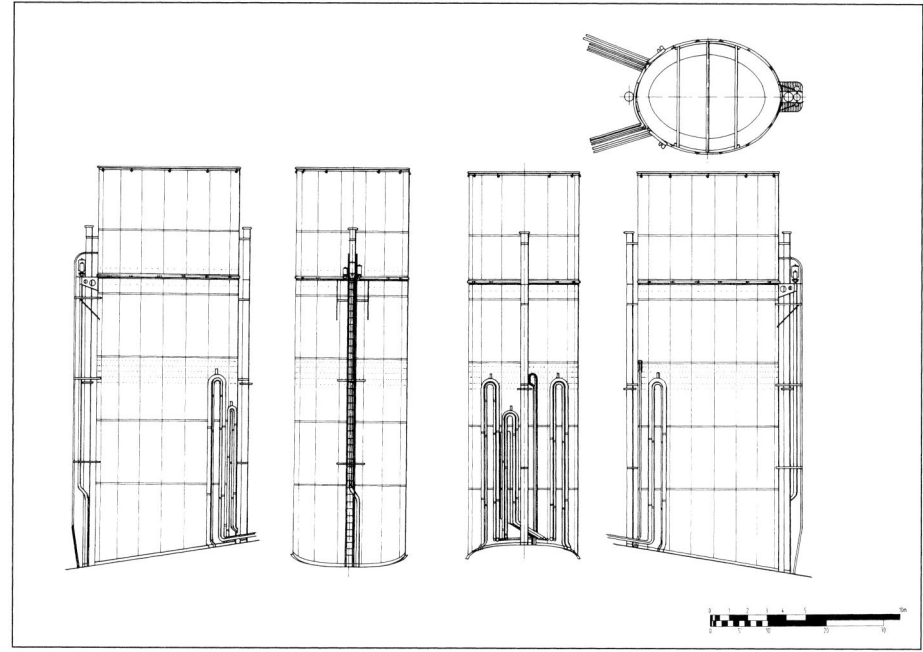

No 3 funnel.
(Scale: 1/384.)

125

FUNNELS

No 4 funnel.
(Scale: 1/384.)

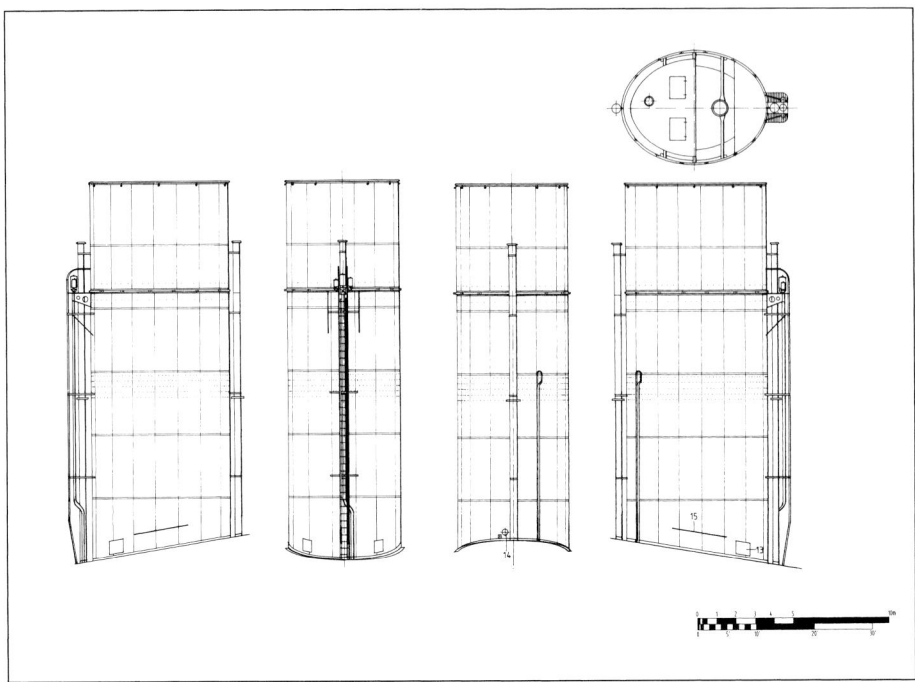

Olympic's funnels being repainted after her first arrival in New York in June 1911. The rivet pattern can be seen in this picture. *Titanic* did not have the eyelets that were attached to the sides of *Olympic's* funnels.
(Photograph: Brown Brothers)

and cemented to the oval, 2mm (0.07in) inside the outer edge. When viewed from the side the angle of the upright flange had the same angle as the funnels. The finished oval was painted satin black and the funnel attached to it, giving us a perfect L-beam at the bottom edge of the funnel.

Because of the plank-on-frame system adopted, the funnels were not hollow tubes as on the real ship. The top frame was approximately 25mm (1in) lower than the bottom band and was clearly visible when looking into the unfinished funnel from above. To avoid too much of the interior being seen, it was completely painted a sooty matt black. The inner sleeve was then added which was an oval plate, approximately 25mm (1in) less in diameter than the funnel to which a sleeve was cemented, which ended about 25mm (1in) lower in height than the top rim of the funnel. This too was painted sooty matt black and cemented to the top of the frame. Three H-girders were attached inside the top rim of the funnel by first gluing two L-beams to the inside edge and then attaching the girders to them.

Steam pipes

These were made from aluminium tube and thick brass rod. The brackets were cut out of thick styrene after drilling in the hole for the tubes. The master whistle was made from different materials such as wood, brass rod and styrene. I planned to cast the whistles for the model, but the resin castings turned out to be extremely delicate, and many of them broke while I was removing them from the rubber mould. The solution was to drop thin steel rods

FUNNELS

Also taken in June 1911 after *Olympic*'s arrival in New York. The funnel rigging can be seen to advantage in this image.
(Photograph: Brown Brothers)

(Far left) The outer skin of No 1 funnel. For all funnels the outer skin was made of one large sheet of styrene, which was wrapped around the funnel after riveting was completed. On the real ships this outer skin consisted of 15 vertical strakes of six steel plates all of equal width, though the height of the plates varied on each funnel, due to the different heights of the funnels.

(Left) The funnels for the model were also made as a plank-on-frame structure. This picture shows the interior with one side of the inner skin already attached. This inner skin was made of plywood into which grooves were cut to make the plywood flexible, so it could be wrapped around the plank-on-frame structure.

into the mould before the resin had set. These rods were inside the thinnest part of the whistle, where it is attached to the mounting bracket, and gave the cast items enormous strength.

Platforms and ladders

The platform gratings were built up the same way as I described the anchor well grating in Chapter 7. Handrails were added from rod, formed over steam using a Perspex jig.

The funnel ladders were built up in a long wooden jig as described in Chapter 5. These long ladders were very flimsy, but proved to

FUNNELS

Olympic's fourth funnel being moved out of the shed in preparation for moving it to the outfitting wharf where the funnel would be lifted onto the ship. The fourth funnel on the Olympic class liners was a dummy.
(Photograph: Harland & Wolff – Claes Göran Wetterholm collection)

Olympic in 1913. This photograph was taken from the top of No 4 funnel. The water overflow pipes behind No 3 funnel were slightly different on *Titanic* to the way they were on *Olympic*.
(Photograph: Günter Bäbler)

The outer skin of No 1 funnel wrapped around the wooden structure.

The steam pipes were made from aluminium and brass rods. Here they are seen prior to painting.

be pretty strong after they had been attached to the funnel.

Water pipes

The funnel water pipes were all bent from thick brass rod. Small slices of styrene tube were pushed over them, to which small pieces of strip were attached to the rear as the mounting brackets. These were cemented to the funnels when the pipes were being attached.

The water pipes behind No 3 funnel leading to the tank room proved to be very tricky. No 3 funnel was placed on a table and the outline of the tank room drawn on the table. This served as a kind of jig for bending the rods. The pipes were all made in one piece, and in some cases several attempts were required before I got a satisfactory result.

Painters' lines pulleys

The painters' lines were ropes fed around a pulley at the top rim of the funnels. Though there were five pulleys at the top edge on each side, it appears that only two lines on each side were attached at any one time.

The pulleys were made from a styrene disc with a short piece of rod folded over it and both ends cemented to the axis. These were attached to the funnel top rims with small eyelets bent from thin steel wire.

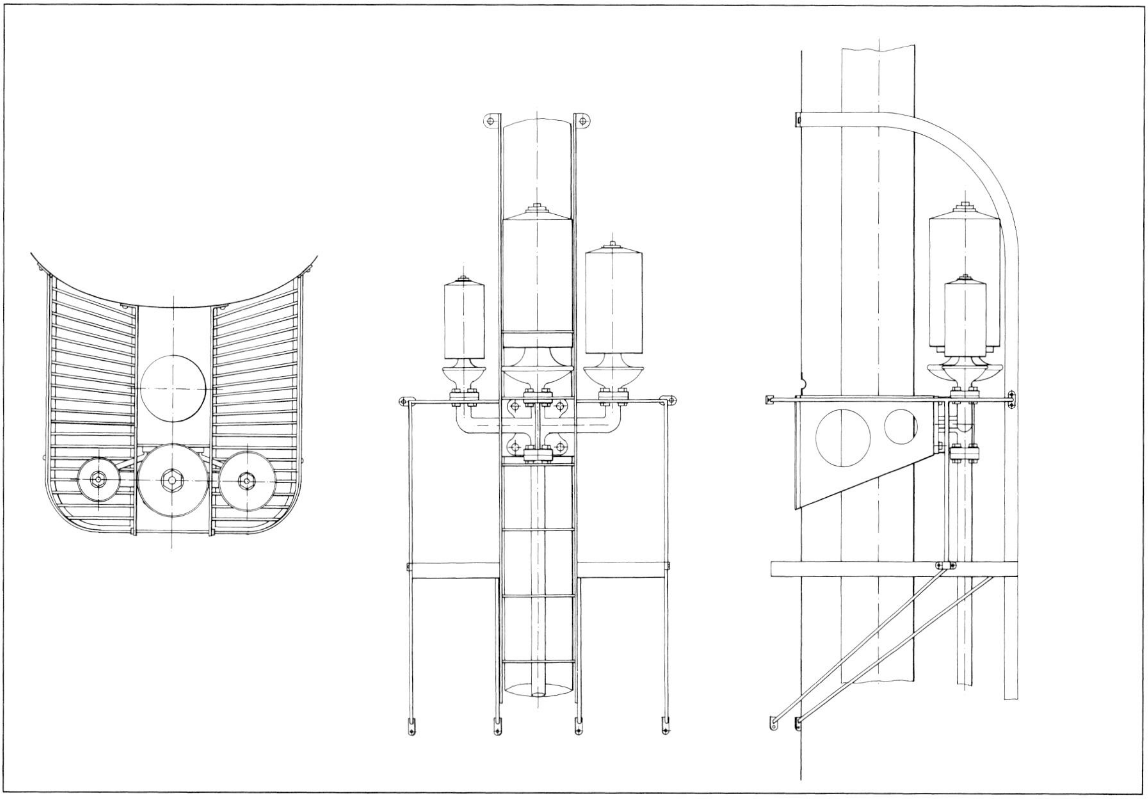

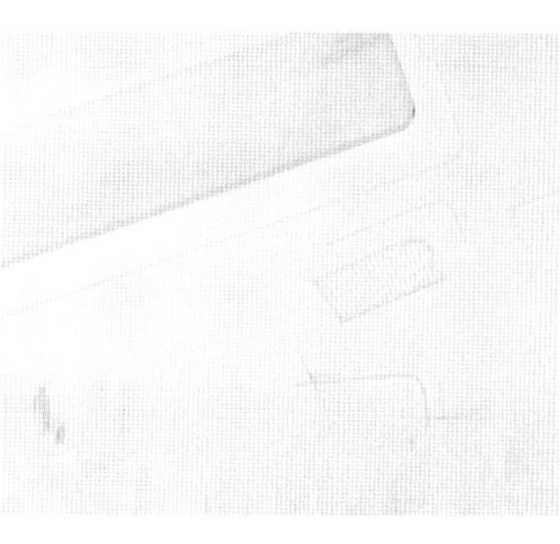

FUNNELS

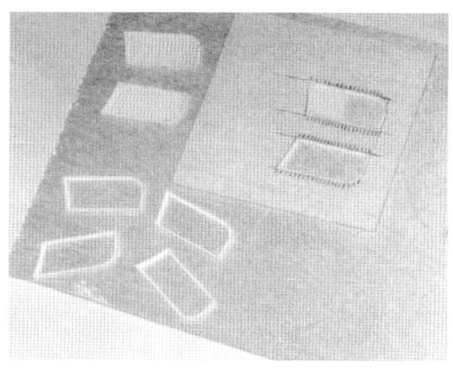

Whistle platform.
(Scale: 1/48.)

(Far left) The gratings for the platforms were made in a wooden jig.

(Far left) The platform handrails were formed to shape over boiling water using a perspex jig.

The platforms completely assembled and ready for painting.

129

FUNNELS

(Below) The complicated overflow pipes behind No 3 funnel were bent from thick brass rod. As a guide the outline of the tankroom, onto which the aft ends of the pipes were mounted was drawn on the workbench.

Funnel stay brackets

These were the last items added to the funnels. They were also eyelets bent from steel wire and inserted into small holes drilled into the bottom funnel band; six on each side. They were secured with superglue to ensure that they would withhold the strain of the guy-wires and were painted satin black.

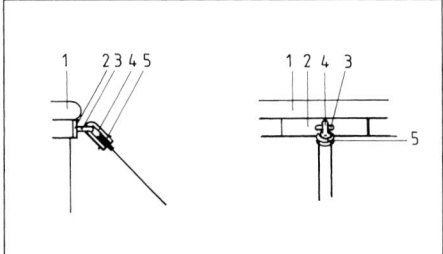

Painters' line block. (No scale.)
Key:
1. Funnel top band.
2. Block bedplate.
3. Bedplate eye.
4. Shackle.
5. Block roller.

(Right) One of the completed platforms.

(Below) Guywire deck bracket. (No scale.)
Key:
1. Seizing on guy wire.
2. Gammon lashing.
3. Guy wire deck bracket.

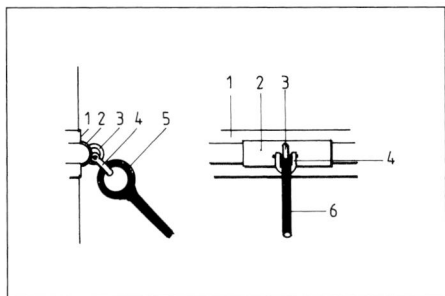

(Above) Guy wire funnel bracket. (No scale.)
Key:
1. Funnel band.
2. Guy wire bedplate.
3. Bedplate eye.
4. Shackle.
5. Guy wire eye.
6. Seizing on guywire.

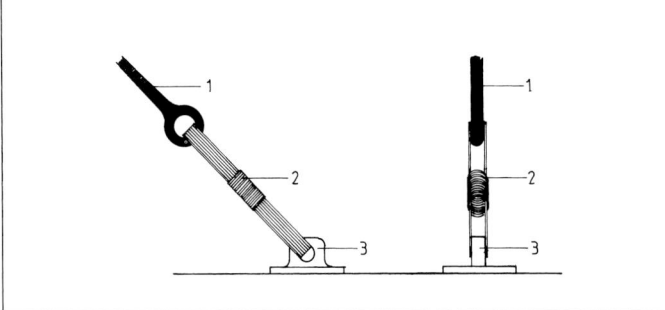

13 Lifeboats and Davits

Titanic had fourteen 30ft lifeboats, two 25ft emergency cutters and four 27.5ft Engelhardt collapsible boats. Eight 30ft boats were placed in the Second Class deck space aft while four were in the First Class area. Two 30ft boats, the two emergency cutters and the four Engelhardts were in deck space allotted to officers and crew only. There were no lifeboats in the Third Class area.

The 1912 Board of Trade rules for the number of lifeboats on an ocean liner were remarkably out of date, not having been revised in 18 years. The Board of Trade grouped passenger ships by tonnage without any reference to the actual number of people on board the vessel. The upper limit of their classification was for a liner of 10,000 tons. Titanic, however, had a gross tonnage of 46,000 tons, nearly five times that limit. According to the Board of Trade rules, Titanic only had to have 16 lifeboats. With 20 lifeboats aboard, the White Star Line had actually exceeded the number of boats required. Nevertheless, she was permitted to sail with accommodation for 3320 people but with a lifeboat capacity for only 1178. Titanic left Queenstown in Ireland bound for New York with 2200 people on board, so half of them could have been saved but only 705 survived the sinking. Many passengers were reluctant to leave the sinking ship and the first boats lowered were more than half empty. In fact boat No 1 was lowered with only 12 people on board. Seven of them were crewmembers.

The boats were numbered 1–16 with even numbers on the port side boat deck. The collapsibles were lettered, with A on the starboard side officers' quarters roof, B on the port side officers' quarters roof, C on the starboard side boat deck and D on the port side boat deck.

When the ship arrived in Southampton on 4 April 1912, the boats were all swung in. This

All that remained of the world's finest ship: Titanic's lifeboats in New York. The two boats in the foreground are 30ft lifeboats, the two boats behind them are the 25ft emergency cutters. The foremost boat has the bow facing to the right, while the boat behind it has the bow facing to the left. Both were from the starboard side. In my original print, I can see that most of the nameplates and the burgees have already been removed. The number 13 can be seen on the second boat. The third boat (Boat No 2) has the bow facing to the right while the fourth (Boat No 1) has it facing to the left.

(Photograph: Brown Brothers)

131

LIFEBOATS AND DAVITS

30ft lifeboat
(boats No 3–16).
(Scale:1/96).
1. Lifeboat nameplate.
2. White Star Line burgee.
3. Specification plaque.
4. Railings.
5. Boat chocks.
6. Gripe.

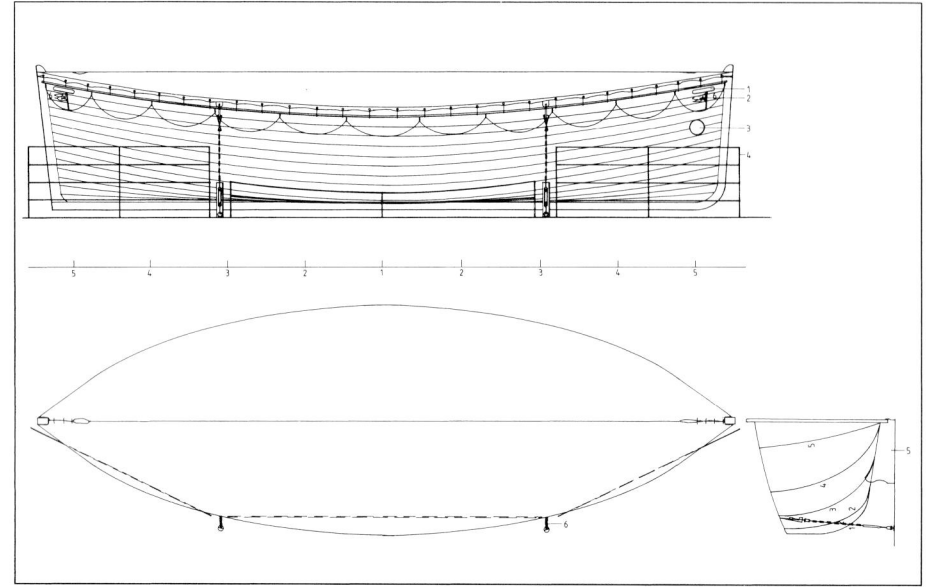

(Below) The completed master lifeboat. This was mounted inverted on a wooden board and a box built around it to produce the silicon rubber mould for casting resin lifeboats.

(Right) At top the master lifeboat; at centre one resin cast boat removed from the mould and at front the silicon rubber mould with a cast boat still inside.

means they were stored on deck with the outer edges of the boats flush with the sides of the promenade deck. After leaving Southampton for New York, via Cherbourg and Queenstown, the stowage of the boats was altered. By the time she reached the Isle of Wight the two emergency cutters (boats 1 and 2) were already swung out and lashed against the hull side. The aft groups of 30ft boats on the starboard side were also swung out, which means that the keels of the boats were flush with the promenade deck sides. When *Titanic* reached Cherbourg, the aft group of boats on the portside were also swung out. This was apparently to give the passengers more promenade deck space.

30ft Lifeboats

Modelmakers building smaller models can heat-mould lifeboats. Small boats can be carved in one piece from wood and when finished a wooden dowel is attached to the top of the boat as a handle. The outline of the boat is drawn on a plywood board and this is cut out. Thin styrene is attached to the board with drawing pins and heated in an oven at about 220° C. After about 30 seconds I remove the heated styrene from the oven and push the master boat into the soft styrene through the hole cut into the board. The boat is then removed from the backing sheet. On larger heat-moulded boats I usually add the keel and the stems from strip.

The master 30ft lifeboat for the Orlando model was built as a solid block, inverted on a board. First I made cardboard templates of the frames and used them to transfer the frames to hardwood blocks of the same thickness as the distance between each frame in the plans. This was very much like building a bread-and-butter hull, the only difference being that we were working with vertical laminates rather than horizontal. Once the frames had all been drawn onto the wooden blocks they were sawn out with a belt saw and a small slot cut into the bottom and the stem and stern to accommodate the styrene keel. Then the blocks were glued together with white glue and after the assembly had dried the boat was sanded smooth. The 30ft lifeboats were planked with 15 planks on each side. To calculate the position of each plank, thin strips of paper were placed on the boat and we marked the top edge of the gunwale and the position of the keel on these strips. The space between the two markings was divided into 15 segments, resulting in the edge of each plank and this was then marked on the boat accordingly by transferring them, using the markings on the paper strips as guides. Due to the shape of the boat the paper strips at the centre were longer than those at the stems but as each was divided by 15, this gave us the strake of each plank on the boat.

The keel was cut out of 1mm (0.03in) styrene including a tongue with which the keel would be inserted into the slot cut into the boat's bottom and stem and stern. Two further keels of the same thickness were cut out without this slot and were glued to each side of the centre keel. This gave us the step which would hold the plank ends in position. After attaching the keel to the boat planking could begin. The lifeboats were clinker planked, *ie* the plank edges overlapped each other like on the hull of a Viking ship.

As on the real boat, planking began alongside the keel and proceeded upwards. For the planking we used styrene strips. A half-round strip was attached to the bottom edge of the gunwale, *ie* the fifteenth plank, and stiffeners added to the extreme ends of the top edge of the gunwale connecting the stem and sternpost.

After completion of the master boat a wooden box was built around it and a mould

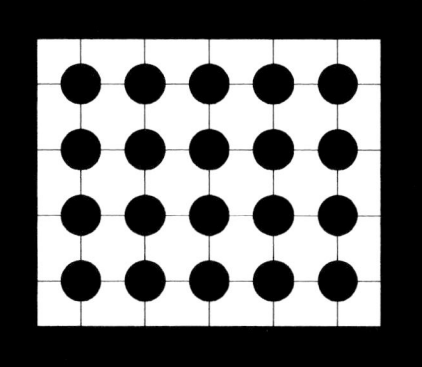

(Above) Lifeboat nameplate. (Scale 1/5) The plates with the name of the ship were attached to the outboard facing side of each lifeboat, well out of reach of souvenir-hunters. The signs bearing the name of the home port 'Liverpool' were attached to the inboard facing side as these were less popular souvenirs.
(Drawing: Ebru Baykal)

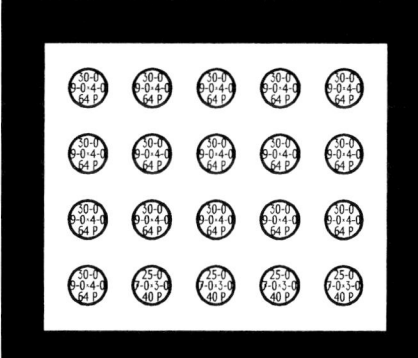

(Left) The drawings for photoetching the specification plaques. Surplus plaques were made in case some were not painted satisfactorily or got lost. The plaques in the bottom row, apart from the one on the left, are for the 25ft cutters.
(Drawing: Ebru Baykal)

(Below) Photoetched nameplates, specification plaques and White Star Line burgees were attached to the lifeboats.

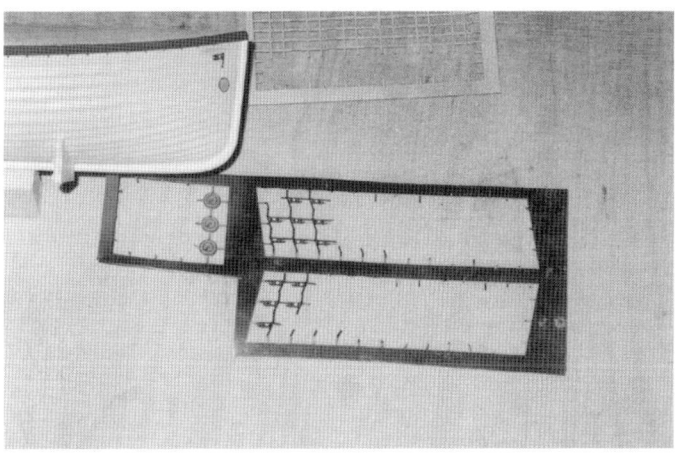

LIFEBOATS AND DAVITS

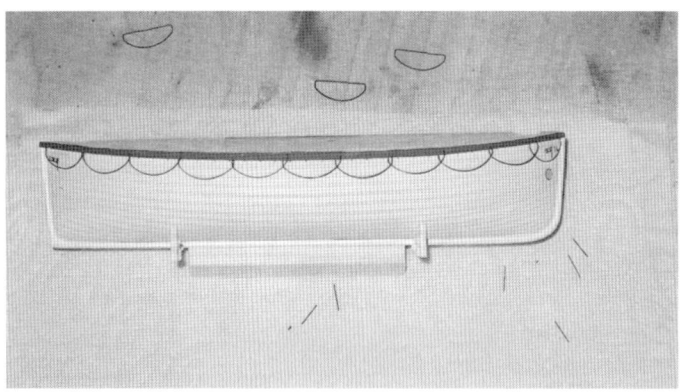

The ropes were made from stretched sprue. Some of these can be seen on the workbench above the boat prior to attaching them to the boat. Excessive material still needs to be removed from these. At first only one end of these ropes was attached to the boat, as can be seen in this photograph. After one end of all ropes for one side were attached; the other end was cemented to the neighbouring rope.

made from silicon rubber. This was used to cast all fourteen 30ft lifeboats. When we removed the cast boats from the mould the top was flat. Excess material was trimmed with a belt saw, taking the inverted 'V' section of the boats into account and the top surface sanded with a smooth disc sander.

Lifeboat nameplates

The only way to produce these to scale, with the letters standing proud of the plates proper, was by photo-etching. The photo-etching process will not be described here as I did not do this myself and it is described in other publications. I asked a friend who studies architecture to draw the items that were to be photo-etched life-size on a computer and to print them out in 1:48 scale. For each item two drawings were required, one with the letters and the second with the backing plates. These had to mate up perfectly when the two drawings were placed on top of each other. For the lifeboats the nameplates, specification plates and the White Star Line burgee were drawn. The lifeboat numbers were attached using decals. The drawings were then sent to a company that does photo-etching, and the returned frets were superb. The name 'S.S. *Titanic*' and the homeport 'Liverpool' are still perfectly legible even in 1:48 scale. These were painted in the appropriate colours while still attached to the frets, then cut from the fret and mounted to the lifeboats after painting.

The nameplates with 'S.S. *Titanic*' were mounted to the boats' side facing outwards (out of reach of the passengers – souvenir hunters were at large even in 1912!). The nameplates with the ship's homeport 'Liverpool' were mounted on the inward-facing side as these were less likely to disappear. In addition each boat had a specification plaque giving the dimensions of the boat and the number of people it was meant to carry. Four White Star Line burgees were attached to each boat, two each at the stern and bow. The numbers were also attached to both sides at the bow and stern.

None of these plates, plaques and numbers were attached to the collapsibles.

Lifeboat lines

The lines attached underneath the gunwales of the 30ft boats were formed from dark brown sprue stretched over boiling water with a wooden dowel that was sanded oval on one side and flat on the other. After trimming the flat side off, the lines were attached to the boat but on one end only until all the lines on one side had been attached. We then glued the other end of the lines to the gunwale, securing

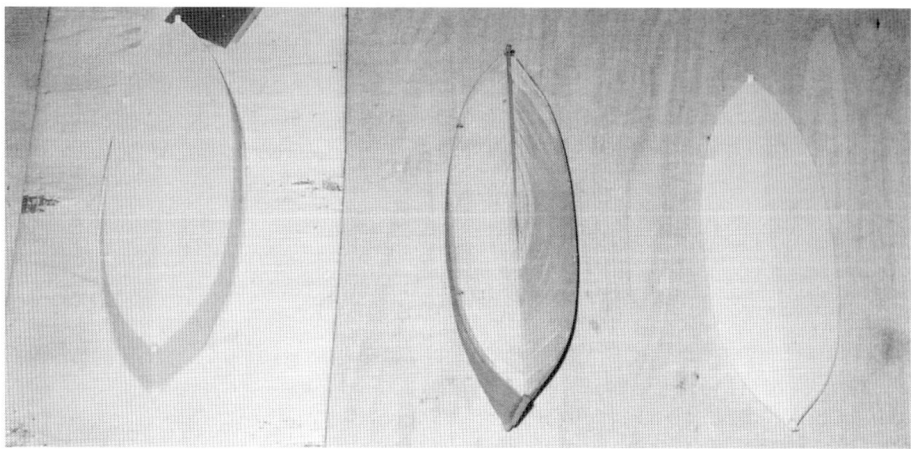

The lifeboat covers were heat-moulded from sheet styrene using a resin cast boat as a former (centre).

it to the already fixed end of the neighbouring line. The 25ft cutters and the collapsibles did not have these lines.

Lifeboat covers

Apart from the two emergency cutters, the lifeboats were all covered with canvas. This canvas cover was heat-moulded thin styrene which was painted off-white like the cargo hatch covers. For heat-moulding the covers, we used a resin-cast lifeboat as a former which had the rounded tops of the stem and the stern post attached from wood as these could not be cast with the resin boats in one piece. We also attached two small wood semi-ovals to one side of this boat to give an impression of the chain clamps securing the boats to the deck and also the stem and stern post underneath the boat cover. The covers were painted in a dirty off-white before they were cut from the backing sheet.

At first we planned to sew these covers to the boats as in reality, but we then realised that it was impossible to produce the small hooks to the bottom edge of the gunwale even in 1:48 scale. Before the canvas covers could be attached, large holes were drilled into the forward and aft end of each boat from the topside to give access for the tackles. Two squares were cut out of each cover in the same area as the holes drilled into the boats also for the tackles. These cut-outs were the same size as the triple blocks that would be pushed into them when boats were being tackled. We used a square hole opened up in a spare cover as a template for this to ensure that all openings were in the same position on each boat cover. The covers were then secured to the boats with strong double-sided tape. Small holes were drilled into the boat side underneath the gunwale and in the side of the cover above. Heat-stretched hemp-coloured sprue was then heated to a 'U' shape, and the ends of these were then pushed into the small holes to give the appearance of lines holding the cover down.

Boat chocks

Each of the 30ft lifeboats rested on two chocks which were secured to the decks. Steel clamps were attached to the outer edge of these chocks into which the boat keel was inserted to prevent the boat from slipping off the chock. To allow free movement of the boat when being lowered, the upper half of the chocks was hinged to fold down.

A master chock was made for each end of the boat as these too were handed. Small steel wire hooks were added to one side; the hinges on the opposite side were made of styrene strip and rod. The chocks for the model were all cast in resin and glued to the bottom of the boats. Unfortunately the joint was not very strong, and while working with the boats some of them came off. As the model would have to survive transportation to the United States, the joint would definitely need to be stronger. Once the chocks were glued to the boat with superglue, small holes were drilled through the bottom of the chocks and into the boat's hull. Steel rods were then pushed into these holes, into the boats giving the joint adequate strength. It probably would have been better to cast the chocks and the boats in one piece.

25ft Cutters

These boats were carried without covers so they could be lowered as quickly as possible in the event of an emergency. Therefore, the interior of these boats had to be included, and

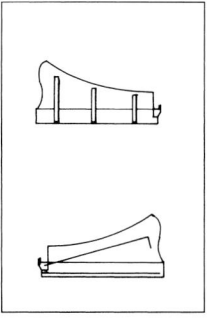

(Above) Boat chock. (Scale: 1/48.)

The boat chocks were cast as individual items. However, after they were glued to the boats the joints were very weak. Small holes were drilled through the chocks into the boats and steel rods inserted into these holes to give the joint extra strength. If I were to build another model like this, I would cast the boats with the chocks in one piece.

LIFEBOATS AND DAVITS

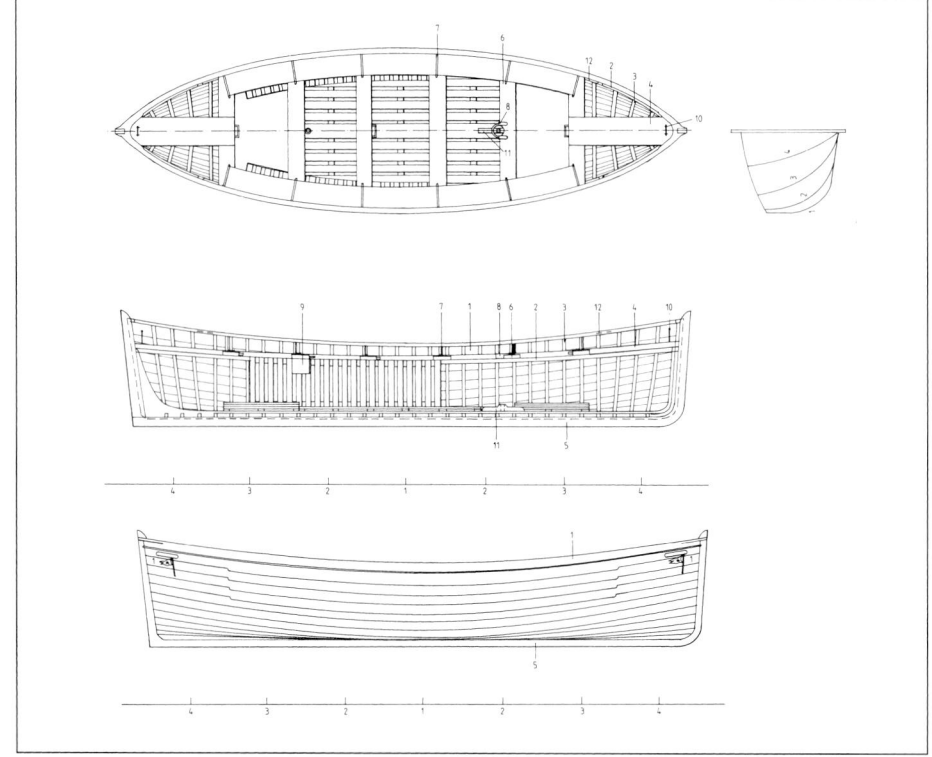

25ft emergency cutter (boats No 1 and 2). (Scale: 1/96.)
1. Gunwale.
2. Stringer.
3. Frame.
4. Gangplank.
5. Keel.
6. Thwart.
7. Iron knee.
8. Mast bracket.
9. Biscuit box.
10. Fall bracket.
11. Mast step.
12. Rigging clamp.

they also had to be as lightweight as possible as they would be hanging from the styrene davits on the finished model.

The master boat was made as described above. To produce the boat shells or hull halves we initially tried vac-forming them, but the results were not satisfactory as we never got really sharp edges for the hull planks. I then tried casting thin hull halves from resin. A silicon rubber mould was made for the outside of each hull half. First the master boat was cut in two halves along the keel. Each half was then mounted on a wooden board and a box built around it and silicon rubber moulds made for the hull halves. After the mould had cured the master was removed and a thin sheet of styrene placed on top of the mould and heated. Once the styrene was soft it was

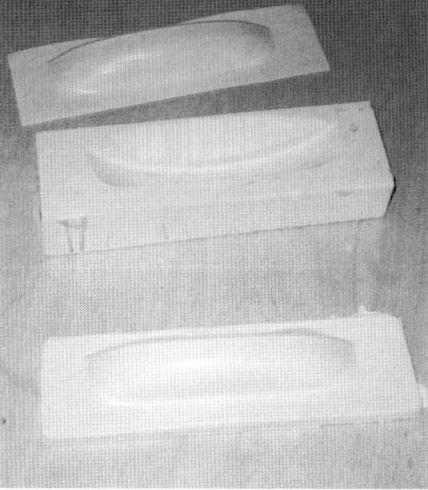

(Right) Silicon rubber moulds for casting the hull shells of the 25ft cutters. At the top is the piece of sheet styrene that was placed over the mould for the shell's outer side (the female mould, at centre), heated and pressed into the mould to give the required thickness of the shell half. Silicon rubber was then poured onto this to give us the mould for the shell's inner side (the male mould), which can be seen at the bottom.

(Far right) One resin-cast half-shell of a cutter.

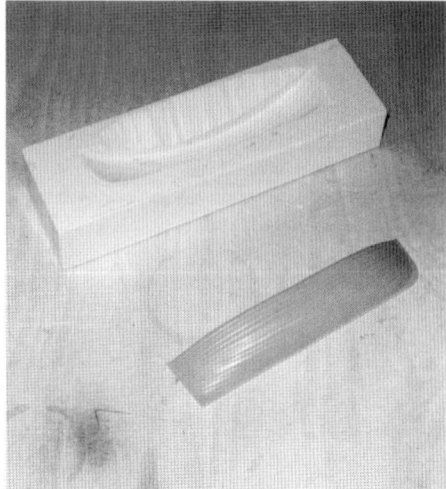

LIFEBOATS AND DAVITS

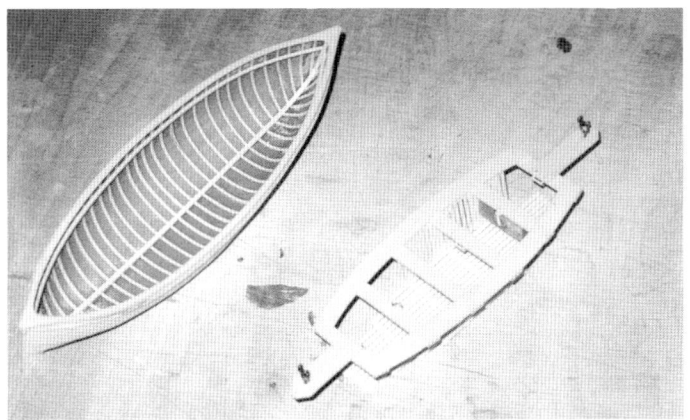
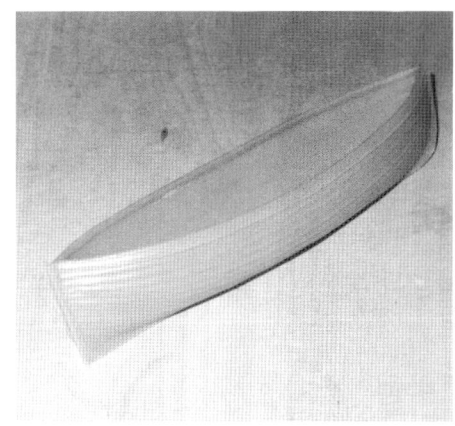

(Above) The hull of a 25ft emergency cutter.

(Top left) The frames have been added to the inside of the hull shell and the boats interior (at right) is completed and ready for painting.

pressed into the mould of the hull half and left to cool. A box was then built around this assembly and a second silicon rubber mould poured on top of this. After the second mould had cured, both moulds were separated. This gave us a two-part mould for a very thin lifeboat hull half, the thickness of the styrene giving us the thickness of the cast hull. The mould for the outside of the hull was placed on a bench with the open end facing upwards and resin was liberally painted on the hull half, making sure no air was trapped inside the resin. Before the resin cured the mould for the boats' inner side was placed on top of it, pushing out excess resin in the process. It worked perfectly. After about an hour the hull halves could be removed from the moulds. They were extremely lightweight and so thin that when held against a light one could see the light shining through. Some flash needed to be removed and the two halves were cemented to each other. The frames were all added to the boat interior, and when they had all been attached the false keel was added to the boat floor and stringers to the sides.

The rest of the interior was made as a separate unit and attached to the inside of the boat when completed and painted. The bottom boards were made from strip on a paper template. The side boards were made separately and attached to the bottom boards after completion. As these side boards only covered the aft section of the boats, they were handed, so two sets of reversed side boards were needed for each boat.

The thwarts were made from 2mm (0.07in) styrene and these were cemented onto the side thwarts. Small biscuit boxes were made from styrene and attached to the bottom of the second aft thwart. The mast step was added to the keelson and this area cut out of the floorboards to allow the step to pass them while the interior was being attached. The mast ring-

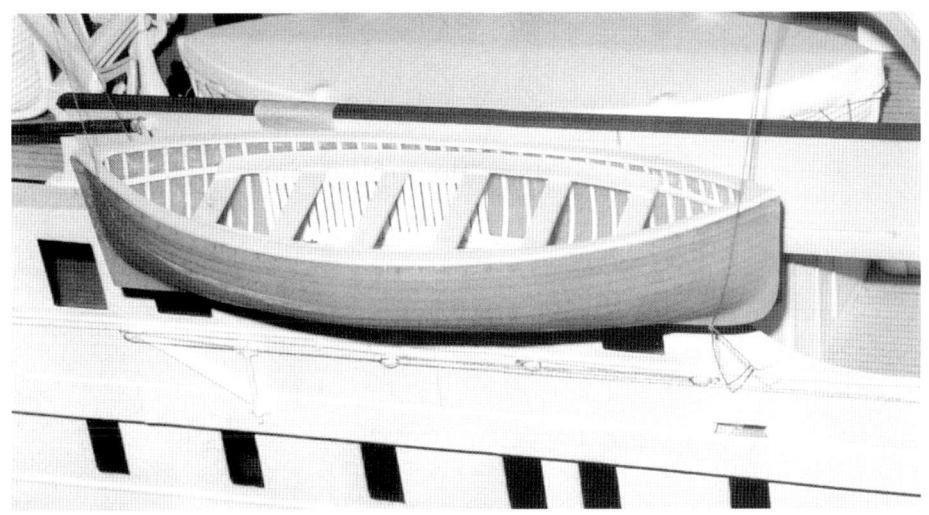

Here the interior is installed into Boat No 1.

LIFEBOATS AND DAVITS

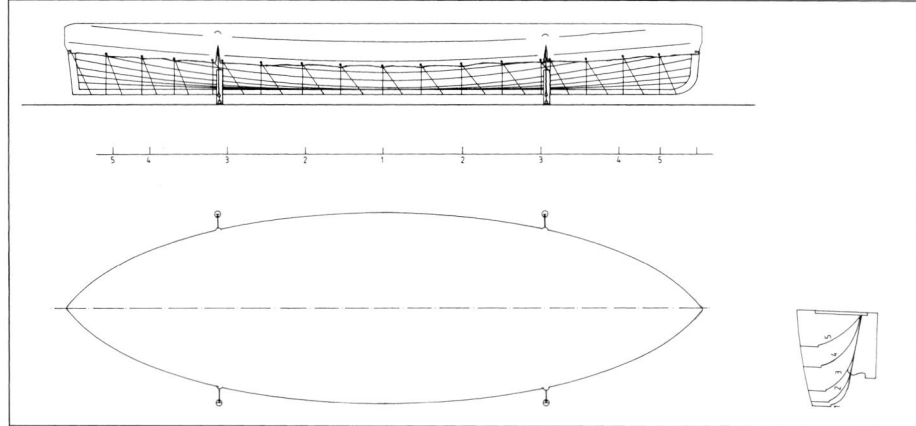

27.5ft Engelhardt collapsible boat. (Scale: 1/96.)

bolts were added from rod and sprue. The floor- and side boards were then cemented to the thwarts and two falls shackles made from brass wire. These were inserted into holes drilled into the gang planks connecting the thwarts to the stem and stern. The interior of the open cutters was painted Humbrol mid-stone.

27.5ft Engelhardt Collapsibles

As these also had canvas covers, there was no need to add the interior to these boats. The master collapsible was made as described above, as was the canvas cover. On these, however, the covers were sewn onto the boats. Small holes were drilled into the bottom edge of each cover and these were reinforced with small eyelets from sprue formed over boiling water. The eyelets were attached to the cover with liquid poly. A long piece of rigging thread was tied to one of the aft-most eyelets and the cover was then attached to the boat with double-sided tape. The thread was then slung underneath the hull and threaded through the adjacent hole on the opposite side. It was then threaded through the neighbouring hole and slung underneath the hull again to the next eyelet. This was continued until the complete cover was tied down. It took me about four hours to sew each cover to each collapsible.

Blocks and Tackle

The emergency cutters were tackled with double blocks and the 30ft boats with triple blocks. The blocks were made of small styrene ovals and discs as the wheels. These were cemented to each other and the gaps at the top and bottom filled with small pieces of scrap styrene. After the cement had dried the block was filed and sanded to shape. Silicon rubber moulds were made and the blocks required cast in resin. Two holes were drilled into each end and bent steel wire inserted into these holes as the eyes.

It was clear from the beginning that the styrene davits would not withstand the boats being rigged with the tackles attached to the davits and the boats. Instead a wooden frame was built in which the blocks were tackled. After rigging was complete the lines were painted with matt varnish so that they would remain straight when removing them from the frame.

The Davits

The davits were all made individually from sheet styrene as they were too thin to cast in

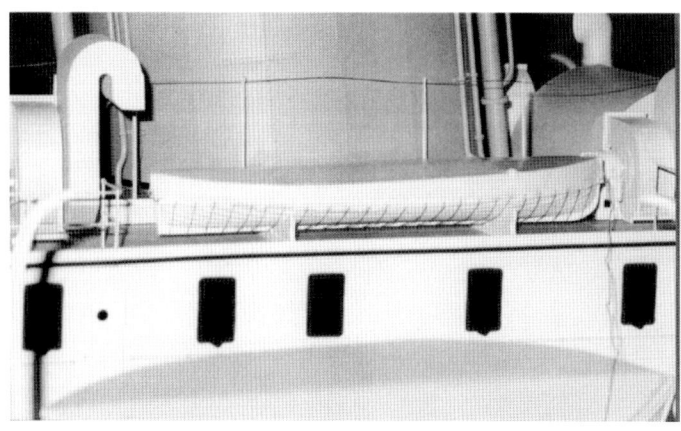

The canvas cover sewn on Collapsible 'A'.

LIFEBOATS AND DAVITS

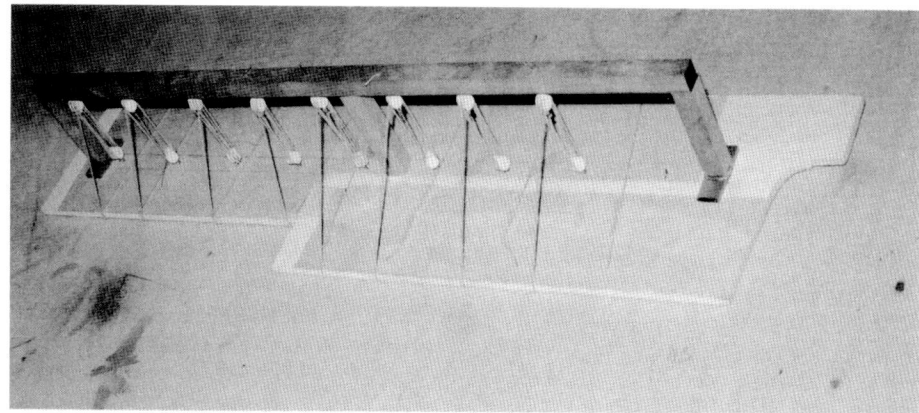

(Left) The falls were rigged in a jig as the styrene davits would not take the strain on rigging the falls *in situ*. After the falls were completed the lines were painted carefully with matt varnish to ensure that they remained in shape and that the lines would not slacken.

(Below) Welin double-acting davit with two arms. This type of davit was located behind boats No 1–6 and 9–14. (Scale: 1/96.)

resin. We started with the bedplate which had an outline of an elongated 'H'. Two further plates were attached at the ends of the bottom of the bedplate. These would be cemented to the deck when the davits were installed. The centreplate was then cemented to the bedplate and the end pieces added. Apart from this being an enormous amount of work, one of the difficulties lay in the tooth-gear at the bottom of the davit arms and the bedplate. A large strip of tooth-gear was made from styrene strip in two different sizes, continuously placed next to each other and once this had dried thin slices were cut off this strip and attached to the bedplates and the davit arms. Wheels and rods were added from styrene and also the operating lever which was also made from rod.

The davit arms were constructed in three pieces: the centrepiece and the two flanges on each side. A master was cut out of styrene and this was used as a template to draw the davit arms onto the styrene. After completing the davit arms, strengthening ribs were added with thin strip. Holes were then drilled into the top of the arm for the shackles. After the davits had all been assembled and painted, they were cemented to the deck. Shackles were bent in brass wire and the blocks and tackles attached to the davits. After completing the lifeboat railings the lifeboats were also cemented to the deck. The boat falls were then guided around the davit wheels and the bitts and fed into the lifeboats through the same openings that housed the blocks. The lower

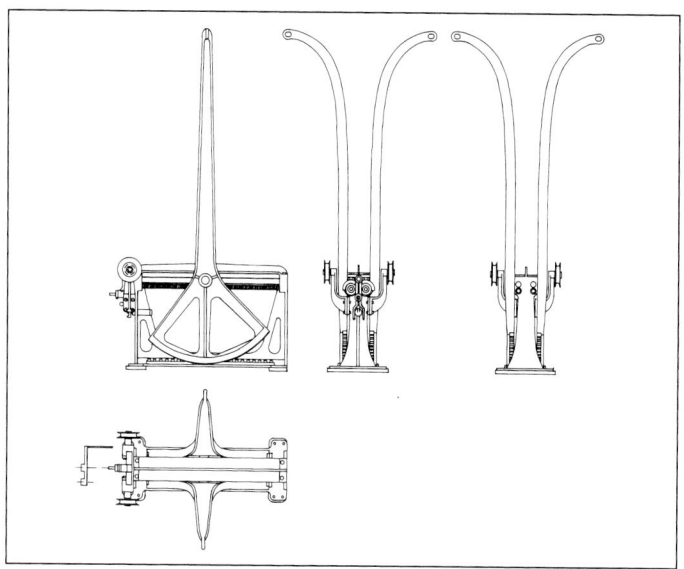

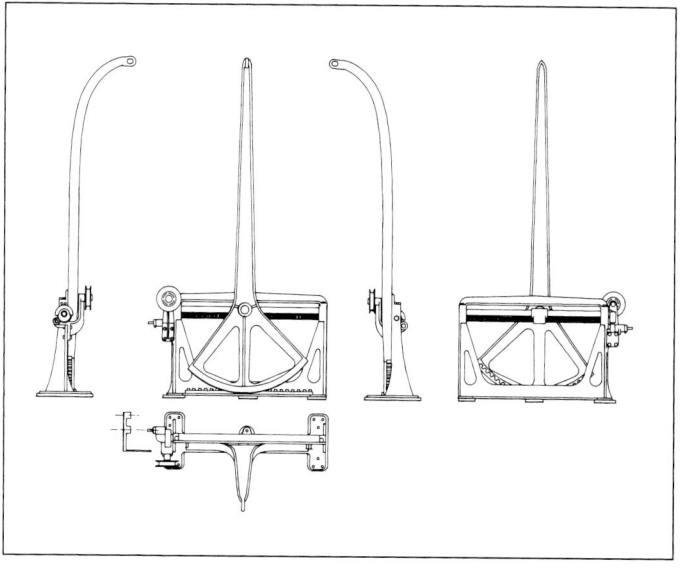

(Right) Welin double-acting davit with one arm. This type of davit was located behind boats No 7 and 15, as well as in front of boats No 2 and 10. (Scale: 1/96.)

139

LIFEBOATS AND DAVITS

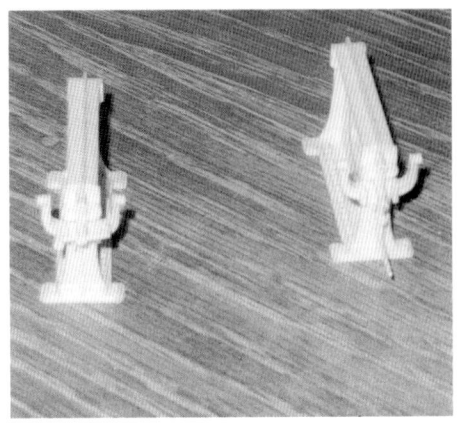

(Above) The lifeboat davits were all built up individually. In the back row the single-arm davits are in preparation.

(Above right and below) Davits with the operating crank in the stored position (left) and with the crank in operation (right).

(Right) Detailed view of the davit working gear.
(*Engineering* – Günter Bäbler collection)

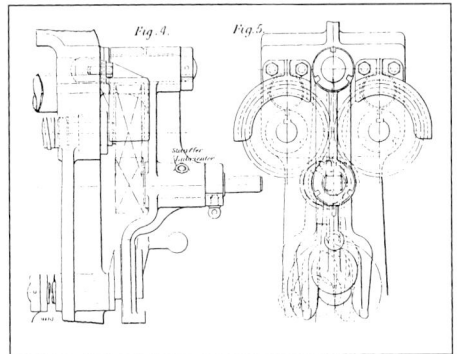

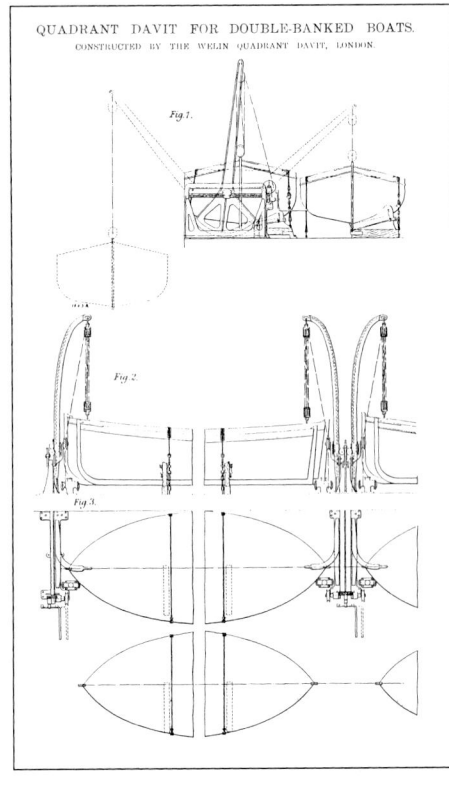

blocks were then secured to the boats with thin wire attached to the bottom eye. This wire was then fed into small holes that had been drilled into the lifeboats. The line between the davit arms was added from grey sprue.

This was the initial idea: two boats could be handled by each pair of davits, but on *Titanic* only one boat for each pair was installed, save for the collapsibles. (*Engineering* – Günter Bäbler collection)

LIFEBOATS AND DAVITS

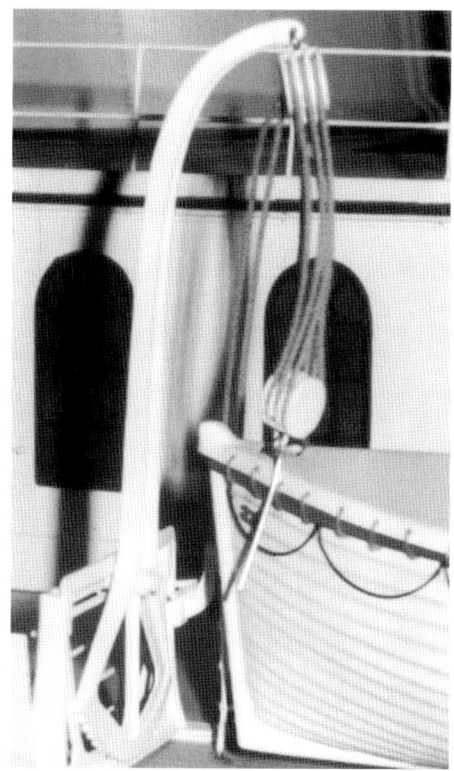
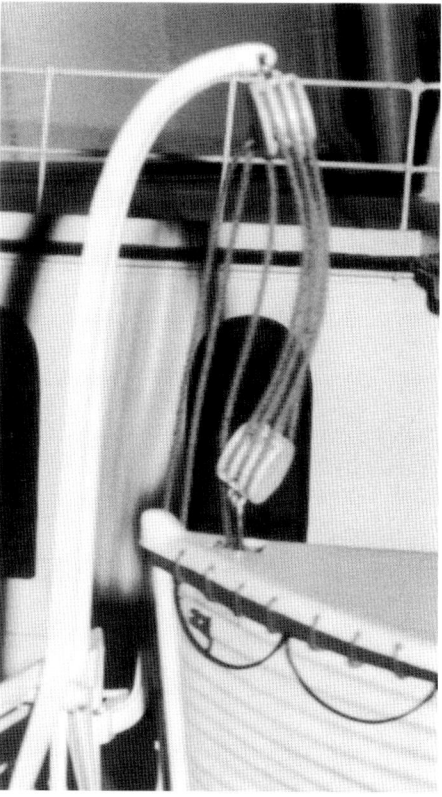

Attaching the lower block to a lifeboat. A short piece of brass rod was attached to each lower block. This was then inserted into a pre-drilled hole into each boat.

(Below) The rope for the falls of boat No 1 stored on deck behind the bulwark.

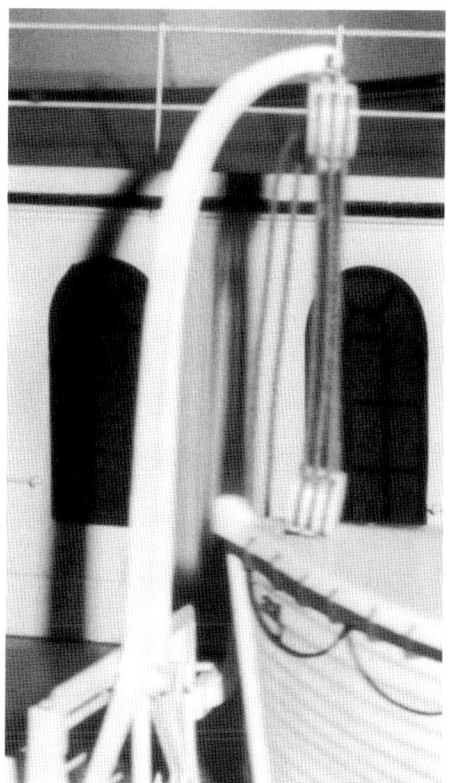

(Left) The block in place and the tackle lines taut.

141

14 Masts, Rigging and Flags

(Far right) Foremast.
(Scale: 1/384.)

(Right) Mainmast.
(Scale: 1/384.)
Key (both masts):
1. Electric lamp.
2. Docking lamp.
3. 15in dia. bell.
4. 25in dia. bell.
5. Double iron block.
6. Teak pole mast top.

Masts

The masts of the *Olympic* class liners were made of steel and were hollow inside. There was a ladder inside the foremast to give the watch access to the crow's-nest. The mast tops were teak poles, 15ft long. The Marconi aerials were attached between the masts.

The masts for the model were turned from boxwood. This was done very slowly to prevent them from breaking as they were very thin at the tops. Masts for smaller models can be made from wood by attaching wooden rods to a hand drill and holding them to a disc sander, pressing the rotating rod slightly to the rotating disc with a wooden block.

After the masts were turned the mast plates were attached using very thin sheet styrene. Each plate was rounded over a wooden dowel before attaching them to the masts. The masts consisted of three vertical strakes, each strake covering one third of the circumference with the overlaps in plan view being at 10, 2 and 6 o'clock when viewed from above with the bow facing upwards. Above the second highest mast-band up to the wooden mast-pole the masts consisted of two strakes covering half the circumference with the overlaps being at 9 and 3 o'clock.

A large hole was drilled into the forward mast behind the crow's-nest. After the mast plating had been completed the opening was cut out of the plating. Two steel grips were

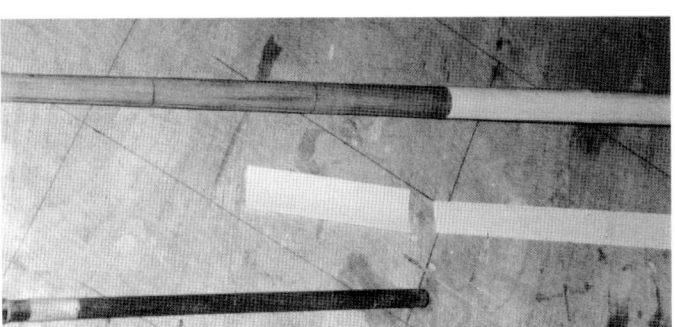

Plating the mainmast. A wooden dowel (bottom) was used to form the styrene plates before attaching them to the masts.

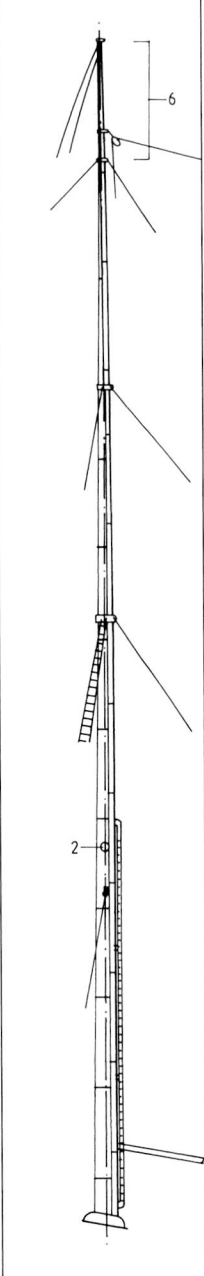

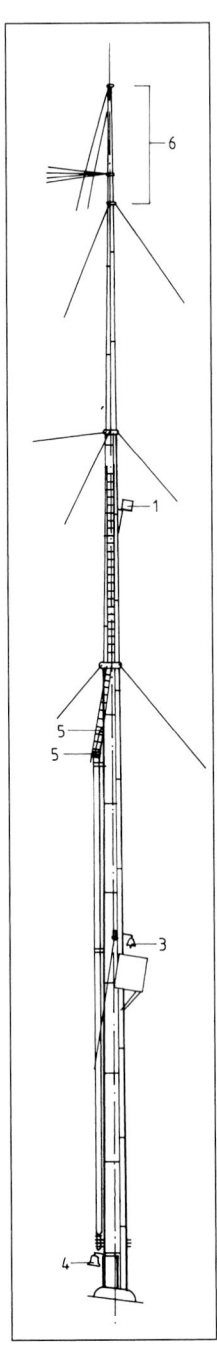

MASTS, RIGGING AND FLAGS

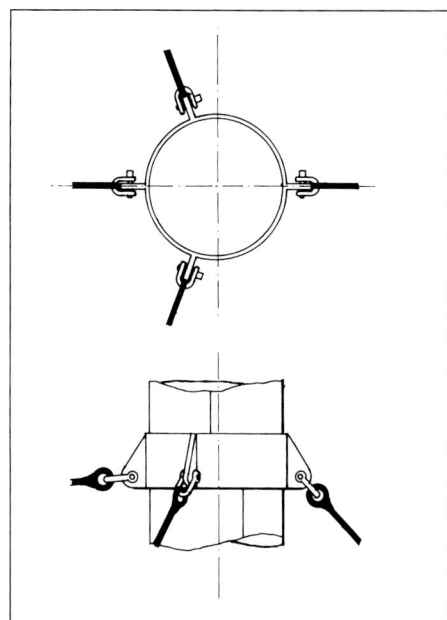

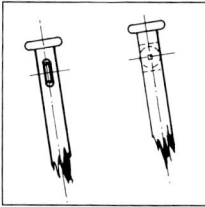

Mast head. (Scale: 1/48.)

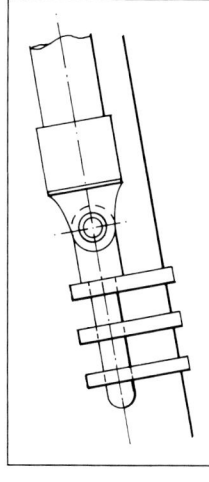

Derrick mount. (Scale: 1/24.)

Mastband. (This drawing applies to all mastbands, even though the number of stays and shrouds altered; the attachment was the same.)(No scale.)

added from styrene rod. Mast bands and eyeplates were added from styrene strip and also various eyelets heat-formed from rod. The mast tops or caps were added from small wooden discs filed and sanded to shape. Once completed the masts were painted in Humbrol Natural Wood.

The derrick was also made from a wooden rod with bands made from styrene and slings formed from steel wire. The crow's-nest was made from sheet styrene with awning struts of brass wire. Two brass telephone boxes were added to the rear wall and a grating covered the floor. For the mast light glazing we used clear tubes, that come with paintbrushes to protect

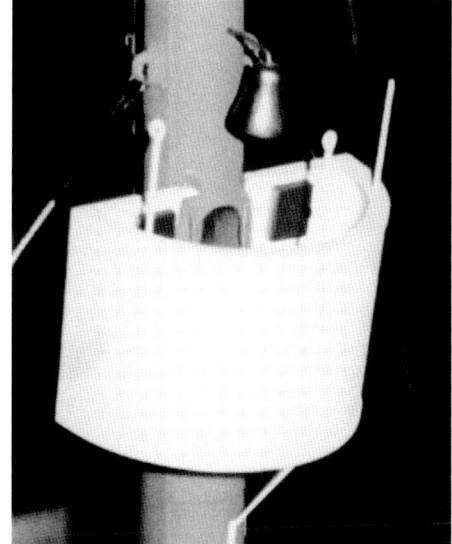

The most famous bell in maritime history. According to the Harland & Wolff rigging plan this was a 15in diameter bell. The bell raised from the ocean floor does not match any of the dimensions of bells given in the *Titanic* rigging plan. Two telephone boxes were added to the rear wall of the crow's-nest.

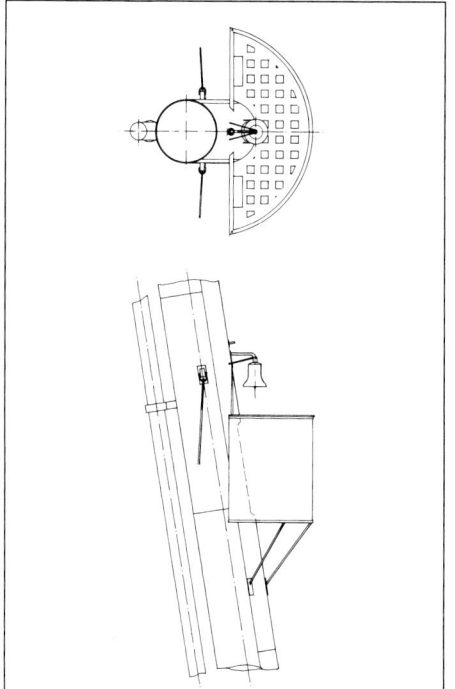

(Above) The fully-plated foremast. Note the cut-out to give the watch access to the crow's-nest.

(Left) Crow's-nest. (Scale: 1/96.)

MASTS, RIGGING AND FLAGS

(Right) Electric lamp. (Scale: 1/12.)

(Far right) Docking lamp. (Scale: 1/48.)

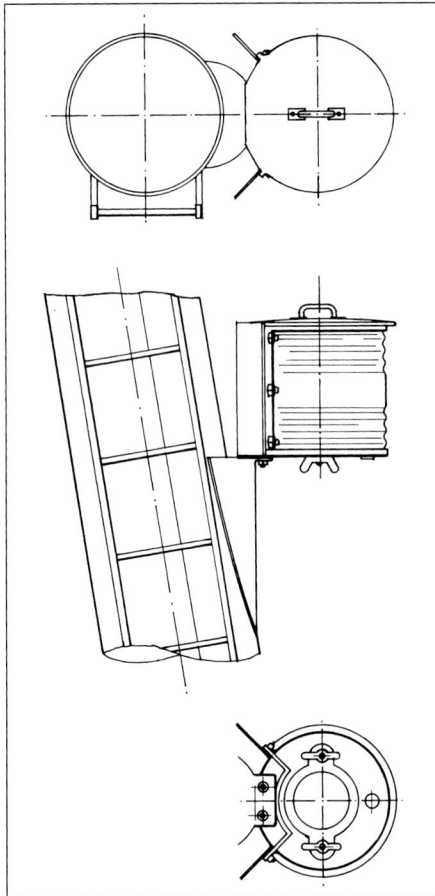

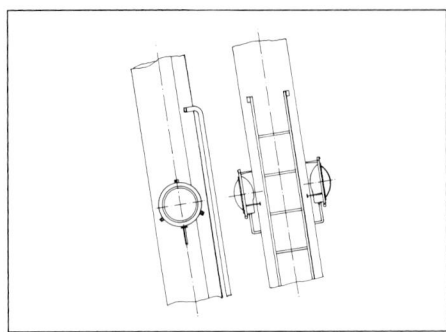

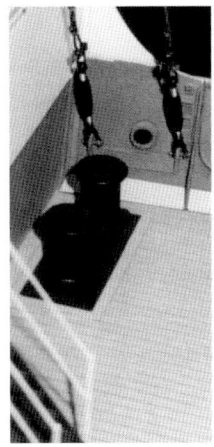

Turnbuckles attaching the starboard-side foremast shrouds to the forward well deck bulwark.

the brushes. The bells were heat-moulded, the formers made from wooden dowels filed to shape in a drill.

Rigging

Stainless-steel thread with memory was used for most of the rigging. The gauges were taken from the Harland & Wolff rigging plan. After the lines were cut to the correct lengths small eyes were formed at one end by bending the line at approximately 7mm (0.27in) beneath the end and then forming a round turn. This was then kept in the required shape using a sharpened clothes peg, holding the end parallel to the line and the seizing made from very thin rigging thread was wrapped around it. The seizing was treated with superglue and after it had dried the clothes peg was removed. The eye and seizing was then painted black, held approximately 2.54cm (1in) from the eye.

After all lines received one eye at one end they were attached to the masts with small shackles bent from thin steel wire. The masts could now be attached and were inserted into their openings in the decks, slotting them into mast-steps which were attached before the upper decks were installed.

All stays were attached to the decks or the inside of the bulwarks with turnbuckles. We used turnbuckles 6mm (0.23in) long, intended for radio-controlled First World War aircraft rigging wires. Shackles needed to be added to each end of the turnbuckles and these were formed from brass wire and each assembly was then painted satin black.

We attached the turnbuckles to their brackets with short pieces of thick brass wire as thimbles, by inserting the wire into a shackle eye, then though the eyeplate on the bulwark or deck and then through the other shackle eye. This was secured with superglue. At this stage the thimble on the other end of the turnbuckle was added as well and all remaining brass parts were painted satin black.

Now was the time to attach the stays to the turnbuckles. This was basically the same method as described above. The turnbuckle was adjusted to its extreme length and the end of the stay bent around the top thimble forming the eye. This was again held to shape using a clothes peg and the seizing added and painted as described above. The upper thimble was then removed from the turnbuckle and the stay attached by inserting the thimble into one shackle eye, then through the eye of the stay and finally through the other shackle eye. Because the turnbuckle was adjusted to its extreme length the stay was rather loose, but by readjusting the turnbuckle to its shortest length, the stays tightened accordingly. All stays were then tightened making sure that the masts remained straight while doing so.

MASTS, RIGGING AND FLAGS

The shrouds

A cardboard template was made onto which the ratlines were drawn. This template was then attached to the inside of the shrouds with tape. Using the drawn ratlines as guides, thin steel rods were then attached to the shrouds with superglue. The length of each line was taken by holding the rod against the shrouds and marking the required length. After completion liquid superglue was run along the outer edge of each shroud, touching the ratlines to ensure a rock-solid joint. After the glue had dried the complete shrouds were overpainted with matt varnish.

Marconi antennae

The Marconi antennae was rigged on a table and installed on the model after it was completed. First the spreader bars were made from thin wooden rods which were tapered towards the ends. These were also painted Humbrol Natural Wood. Four holes were drilled into the rods through which the aerials were fed.

Three long nails were then partially driven into the workbench, for each mast top, in a triangular shape, the extreme outer nails serving as the mast tops, the two inner nails acting as supports for the spreader bars while the antennae was being rigged. Two lengths of black rigging thread were then needed for each spreader bar. These threads had a small steel eyelet attached to one end. The other end was fed into a hole in the spreader bar and then into the adjacent hole on the opposite side. To this end another steel eyelet was attached and the spreader bar mounted to the nails on the workbench, the tightness of the lines slung around the outer nails holding the bars into place.

Four thin steel threads for the Marconi antennae were cut to the required lengths and eyes formed at the ends as described above. These eyes were then tied to the steel eyelets of the forward spreader bar using gammon lashings. First a thin piece of black rigging thread was tied to one eye of the steel thread. This was fed through the steel eyelet and then past through the steel's eye. This was repeated about nine times for each aerial, keeping the distance between the spreader bar and the aerial at about 1.5cm (0.58in). The ends were then seized around the gammoning and secured with matt varnish.

Belaying bar on the model with one rope-coil attached.

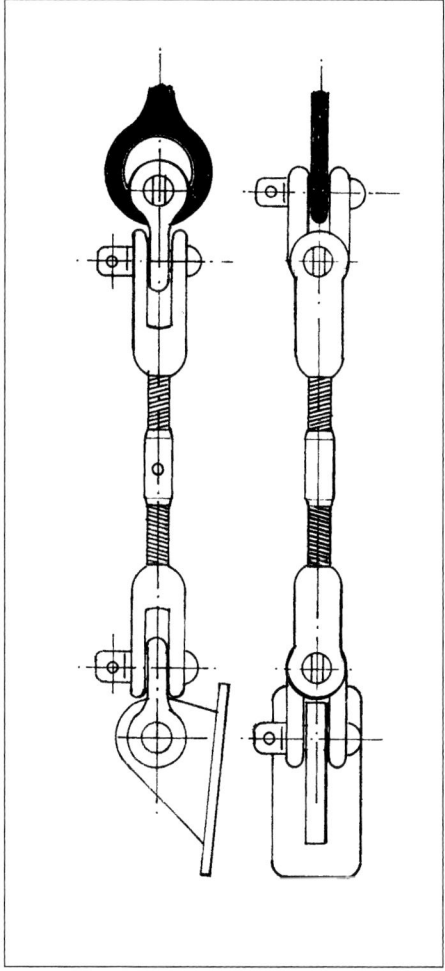

Turnbuckle; stay or shroud to deck or bulwark mount. (Scale: 1/12.)

145

MASTS, RIGGING AND FLAGS

(Right) Belaying bar.
(Scale: 1/48.)

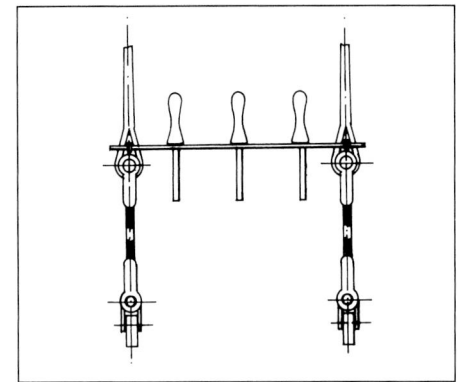

(Below) Making rope coils using a wooden jig. Rigging thread is lashed around two toothpicks attached to a square wooden strip. Once completed the coil is painted slightly with matt varnish, removed from the jig and the ends cut off. The coils were then placed onto the belaying bar

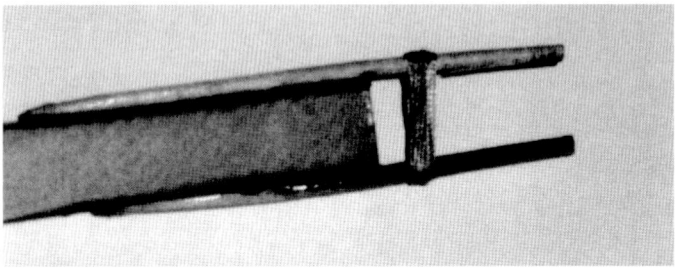

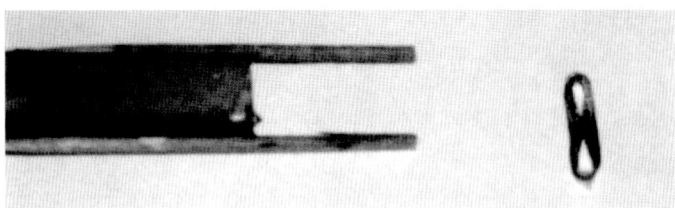

The aerials did not cover the complete distance between the masts. The aft quarter, filling the gap, was normal rigging line. For this too, we used dark brown rigging thread which was also gammoned to the aerial wires and the rear spreader bar eyelets. A block was attached the rear mast top through which the aerial fall was fed, the fall being attached to the starboard belaying bar at the foot of the shrouds in the aft welldeck.

The ends of the aerials were attached to the mast heads with small steel eyelets. Four lines leading down from the aerials to the aerial trunk were attached and these too were seized together at the bottom end. Two of these lines passed through the seizing and were fed into the aerial trunk. Each end of the spreader bars received a stay made from thin thread which was attached to the belaying bar at the foot of the shrouds.

The belaying bar was made from brass wire bent to shape forming four holes for four belaying pins. The extreme length of each bar was approximately 7mm (0.27in) wider than the shrouds at each end, to which the bars would be attached. One end was bent to a U-shape so one of the shrouds could slot into it; after attaching the bar, the other end was bent around the opposite shroud, thus attaching the belaying bars to the shrouds. We used 7mm (0.27in) brass belaying pins that we purchased from a mail-order shop. The flag falls were also attached to these belaying bars.

To reproduce the rope coils wrapped around the belaying pins, two toothpicks were attached to a square wooden strip as a jig for the rope coils. Rigging thread was then wrapped around the ends of these toothpicks several times and this was secured with matt varnish. After this had dried the coil was removed from the jig and after the ends were cut off the coil was attached to the belaying pin, one for each line attached to the pins.

Funnel guy wires

These were basically the same as the stays. Eyes were formed at each end of the lines, seized and painted black. They were attached to the funnels with small shackles bent from thin steel wire, the bottom ends gammoned to the guy-wire brackets with thin black rigging thread. The thread for the gammoning was first tied to the bottom eye and then passed through the opening in the bracket and then back through the eye. This was also repeated nine times for each stay and the ends then seized. We tightened the stays in turns: first the aftmost pair, then the foremost. After that the second aftmost pair, and then the second foremost etc, taking care not to mis-align the funnels.

Painters' lines were added, two on each side of each funnel, fed around the blocks on the funnel tops and lashed around the funnel stays slightly above deck-level. For the painters' lines we used hemp-coloured rigging thread.

Flags

On British merchant ships, in 1912, the flag of the nation to which the ship was ultimately bound was raised at the foremast when the voyage began. The flag remained at the mast irrespective of how many countries were called at while the ship was on her way. On

MASTS, RIGGING AND FLAGS

Titanic the Star Spangled Banner of 1912 with 46 stars was at the foremast.

Before the final destination was reached, the flag of the nation from which the ship sailed was raised at the foremast which would have been the Union Jack on *Titanic*.

The White Star Line house flag was flown on the rear mast, a red sparrow-tailed pennant with a white five-pointed star in its centre.

On the flagstaff at the stern was the Blue Ensign, a flag of the Royal Naval Reserve as Captain E. J. Smith was in the Royal Naval Reserve.

It is of course impossible to produce cloth to 1:48th scale or even smaller. I paint the flags on tin foil with acrylic paint, applying the paint in several coats crosswise. The acrylic paint allows the flag to be slightly bent to the required shape while the flag is being attached. On all flags the white paint was applied first, larger than the flag proper. Once several layers had been applied, the flag outline and contours of the remaining colours were carefully drawn on the white painted area witha sharp pencil on my drawing table. Then the other colours were applied, also crosswise and also in several layers.

The flags are made slightly longer at the side where the line is to be attached. This is so I can bend the tin foil at this side over the fall and secure it with contact cement.

The lines for the nation flag and the White Star Line burgee were attached to belaying pins at the foot of the shrouds.

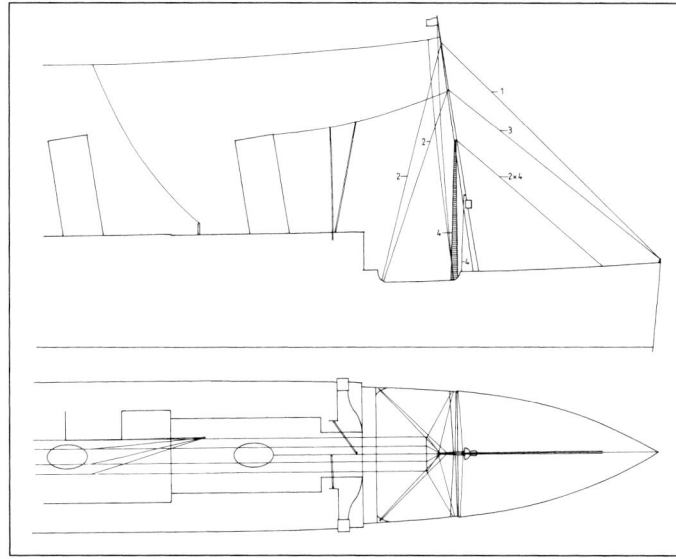

(Above) Foremast rigging diagram. (No scale.)

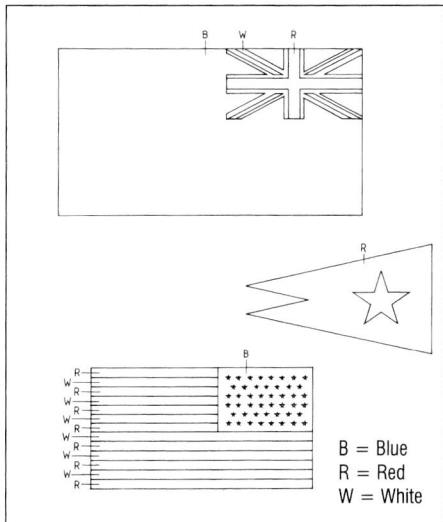

The flags were painted on tinfoil.

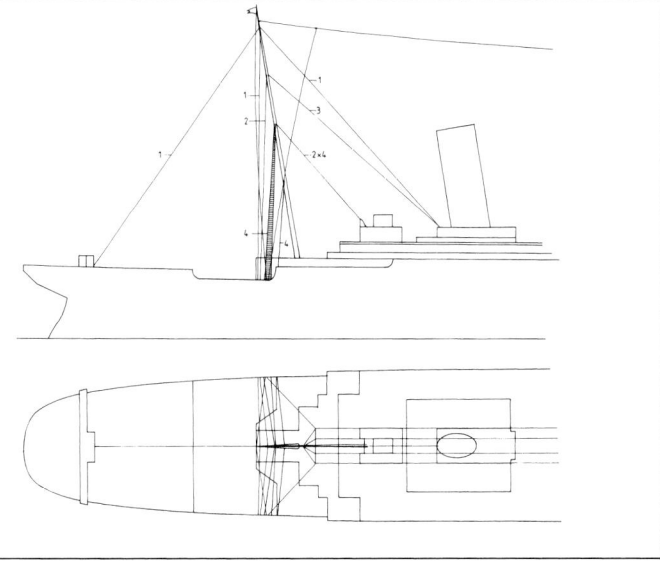

(Below) Mainmast rigging diagram. (No scale.)
Key: (Both masts)
1. 3in steel wire.
2. 4in steel wire.
3. 4¼in steel wire.
4. 5½in steel wire.

Appendix I Model Kits

In 1975 the American plastic kit manufacturer Entex released a 1:350 scale model of *Titanic* that stunned the modelling fraternity. As the plan situation in those days was pretty poor (Harland & Wolff stated that all plans were destroyed by bombing during the Second World War) Entex called the Titanic Historical Society and the noted *Titanic* artist Ken Marschall advised Entex on constructional details of the ship (he also supplied the stunning artwork for the kit's box-top). The model was pretty accurate and it is today still the best plastic model of *Titanic* that is available. A year later Entex released their *Lusitania* to the same scale which was even better than the *Titanic* model. The Entex *Lusitania* might rate as the best plastic model of an ocean liner to date – not bad for a kit that was designed nearly thirty years ago. It is still available under the Gunze Sangyo label.

After the sad demise of Entex the moulds went through several hands, and the 1:350 *Titanic* was initially available from Anmark and Revell and finally from Academy/Minicraft. After Academy and Minicraft decided to go their own ways, Academy released their own 1:400 kit, which they would have been better off leaving well alone as not only were the Entex mistakes copied but new mistakes were added which are almost impossible to correct. The promenade deck and B deck are far too high and this results in a model that does not really look like *Titanic*. Probably the biggest mistakes are that two lifeboats have been forgotten and the overlaps of the shell plating face the wrong direction.

Minicraft meanwhile decided that the old Entex moulds were in dire need of a facelift. An upgraded version was released, which had some of the mistakes taken care of such as the reserve anchor and the crew galley skylight added and the kit also features photo-etched brass railings and fittings. It is sold as the 'Deluxe Edition' and is still available today – a fitting testimony to Entex's efforts in the mid-1970s.

In 1976 Revell released their own 1:570 scale kit which was a crude, scaled-down copy of the Entex kit. The most unfortunate feature of this kit is that the railings are moulded on the decks and superstructure as solid wall rails. Correcting this would be an enormous undertaking. But at least the finished model actually looks like *Titanic*.

Coinciding with the 1997 release of James Cameron's blockbuster feature film, Revell released another new model which was in 1:400 scale. This kit is also very crude and alas without solid wall railings, but at least the completed model looks somewhat like *Titanic*. It is not produced from the same moulds as the Academy kit to the same scale.

A large number of other kits have been released, mainly from Far Eastern companies, but most of these are also copies of the old Entex achievement. The ultimate *Titanic* kit still has to be produced though.

A number of cottage-industry companies have come out with photo-etched and resin items to upgrade plastic models.

I received samples from Tom's Modelworks, 1050 Cranberry Drive, Cupertino, CA 95014 U.S.A. (www.tomsmodelworks.com);

Loren Perry's Gold Medal Models, 1412 Fisherman Bay Road, Lopez, WA 98261, U.S.A. (www.goldmm.com);

Tom Nicolai's Ocean Liner Models, P.O. Box 2608, Long Beach, CA 90802-9998, U.S.A.;

Robert Hahn, Kestenzeile 21a, 12349 Berlin, Germany (www.titanic-plan.de) e-mail: hahn@titanicplan.de;

Dan Reed, 18641 East Powers Pl, 80015 Aurora Co, U.S.A.

Airbrushing these items is the best way to paint them as painting them with a brush is bound to clog up some of these very delicate little pieces.

Here is a list of brass frets I have received and what they include:

Tom's Modelworks 1:350 Scale set #3511 *Titanic* Rails
All railings needed for a 1:350 scale model, barrier gates, stairs and shrouds.

Tom's Modelworks 1:350 Scale Set #3521 *Titanic* Windows
This includes all types of windows needed for the superstructure of the ship. A very delicate little fret. It appears that the master drawing was done by hand, but this is in no way intended as a criticism. The veranda cafe windows are a delight.

Tom's Modelworks 1:350 Scale Set #3533 *Titanic* Benches
Forty-eight bench seats, all of the long type. Items like these should be folded to shape using wooden jigs as guides, as trying to fold them by hand is impossible and would only ruin them.

Tom's Modelworks 1:350 Scale Set #3523 *Titanic* Detail Set
This includes compass platform crutches and ladder; propeller shaft spanners; crane crutches; lifeboat railings; skylights; crane hooks; funnel ladders and platforms; wheels; chain capstans; fidley gratings; stokehold vent mesh; crane jibs; lifeboat tackles; rails for crane platforms, ladders and the anchor well gratings

Tom's Modelworks 1:350 Scale Set #3533 *Titanic* Deckchairs
Forty deckchairs; only a handful of the several hundred deckchairs that were on *Titanic*'s promenade deck.

Tom's Modelworks also has 1:144th scale etched brass items in their catalogue. These include bench seats, deckchairs and railings (the railings are very delicate). Robert Hahn has produced three 10in brass frets also in 1:144th scale which include nearly everything one would need that lends itself to the photo-etching process, from stairs, ladders, windows and boat davits to the shrouds.

Also in 1:144th scale are resin lifeboats, funnels (all the same height), and a complete vent set which is slightly crude and some of them are incorrect. These were produced by Dan Reed who also has a 1:144th scale hull on his list.

Gold Medal Models 1:350 Merchant Ship (*Titanic* & *Lusitania*)
Consists of railings, shrouds, stairs and ladders for both the 1:350 scale *Lusitania* and *Titanic*. Beautifully etched.

Gold Medal Models Gold Plus Detail Set for 1:350 *Titanic* & *Lusitania*
Consists of *Titanic* bench seats (much smaller than the Tom's Modelworks offerings and also a little more complicated to fold to shape), coaling outriggers, railing gates, lifeboat lines, bow anchor well grating, *Titanic* cargo crane platform railings, deckchairs, crane boom supports, crane

APPENDIX I - MODEL KITS

boom girders, *Lusitania* and *Titanic* docking bridge supports, *Titanic* compass platform, ship's wheels, *Lusitania* and *Titanic* wireless antennae spreaders.

Gold Medal Models 1:350
Ocean Liner Figures
For those who wish to add passengers and crew to their model, here is a fret with more than 200 people onboard, including Captain Smith and the ship's orchestra.

Gold Medal Models 1:350
***Titanic* Lifeboat Davits**
This is a must for those who wish to improve their 1:350 model kit. With care some stunning small davits can be built; it comes with templates to bend the davit arms uniformly. The instruction leaflet is very good.

Gold Medal Models 1:600 Merchant Ship
Identical to the 1:350 merchant ship offering with the same name, but in smaller scale. The finesse of the items is amazing.

Gold Medal Models 1:700 Merchant Ship
Same as above.

Tom Nicolai's Ocean Liner Models has produced a conversion set for the 1:350 scale model to be converted into *Britannic* and *Olympic*. The *Britannic* set comes with promenade deck walls, B and C deck walls, a full array of gantry davits, red crosses and additional deckhouse walls. A set of resin *Britannic* lifeboats and deckhouses is also available, although I have not seen them yet. The *Olympic* conversion set is every bit as impressive. The major features are, as was to be expected, the promenade and B and C deck walls.

Both come with a very comprehensive instruction 'booklet' which guides the modeller through every building stage. It is very well drawn and easy to understand. Highly recommended. Tom also released a small fret with the correct staircase skylight covers for *Olympic* and *Titanic*.

1:48 scale railings were purchased from **Display Models**, James Lane, 30 Broadway, Blyth, Northumberland NE24 2PP, U.K. He also has brass stanchions for railings in 1:96, 1:72, 1:48 and 1:32 scale, as well as etched fittings such as ladders, ships' wheels and wire mesh suitable for *Titanic* models.

My thanks to all for the review samples.

(Top) 1:350 scale *Britannic* built by Remco Hillen from the Netherlands. He used Tom Nicolai's conversion set to build this stunning model from the 1:350 kit.

(Above) Loren Perry's 1:350 scale *Titanic* model.

Appendix II Colour Chart

The exact colours *Titanic* was painted in have always been, and most probably always will be, cause for debates amongst historians. Obviously no colour images of *Titanic* were taken and none of *Olympic* have yet surfaced. Quite a number of colour prints of later White Star liners are around, but these cannot be relied upon either, as the colours of these images have doubtlessly changed throughout the years, as well as the paint fading on the ships after several years in service. When comparing two colour images of the same ship (sometimes even the same image) the colours differ enormously.

To get as close as possible to the real *Titanic* I used Ken Marschall's latest paintings as a guide. Ken has also changed some colours throughout the years as his research progressed. It is known that a print of an artwork, particularly in a book, does not show exactly the same colours as the original painting.

In addition to this colour images of the builders models were also used as colour guides. These, however, were also of VERY limited use as the pictures showed many models in various stages of neglect (*Olympic*, *Teutonic*, *Oceanic*) and the models were extremely dirty. The white deckhouses were a shade of dirty-brown which was apparently on all parts of the model, changing all the colours.

The colours used for the Orlando

model were very well received by all renowned historians who have seen the model so far, particularly the funnels, so I can safely say that I got it as close as I could get.

It is, of course, up to each modelmaker to decide if he is happy with the colours I used or not.

Unfortunately, a conversion chart, for converting RAL (German) paints into Pantone does not yet exist, so I can only list the RAL paints used with the according RAL number.

The hull beneath the waterline:	RAL 3016 Korallenrot
The hull above the waterline:	Humbrol 85 Coal Black
Hull white and deckhouses:	Humbrol 130 Satin White
Dadoes in the well decks:	Humbrol 62 Matt Leather
Masts:	Humbrol 110 Matt Natural Wood
Electric winches:	Humbrol 149 Matt Dark Green
All wooden and brass window frames:	Humbrol 10 Service Brown
Lifeboat burgees:	Humbrol 19 Bright Red
Steel deckhouse roofs:	Humbrol 145 Matt Medium Grey
Funnels (White Star Buff):	RAL 1001 Beige
Yellow trimline	Modelmaster Insignia Yellow

Appendix III Recommended Reading

There must be hundreds of books written about *Titanic*. The variety of subjects is quite astounding ranging from a book about premonitions of the disaster to the life of the survivors after the sinking.

As a modelmaker I am interested in books dealing with the ship in technical terms so every book with a large number of illustrations of *Titanic* and *Olympic* is appealing to me. I will list books here which I am sure will also be interesting to fellow modelmakers, as well as a few books dealing with detailed narratives of the sinking.

Archbold, Rick & Ken Marschall,
Ken Marschall's Art of Titanic (Hyperion 1998)

Ballard, Dr. Robert,
Exploring the Titanic (Scholastic 1998)
—, & Rick Archbold,
Discovery of the Titanic (Warner Books 1998)

Bonsall, Thomas,
Titanic. The Story of the Great White Star Line
Trio: The Olympic, the Titanic and the Britannic
(Gallery 1987)

Chirnside, Mark,
The Olympic Class Ships
(Tempus Publishing 2004)

Cinefex #72, *Titanic* Issue (1997)

Eaton, John and Charles Haas,
Titanic: Triumph and Tragedy (Newton 1996)

Hall, Steve and Bruce Beveridge,
Titanic and Olympic, The Truth behind the Conspiracy (Haverford 2004)

Hutchings, David,
RMS Titanic - 75 Years of Legend
(Kingfisher Railway Productions 1987)

Lord, Walter,
A Night to Remember (HR&W 1976)

Lynch, Don & Ken Marschall,
Ghosts of the Abyss (Madison Press 2003)
—,
Titanic, An Illustrated History
(Madison Press 1992)

McCluskie, Tom,
Anatomy of the Titanic (PRC Publishing 1998)
—, & Michael Sharpe & Leo Marriott,
Titanic and her Sisters Olympic and Britannic
(PRC Publishing 1998)

O'Donnell, E. E. (editor),
Father Browne's Titanic Album
(Wolfhound Press 1997)

Shipbuilder Magazine.
Ocean Liners Of the Past. Volume 1: White Star Triple Screw Atlantic Liners *Olympic* and *Titanic* (PSL 1970)

I must point out my reservations in regard to Tom McCluskie's books. A large number of the captions in his books contain fundamental errors in regard to which ship is actually shown. The worst is a photo of the Cunard *Aquitania* which is captioned as *Britannic*. Nevertheless, these books have been listed here too, as the photographs alone in these are worth having.

Selected prints of Ken Marschall's amazing artworks are available from:

Trans-Atlantic Designs, inc.
P.O. Box 539
Redondo Beach, CA 90277
USA
http://www.transatlanticdesigns.com

The author can be contacted at Pandavies@aol.com

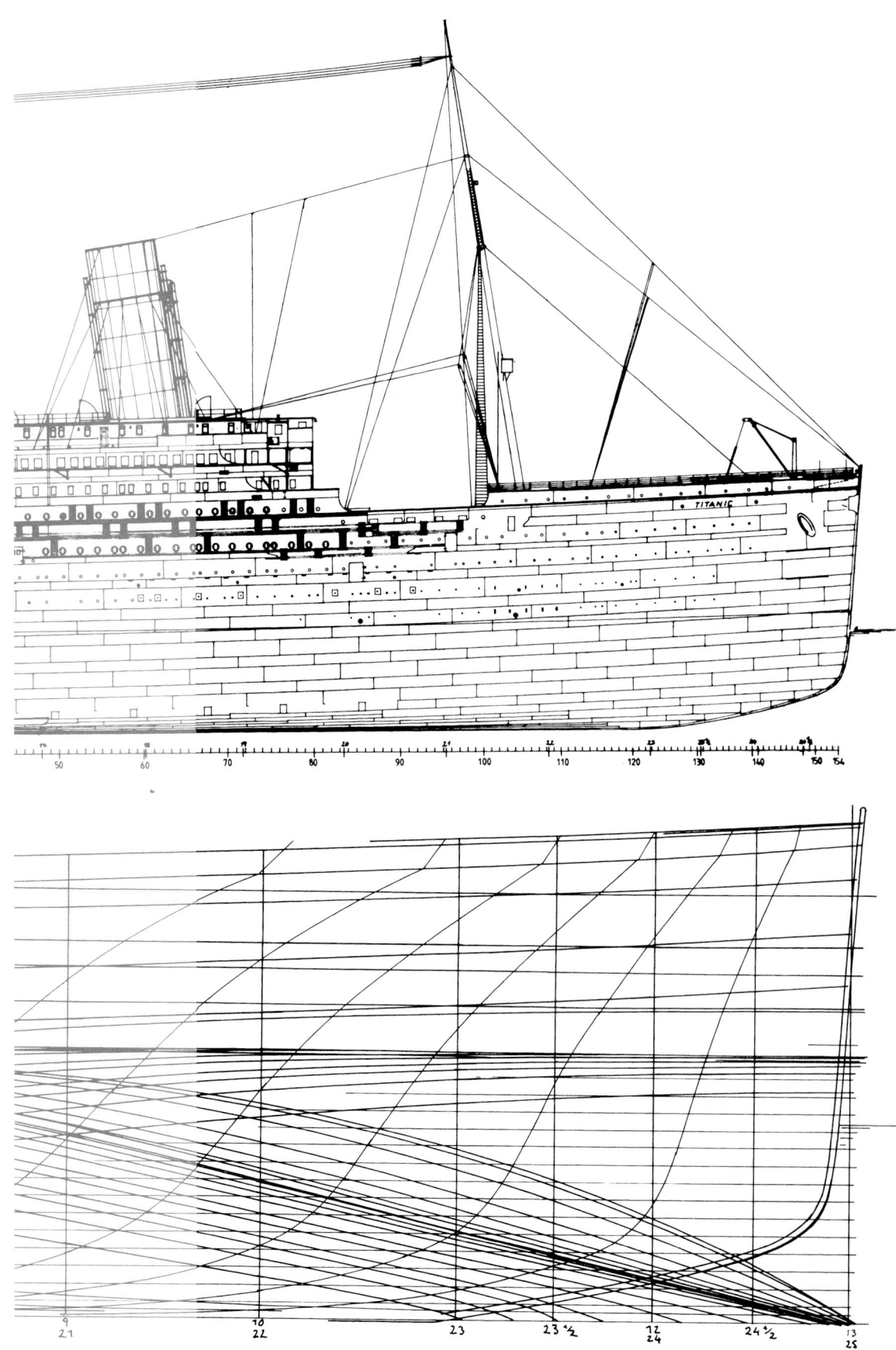

Harland & Wolff Yard No. 401
Triple Screw Steamship
R.M.S. (Royal Mail Ship) *Titanic*
White Star Line, 1912

Length overall:	882ft. 9in.
Length between perpendiculars:	850ft. 0in.
Breadth extreme (at the waterline):	92ft. 6in.
Gross tonnage:	46,328

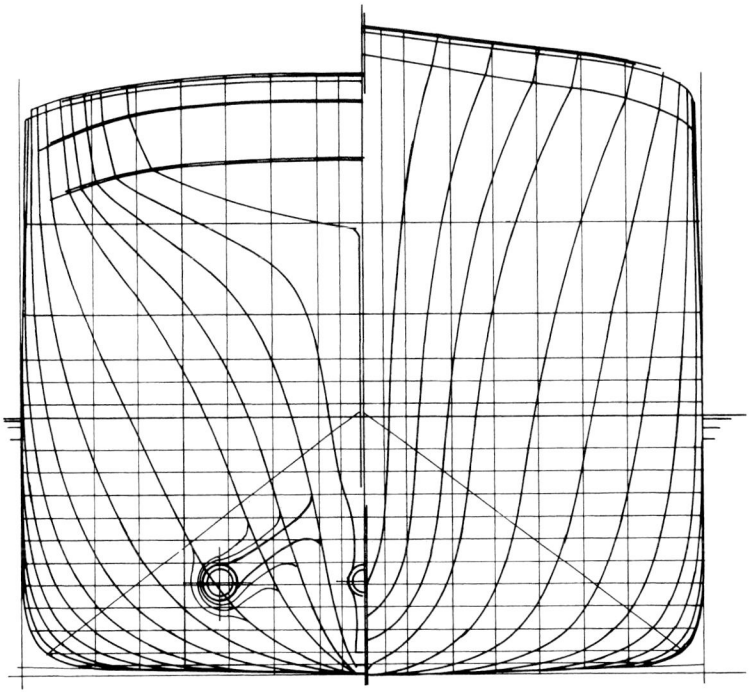